MW01625874

Praise for ***Secrets of the Art World***

"Finally! A book that guides an artist through development, sales, and representation. Be true to yourself and at the same time, appeal to your audience. Litsa Spanos brings her "Super Star" experience in representing artwork and artists via a step-by-step chronology. This is a must read for artists, gallery owners, and publishers."

—Rick Barnett
Author, Lecturer, and Television Personality - Managing Director
Redwood Media Group

"Litsa, with her passion for beauty and excellence, walks firmly on the cutting edge of the U.S. Art Market. For her to share her 'secrets' is a stunning gift to all of us in the industry! I am humbled by her generosity of spirit and feel privileged to traverse this complicated, yet richly-rewarding business, along- side my colleague and friend. This book is a bible for anyone who wishes to "make it" in the Art World!

—Bette Ridgeway
Artist & Author, *Talent is Just the Beginning*

"This is the go-to-book on how to navigate the business of art with insights from Litsa and other art professionals. Every aspect is covered for those just beginning up to the seasoned pro. There is valuable business guidance in these pages and priceless wisdom for the inner artist. Get this book and get going now!"

—Ken Elliot
Artist & Author, *Manifesting 123* and *You Don't Need #3*

"Litsa offers a connective, empowering and passionate gift to fine artists who are truly committed to their artistic practice and financial well-being. This content-rich book breaks down the various steps of creative business building, gives you the tools necessary to reach your goals, then carefully guides you, like a trusted and confident friend to a greater opportunity for success."

—Andrea Rosenfeld
Founder/CEO, Detroit Art and Business Institute

"Having recently completed a large project with Litsa, I can tell you that this book is a wonderful reflection of the qualities and energy she brings to her work. This book, like the author herself, is inspiring, passionate, wise, creative, and practical. It is a generous gift to those artists who might apply her thoughtful insights and embrace her optimistic, can-do attitude for what is possible!"

—Paul Darwish
Chief Business Development Officer & Director of Marketing, Graydon

"This inspiring book is an invaluable guide on many levels. Sharing her own life journey as an immigrant family to the United States to becoming a successful business woman in the arts, Litsa outlines in detail the many aspects that will support aspiring artists to be successful. She provides helpful instruction of how to nurture creative selves into thriving working artists. From practical tips of how to get comfortable with taking risks to engaging in social media, these pages include everything you always wanted to know about how to carve out your unique place within the fast paced art world.

—Raphaela Platow
Director, Contemporary Arts Center

"Litsa runs one of the most unique galleries in Cincinnati. In this book she provides clear vision for any artist looking to achieve both practical and 'out of the box' ideas in selling your work. Read this book, you will learn from the best!"

—Jeanne Porter
Founder, Women in Business Networking
Author, *SUCCESS Powered by Relationships*

"This is a true work of art. Litsa is a passionate, creative, and has achieved her many successes through risk-taking and determination. This book is perfect for all of us looking to hone our talents to find happiness professionally and personally. Must-read!"

—Patty Brisben
Founder & Chairwoman, Pure Romance

"Litsa's dream for her career was to bring beauty to others, and she has been hugely successful in reaching her dream. With this book, she empowers artists with the direction, resources and inspiration for sharing their art-their beauty-with us."

—Barbara Perez
President & CEO, YWCA, Cincinnati

"I have known Litsa professionally and personally for 10 years. What she has created in our community through ADC is nothing short of remarkable. She provided a much needed shot of energy into the art community. The quote, "The rising tide lifts all boats" is just what she accomplished. No one I know is better at marketing and promotion than Litsa. Her thinking is created out around the edges, so things feel fresh and new. Many have benefited from her genius."

—Deni Tato, President
Corporate Consciousness

"Litsa's joyful philosophy and disciplined approach have launched hundreds of artists like the ones in Cincinnati Financial Corporation's collection. Now she has put all of that wisdom and experience into this book, a veritable treasure map for the aspiring artist."

—Joan Shevchik
Cincinnati Financial Corporation

"Litsa has captured my mind, heart, and soul with Secrets of the Art World: Getting Real about the Process, Business, and Selling of Your Work. *Litsa is an inspiration to everyone."*

—Earl L. Walz
CEO, The Urology Group

"Secrets of the Art World *is more than a book. It is a superior tool to help all artists, and I would dare to say non-artists as well to be inspired and dare to dream big."*

—Katie Brass
Executive Director, The Carnegie

"Secrets of the Art World is a must read. Beyond being an indispensable guide to the business of art, it captures the essence of Litsa: energy, grace, dynamism, entrepreneurism, humility, and success. All will come away inspired from Litsa's work."

—Gary M. Kirsh, M.D.
President, The Urology Group

"For emerging artists, gaining access to quality advice and resources can be very difficult. This book fills that gap and provides vital insight into how to be a working, professional artist."

—Sara M. Vance Waddell
Art Collector, President, SMV Media

"Litsa Spanos can write a book on how to successfully integrate knowledge of fine art, business acumen, commitment to her community, strategic thinking, belief in collaboration and inclusion, and a pioneering spirit. Thank goodness she has. A great primer for artists, gallery owners, and anyone looking to follow their passion."

—Patty Beggs
The Harry Fath General Director & CEO, Cincinnati Opera

The Secrets of the Art World

The Secrets of the Art World:

Getting Real about the Process, Business, and Selling of Your Work

Litsa Spanos,
President, ADC Art Design Consultants, Inc.
Publisher, Blink Art Resource

Foreword by **Robert Probst,**
Dean, College of Design, Architecture, Art, and Planning (DAAP),
University of Cincinnati

To Lillian, Wishing you much success! Litsa

adcfineart.com

Printed and bound in the United States of America.

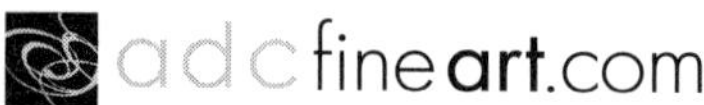

Published by ADC Art Design Consultants, Inc.
310 Culvert Street
Cincinnati, Ohio 45202
www.adcfineart.com

Cover Design by Sandy Eichert
Interior Design by Sandy Eichert
Back Cover art by Dimitra Milan
Author Photography by Kate Messer

Library of Congress Cataloging-in-Publication Data is available on file.
Print ISBN: 978-0-9987016-0-8
Ebook ISBN: 978-0-9987016-1-5
10 9 8 7 6 5 4 3 2 1

This book is dedicated to my husband and children.

age

xvii **Foreword** by Robert Probst, Dean College of Design, Architecture, Art, and Planning (DAAP) University of Cincinnati

1. **Introduction—*Follow Your Passion***
3. More than Luck
8. Taking Risks
10. Living the Dream
13. Growing Pains
17. My Hope for You, Reader
20. So How Can this Book Help Supercharge Your Art Career?
23. First Steps

29. **Chapter One: *So You're an Artist***
31. What's Your Dream?
37. Do You Have What It Takes?
46. Taking the Leap of Faith
50. A Word about Gratitude
    The Most Essential Quality of Every Artist and Entrepreneur
53. **Artist to Artist** Brian Goodman
58. Action Steps

63. **Chapter Two: *You're a Working Artist, Now What?***
65. The Most Important Secret
69. Litsa's Not-So-Top-Secret Steps to Think More Positively
72. Doing the Work of Positive Living
76. Self-Care and the Artist's Life
77. Litsa's Ten Tips for Higher Performance
85. **Artist to Artist** Chin Yuen
    The Importance of Self-Care
88. Action Steps

page

109. **Chapter Three:** ***So How do I Make Money?***

111. **Separating Yourself from Your Art:** You Are Not Your Work

113. **Pricing Your Art**

114. **Factors to Consider When Pricing Art**

120. **Do Your Homework**

Practical Exercises to Do Today to Help You Price Your Work

124. **Selling Your Art**

Getting Real About Selling Your Work in Six Easy Steps

128. **Artist to Artist** Lisa England Schuster

Working with Designers and Galleries

131. **Gallery Owner to Artist** Roy Saper, Saper Galleries

Working with Designers and Galleries

134. **Gallery Owner's Advice** Sylvia Rombis, Malton Gallery

Submitting Work to Galleries

138. **The Importance of Shows**

How, When and Where to Show Your Work

Open Studio Events

Juried Competitions

Nonprofit galleries

Art Fairs and Tradeshows

144. **Artist to Artist** Mary Johnston

The Importance of Featuring Art at Fairs, Conferences and Tradeshows

148. **Trade Show Owner to Artist** Eric Smith, Redwood Media

Showing Your Work for Maximum Impact

153. **Understanding Contracts**

156. **Payments and Receipts of Authenticity**

156. **Bookkeeping 101**

157. **Litsa's Not-So-Secret Tips to Being a Working Artist/Businessperson**

159. **Investments**

161. **Financial Professional to Artist** Francie Henry, Bank Executive

163. **Action Steps**

Page

165. **Chapter Four:** ***Branding, Marketing, and Relationship Maintenance***
168. **The Difference Between Marketing and Branding**
169. What is a brand?
172. Steps to Help You Understand Your Brand
175. Testing Your Brand
176. Creating Your Artist Statement
180. Now You're Ready to Execute Your Brand
183. Marketing: Getting the Word Out
189. **Social Media**
194. **Artist to Artist** Nicholas Teetelli
The Power of Ad Campaigns on Facebook
197. **A Word About # (Hashtags)**
199. **Artist to Artist** KX2 Ruth Avra & Dana Kleinman
The Power of Instagram
201. **Let's Put a Pin in It**
202. **Artist to Artist** Kevin Grass
The Power of Twitter
204. **Email Marketing**
205. **Artist to Artist** Cat Tesla
The Power of Newsletters and Social Media to Boost Art Sales
207. **Artist to Artist** Cindy Avroch
The Power of Newsletters to Enhance and Strengthen Relationships
210. **Direct Mail**
210. **Paid Advertising**
212. **Search Engine Optimization (SEO)**
213. **Artist to Artist** Nicholas Yust
The Importance of a Well-Designed Website, Keywords, and SEO
216. **Measuring and Analyzing Your Data Regularly**
217. **Artist to Artist** Scott McHenry
The Power of Using Measurement Tools and Proper Use of Social Media

page

219. **Maintaining Relationships in Real-Time:**
The Importance of Networking and Community Involvement

221. **Gallery Owner to Artist** Jason and Bonnie Mansour, Art Leaders Gallery
The Importance of Marketing

224. **Artist to Artist** Kevin Caron
The Power of Youtube

228. **Online Opportunities to Market and Sell Your Artwork**

229. **Artist to Artist** Amy Meya
The Power of Seeing Your Work as a Product

231. **Artist to Artist** Renato Foti
The Power of Artful Home for Marketing

233. **Artist to Artist** Lea de Wit
The Power of Blink Art Resource

237. **Publishing Your Art**

238. **Art Publisher to Artist** Joanne Chappell, Editions Limited
What Artist's Need to Consider When Submitting Work

240. **Artist to Artist** Don Wunderlee
Success Selling Prints with Editions Limited

243. **Artist to Artist** Karen Hale
How Fine Art America Works for Artists

245. **Trademark, Copyrights, and Other Legal Matters**

246. **Hiring Help**

248. **Action Steps**

253. **Conclusion:** ***You Have What it Takes***

258. **Acknowledgments**

266. **Notes**

Foreword

Litsa Spanos' long-time passion for supporting artists is reflected in this timely, definitive guide to every aspect an artist requires to succeed and sustain their careers.

As a gallery owner, consultant and mentor to artists, Litsa's unabashed enthusiasm for the art world begins with a candid look at her own career challenges and entrepreneurial decisions. Her varied experiences enable her to create a detailed blueprint for a successful art career. From how to forge partnerships with galleries and tradeshows to marketing and selling your work, every one of Litsa's chapters inspire readers to "supercharge" their art careers. Litsa has been a risk-taker but also offers wise advice on self-care to avoid anxiety and burn out.

Her twenty-five years of experience in every aspect of the art industry are invaluable to artists at every phase of their careers who focus on creativity but are less sure about the business end of the ever-changing art world. Her practical tips illustrate how to flourish and still handily pay the bills.

She aptly discusses important details such as pricing work, commissions, taxes, and obtaining the most useful financial software. Litsa has also gathered some of the world's top experts who weigh in on state-of-the-art practices to ensure artists get their work noticed by the appropriate audiences. Their contributions include areas such as branding, marketing, social media, websites, blogging, key words and search engine optimization. Litsa and her cadre of experts provide a thorough, well-thought out checklist of information to ensure *Secrets of the Art World: Getting Real About the Process, Business and Selling of Your Work* becomes a must-read for artists, young and old, who can locate all the information they need for success and motivation in one, comprehensive book.

Robert Probst
Dean, College of Design, Architecture, Art, and Planning (DAAP)
University of Cincinnati

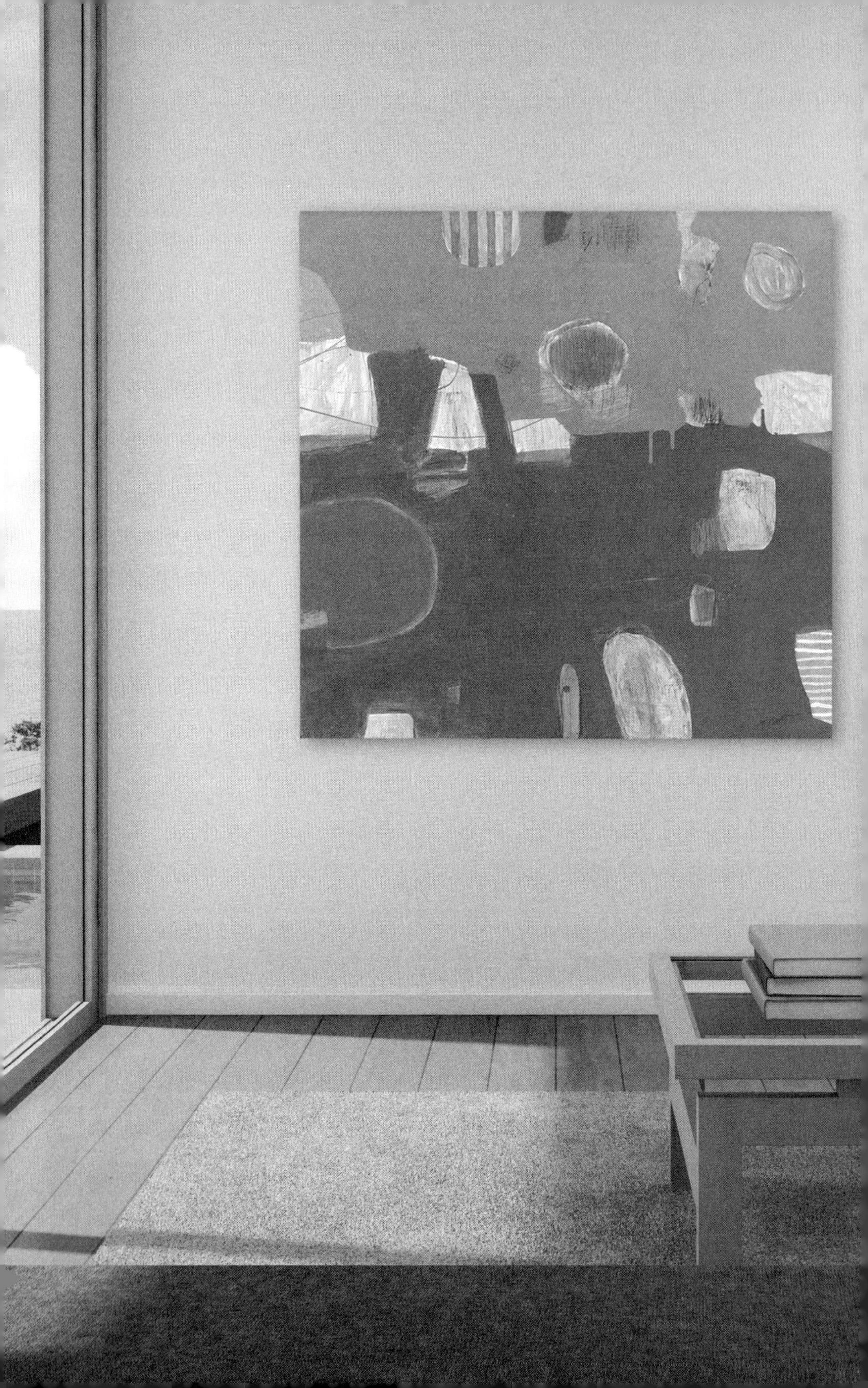

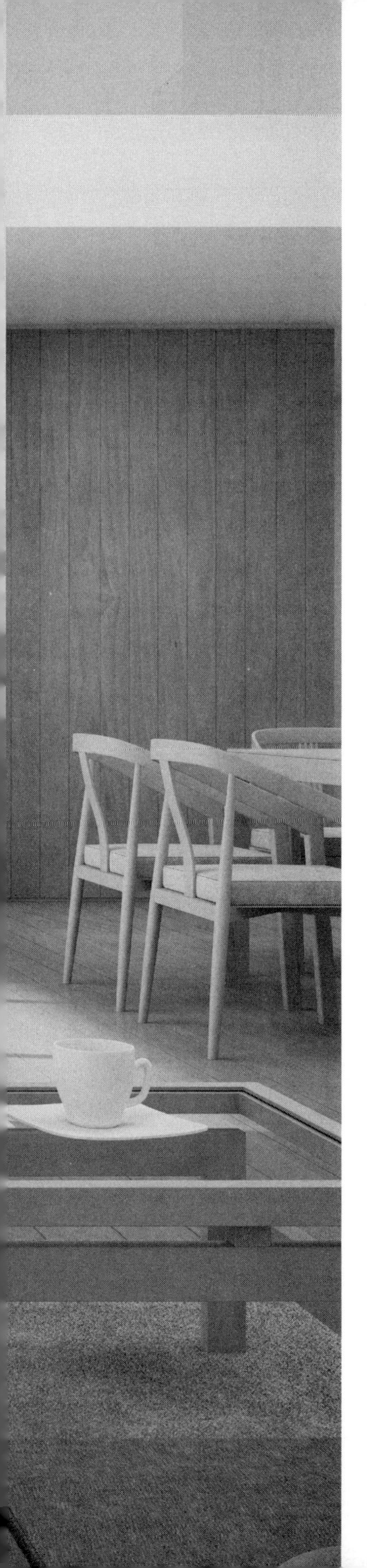

*"PASSION is the genesis of **genius**."*

— Galileo Galilei

Artist: Tom Owen

introduction

Follow Your Passion

"I WOULD RATHER DIE OF PASSION THAN OF BOREDOM."

— Vincent van Gogh

More than Luck

People who don't know me well, often come up to me and say things like:

Lucky you, Litsa!

Lucky you, you get to work in such a beautiful space!

Lucky you, you get to work with artists, interior designers, and businesses seeking art!

Lucky you, you own your own business!

Lucky you, you get to go to glamorous gallery events and get all dressed up!

Lucky you, you get to make a living doing what you love!

I always smile and say, "Yes, I am!" But, a part of me knows that more than luck had to do with my success. It's impossible to explain how all of this "luck" seemed to show up in my life in a split second or during polite, casual conversation, so I don't. However, the life I have today, I assure you, didn't come without its share of obstacles, failures, and life-changing lessons. And, I couldn't have made it at all without two incredible people, my parents, Petros and Sofia.

In 1967, my parents took the ultimate risk and left their small farming village nestled in the mountains of Aetos, Greece (population 800) with nothing more than a few hundred dollars, their two young daughters (my sister, Sylvia and me), and a suitcase for each of us.

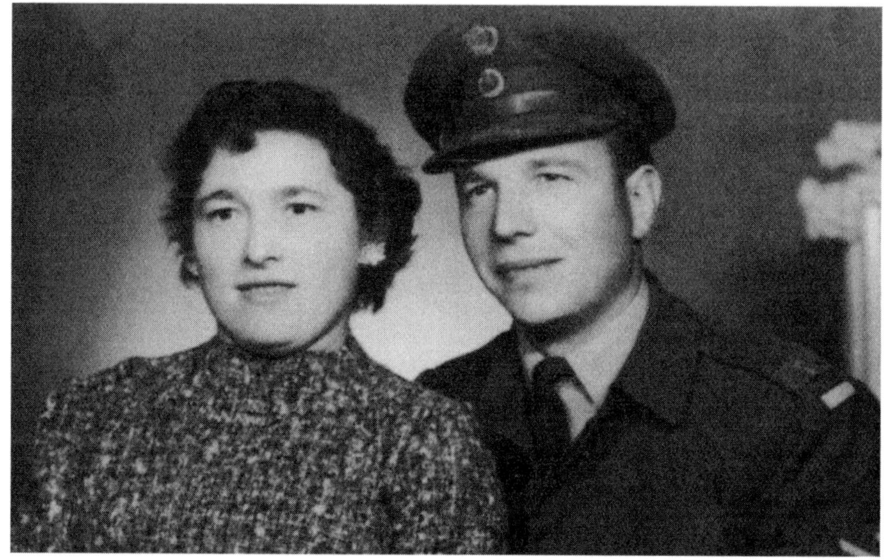

My parents , Petros and Sofia, 1958

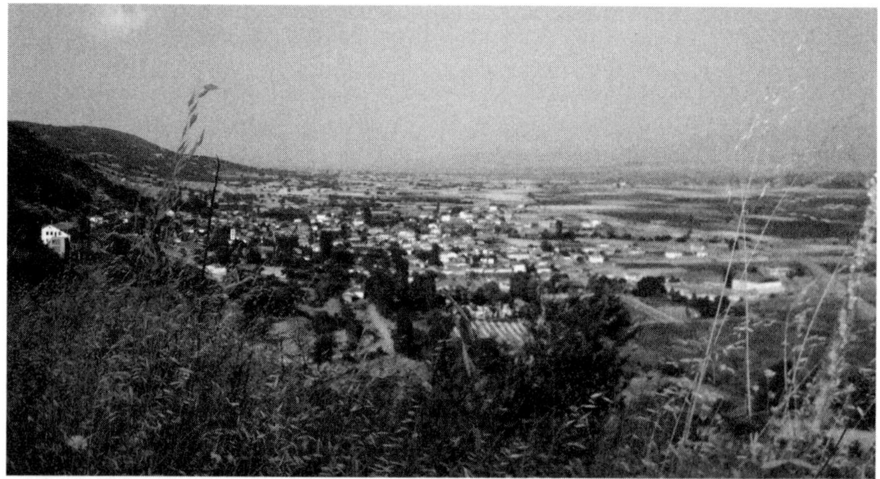

Aetos, Greece, population 800

After a long journey at sea, we sailed into New York Harbor, where the Statue of Liberty, her lighted torch, and the hope it represented, greeted us. Soon after we disembarked the ship, we walked through the majestic hall on Ellis Island, just like countless immigrants before us had, and then we took a ferry to the "land of opportunity" to begin our very own American Dream.

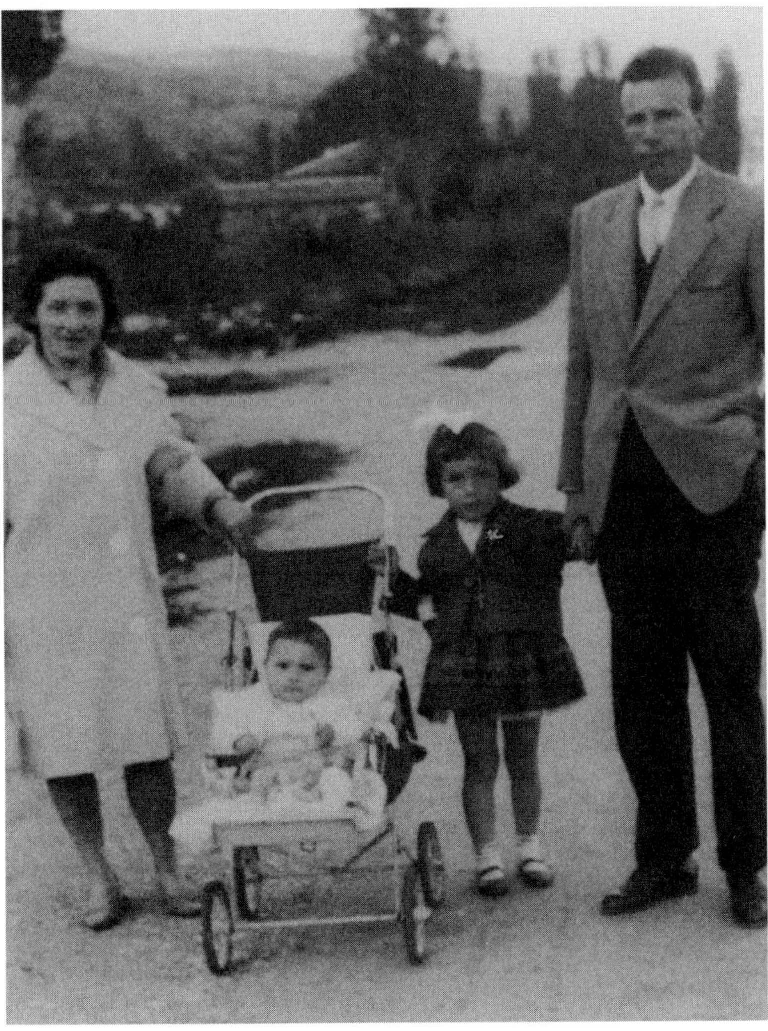

My family in Greece, before moving to the US, 1963

Remembering this humble beginning, while writing this book on the top floor of a building that overlooks another great American city, Cincinnati, in a gallery I own, surrounded by incredible art and talented people, stops me cold. I still need to catch my breath whenever I think of it. What a seemingly impossible journey my parents embarked upon. I don't think in their wildest dreams they could have imagined such an incredible life for their daughters! Back then they had no idea what to expect. They had little money. They didn't even speak English. They simply had a dream to give their girls a better life. I get choked up just thinking about what they did for us.

"There are hundreds of paths up the mountain, all leading to the same place, so it doesn't matter which path you take. The only person wasting time is the one who runs around the mountain, telling everyone that his or her path is wrong."

—Hindu proverb

We were fortunate back then to have some help. My father's younger sister, my Thea Chrissa, who emigrated before us with the rest of my father's family, met us in New York and served as both our translator and ally. She helped my dad get settled and find work. No job was too lowly for my father. Work was work. My dad took a job making $2.04 an hour, unloading and loading mattresses during a night shift for Sterns and Foster. Then after an exhausting night of work, he came home to watch my sister and I during the day so my mother could work as a seamstress. To this day I just find this unbelievable.

I often find myself asking, How did they do it? And, let me tell you, there hasn't been a day that's gone by that I don't think about their work ethic and resolve to put their children first. It has stuck with me.

But, their work ethic isn't the only thing that's stayed with me. They were savers too. Even when my parents were making so little, they were putting a little money away on the side. Eventually, they were able to save up enough money to buy a home for us with cash. My mom and dad never took out a loan (not even to buy a car or put my sister and I through college). "If you don't have the money, you don't buy it," my dad always said. When I look back on it, I think: "This is the definition of impossible!" And, yet, they did it. And they showed me that whatever I put my mind to can be done. Above all they showed me the power of persistence:

If you decide to do it, you'll do it if you work at it hard enough and long enough.

Taking Risks

"The biggest risk is not taking any risk... In a world that is changing really quickly, the only strategy that is guaranteed to fail is not taking risks."

—Mark Zuckerberg

My parents took an enormous risk bringing their young daughters across an ocean to build a life for them. It took incredible amounts of sacrifice, self-discipline, faith, and courage. They left everything they knew—their family, friends, village, and country—to live a life they imagined for their daughters, complete with a nice home, a good education, and meaningful work. (My dad and mom went on to purchase and own a small convenience store, which my dad successfully ran for fifteen years.) But their life, their conviction, their work ethic, their ability to save, and most importantly their ability to take risks is why I am who I am today. It's why I am not afraid to take the risks I do—in art or in business. I do it for the people I care about. I do it for my family of artists. I do it for my employees. I do it for my husband and daughters. I want them all to be as proud of me, as I am of my parents.

I don't take a single day for granted. Yes, it's true I am lucky—lucky to have been born to two individuals who taught me the value of hard work, risk-taking, and living one's dream. I am incredibly grateful for their sacrifice and for the life they helped to create for my sister and me. I don't want to waste a bit of this precious gift. More importantly, I want to pay it forward and give it to others.

A long time ago, I also realized not everyone was as fortunate as I was to have two amazing role models like my parents. I realize most people setting out in life often feel somewhat adrift, especially artists. There is no all-encompassing book or manual that artists can read to help them manage their talent, their gifts, their business, their money, their moods, or how to handle difficult times. After all, (and I should know), there is no ONE way to "make it" in the art world. However, I do know what things work and what things don't (most of the time). I know this because my parents were incredible teachers. They taught me how to live by example. They taught me how to treat others, by how they treated me, and everyone they met. The world could use more people like them. But, since not everyone is going to be able to grow up in the home of Petros and Sofia, and not everyone has had the opportunity to learn from hundreds of artists, gallery owners, consultants, and business owners, I thought I would write a book that could help other people become as "lucky" as I have been.

"To create one's world in any of the arts takes courage."
—Georgia O'Keeffe

But, then again, I've learned this too: Luck and risk-taking will only take you so far. It takes grit and sheer determination to see those risks through. It also takes something else: great people. And boy do I know them. Besides my parents, I have a supportive husband, Van, who has always believed in me. He has always been there for me, both back when I was working fourteen-hour days when I just got started and when I work fourteen-hour days now.

And besides luck, taking risks, grit, and great people, you need something else: A DREAM.

Living the Dream

"To accomplish great things, we must not only act, but also dream, not only plan, but also believe."

—Anatole France

Like my mother and father before me, and like you, I had a dream when I started out in the art world. I have always loved beautiful things and I also loved making things beautiful. And, I have my parents to thank for this too, especially my mom. When my sister and I were children, my parents couldn't afford to take us to department stores to shop for our holiday dresses. Instead my mom designed and hand-sewed many of the dresses my sister and I wore. My mother's attention to detail was impeccable. I still remember the matching sky blue velvet dresses she made for my sister and me with hand-sewn pearl beading and lace. It was the first piece of art I ever fell in love with. Little did she (or I for that matter) know that it was just the beginning of what would become my life's passion. Or that it would affect my sister, too. She had a successful career in fashion design and became a gallery owner as well.

My mother was the first artist I knew. She was able to create something out of nothing—what all artists essentially are called to do. She could turn a piece of fabric and some beads and lace into something awe-inspiring and breathtaking. I remember putting that pearl-beaded dress on for the first time and feeling instantly beautiful. It was the first time I experienced the life-transforming effect that art can have on a person. Wearing that dress instantly made me feel better about myself. It instantly made me feel more alive, more beautiful, more connected, and happier than I had ever been. And, I was just a little girl! I couldn't even articulate it. But, I wanted to bottle that feeling up. To this day, I get chills when I see a piece of art that's been created by someone with a vision. Art has always brought me so much joy, so much life, and I knew, even at a young age, I didn't know how, but I wanted to spend my life making myself and others feel this way.

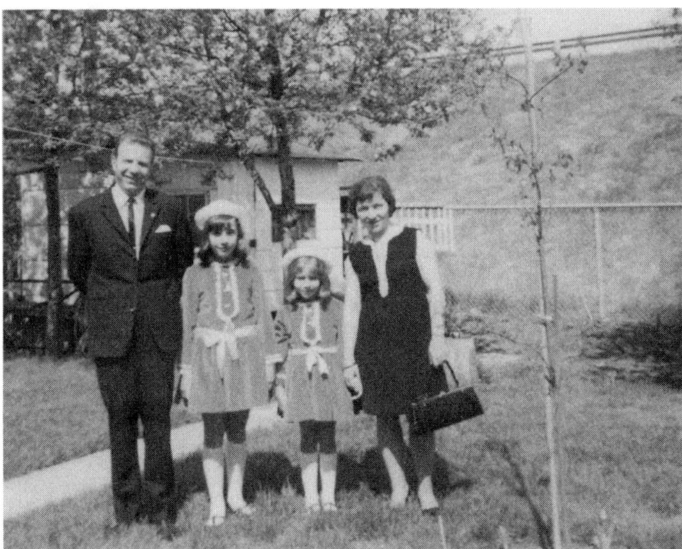

My parents and my sister Sylvia and I, in the sky blue dresses that my mother made, 1970

Armed only with a simple dream to bring beauty to others, I set out, like my father did before me, into uncharted territory and took the biggest risk of my life—to begin my career as an art consultant and gallery owner. My sister Sylvia and I started ADC, Art Design Consultants in 1992. We worked in her small basement. I remember using her washer and dryer as a table for the dry mount press. We had so little, but we made it work, because it's what we had at the time. My first client, Cincinnati Financial Corporation, soon became our best client, and happens to still be a client today.

"Knowing is not enough; we must apply. Being willing is not enough; we must do."
—Leonardo da Vinci

I put in long hours, even as a young mother. Mind you, shortly after starting my company, I had three children in three years. I vividly remember giving clients thirty minute breaks during long art presentations to run to a lactation room. I look back on it now and think, "I was crazy to work that hard." But, I didn't know any different. I just did it. I knew that the work had to be done. As a young entrepreneur with a dream, I didn't think I was doing anything extraordinary. Now, when I see young people working and balancing their career and families—I think to myself, "I don't know how they do it! They're extraordinary!" But, I also realize that when you're in the middle of it, like my father taught me, you do what needs to be done. You do it because people are counting on you.

My girls were counting on me. My husband was counting on me. My employees were counting on me. My clients were counting on me. My artists were counting on me. It's an incredible responsibility. And one I didn't take lightly. Something I learned early on was:

Dreams don't come true without an extraordinary effort by the dreamer.

Growing Pains

In 1993, my sister went back into the fashion industry and I moved out of the basement and into the burgeoning Pendleton Arts Center just north of downtown Cincinnati. For people not from Cincinnati, this was a wonderful warehouse, with many local artists' studios. We initially rented 500 square feet, but by the time we left eighteen years later, we were occupying 14,000 square feet. Those were happy days. We were surrounded by artists' studios. If a client showed up and was looking for something, I could run into a studio and pick a piece to show right on the spot. It was a wonderful environment to get started and to grow. We got to know the artists intimately and it was such an inspiring space. Things seemed to be going as good as they could as we continued to grow.

But on September 29, 2008, everything changed. I remember the day vividly. I was at an art show in Las Vegas. My husband Van and I spent the entire day and night before setting up. All the art was hung, our booth looked superb, and we were ready to sell some art. But, that morning the stock market crashed, and practically no one showed up. I am not exaggerating. The show was a ghost town. Overnight the business world and model I had been operating in (and thriving in) was turned upside down. People panicked. They didn't want to invest in art. Clients that I once counted on for sales put a hold on purchasing art—in fact, many were laying off employees. Interior designers and architects were getting laid off as well. Instantly, many of my clients were all but gone. **It was a scary time.**

"Renew your passions daily."
—Terri Guillemets

I knew I had two options:

1) I could quit. I could close my doors and congratulate myself on a job well done while it lasted and move on. (*But what about my employees? What about my artists? My clients who still needed me? I thought.)*

2) I could use this downturn as a chance to get better, to grow emotionally, give back to others, and in the meantime even improve my business.

Come on, you know what option I picked!

I wouldn't be writing this book right now if I had quit. You could say I bet the ranch on myself and my dream. I doubled down. I cashed in all of my savings, and decided this was the best time to buy a bigger, better, more growth-friendly place. It would be a place that would give people the shivers when they walked in and saw all the beautiful art showcased.

In 2009, I took a dingy, old freight elevator up an abandoned building that had its windows bricked-in. I am sure the realtor, owner, and everyone around me, for that fact, thought I was certifiably crazy. But, what I saw was pure potential. I, like my mother, like all artists do, realized I could create something beautiful out of nothing. The space was dirty and dark, but as I stood there, I imagined windows that overlooked the city. I imagined large moveable white walls displaying gorgeous works of art. I imagined a frame shop. I could see employees sitting in tastefully appointed furniture working. I imagined being able to help these employees live a meaningful and purposeful life—doing great work, in a great space, for an income that would allow them to support their own families. My heart could burst when I thought of the possibilities.

"That which does not kill me makes me stronger."

—Friedrich Nietzsche

I used every bit of my savings making the 10,000 square foot space something beautiful. We added HVAC, electricity, near floor-to-ceiling windows, and lighting. We painted it. We furnished it. We installed the art. When it was completed, it was beyond all of my wildest dreams. And every day, when I walk in here, I still can't believe it's real, and that I still get to work here—that this is my business, my life's work.

But, building a gallery space alone wouldn't bring clients. I knew that. So I invested in talented employees, a new website, in marketing, in a blog, and building a client list. I started from the ground up. And in many cases I learned by trial and error. Those were some tough years. For three years I went without a paycheck and was working long days, but I was determined to keep the gallery open and pay my employees. I knew that great sacrifice always pays off. I saw it before. I saw it when my dad and mom left everything they knew and loved to travel to America to build a better life for their family. If it worked for them, it would work for me.

And, eventually it did. Seven years later, we're bigger than we've ever been. I have a motivated team, represent hundreds of artists, and we're ranked in the top 2 percent of all women-owned businesses. And in 2013, I was awarded "Woman Owned Business of the Year." Our beautiful gallery is now rented out as a space to host charity events, corporate meetings, and even weddings.

Just like wearing a handmade, pearl-embossed dress once did, my gallery makes me extraordinarily happy.

My Hope for You, Reader

Like I've said, I have always felt incredibly blessed and lucky to live the life I have. Not a moment has gone by that I don't stop and say: ***Wow! Thank you!*** So many people, beginning with my parents, of course, have helped me along the way. As a wife, mother, sister, daughter, and friend, I've also benefitted from countless moments of service and love from the people I hold dearest to my heart. As a business owner, I know, without a shadow of doubt, I couldn't be where I am today without the exceptional skills, talents, and dedication of my incredible team. And of course, there are all the artists that inspire me every day to promote and sell their beautiful and jaw-dropping work to my valued clients, who, in turn, are driven to create beautiful, art-filled spaces. I am so overwhelmed with gratitude for every single person who has walked along with me on this twenty-five-year journey. So when I was thinking about how I might celebrate or mark the occasion of ADC's Silver Anniversary, I immediately thought: *I want to give back to those who have inspired me over the years.* I want to give something to all the artists—emerging artists, mid-career artists, established arts—and anyone else seeking to also follow their passion.

By believing passionately in something that does not yet exist, we create it.

—Nikos Kazantzakis

So what could I give? What could I possibly offer artists, visionaries, and would-be world-changers?

Throw a party? (Sure that would be fun. And I will do it, but still I want something that would last a little longer than a one-night celebration.)

Send thank you cards? Yes, but they don't quite seem to say it all.

Then it hit me: I know what I can do. I can share something:

MY PASSION.

I have so much. *I mean, can you feel it right now?* I hope so. I get up every single morning, just so excited to share what I do for a living with others. I eat, sleep, and dream art. I imagine ways I can get more artists in my family of artists. I imagine ways I can get more of their art into the hands of designers, collectors, corporations, hotels, and hospitals. I imagine all the ways to make the places people live and work more beautiful, and in the end, happier. And, yes, I imagine all the ways I can help artists be better, more profitable, more prepared for the less glamorous side of the art world—the business of art.

This passion is something I wish I could bottle up and sell. But, I know I don't need to. I know that every single person reading this book right now has that passion inside them too.

Something beyond you is driving you to get up in the morning. Driving you to create. Driving you to be the artist you are. Driving you to read this book. *(Please tell me! Tell me how to do it! I just want it soooooooo badly.)*

You understand passion. You get passion. You have passion. The reason you're an artist is because there is no other way of life that you can possibly imagine.

There is no greatness without a passion to be great, whether it's the aspiration of an athlete or an artist, a scientist, a parent, or a businessperson."

— Anthony Robbins

I want to sit here with you a while and celebrate that passion that is uniquely, yet ubiquitously yours—this God-given force that connects us all. I want to celebrate that force that has single-handedly saved the planet many times over. Where there is art, there is hope. I also want to help you harness your passion, remind you of that passion (when the inevitable obstacles get in the way), and help you make a living off of your passion.

I know, I know it's scary you say. *Easy for you to say, you have a job, Litsa.* You're not an artist, you say.

Let me tell you, I hear you. Loud and clear. And, whoa, have I been there. I know what it is like to feel a calling so deeply within and wanting badly to share it with the world. I also know well the fear of rejection. The impossible demands on one's time. I also know dedication, sacrifice, and yes, dear ones, let's be real here, *money,* that it takes to make your passion come to life.

So, that's where I come in.

I am here.

I can help.

This book can help.

So How Can this Book Help Supercharge Your Art Career?

Over the years, I have seen it all (and as I write this, I am seeing plenty that I haven't seen yet—so you see, I'm still learning). So I am in a good place to recommend a few things that I know will work to help you create, sell, or manage your art—whatever stage you're at in your career. I also happen to know so many wonderful people—artists, gallery owners, collectors, designers, publishers, trade show exhibit owners, and many more. In fact, many of these fine people agreed to collaborate with me on writing this book. So you'll not only read sound advice from me, but from a number of experts who have breadth and range of experience that neither I nor any one human could possibly possess. Collectively, you're not only getting information from a twenty-five-year veteran art consultant and gallerist, but countless years of experience from a variety of people—who, like me, have also learned a few things along the way.

"The most powerful weapon on earth is the human soul on fire."
—Ferdinand Foch

This book is structured so that depending on what stage you're at— emerging (i.e., just graduating from high school, college, an MFA program or even just deciding after years of sitting behind a desk that you'd rather be standing in front of a canvas), mid-career, but not the sales you're hoping for (like you're sitting next to a pile of pieces that you just can't seem to get in the hands of paying clients), or successful, but ready to up your game and build a legacy or better brand—you can access the info you need here in this book.

For example, if you're just starting out, best to start with Chapter One. It's going to help you identify your goals, your passion, your abilities, and most importantly, it can, if you're ready, help direct you toward the steps you need to be taking today to transition into a career as an artist. It will even include a list of resources, websites, and action steps for you to record and hold yourself accountable. For many of you seasoned professionals, you might want to skip this part. However, there are those of you out there who might benefit from a little refresher or some inspiration. In each section you'll hear from artists, gallery owners, and other appropriate experts who have valuable tips and insights that you may not want to miss.

"Your time is limited, so don't waste it living someone else's life."

—Steve Jobs

Chapter Two is for everyone. I've seen a lot of artists crash and burn over the years, and not from lack of passion or business acumen, rather it's lack of self-care, lack of discipline, and in many cases, the inability to accept criticism, ask for help, or let go of long-held, negative mindsets about selling art. Even the most advanced artist might benefit from a refresher here—and it may be helpful to hear what other artists do to stay inspired, healthy, and working.

Chapter Three is where we get down to business. In the past couple of decades, a lot has changed in the way artists share and sell their work, and every year there is a new platform to showcase (and compete) with other artists to sell your work. I am going to walk you through every single step of the process—from pricing your art to who to network with, who to talk to, who to submit work to, and how to keep tabs on your expenses—along with tips on bookkeeping software.

Finally, in Chapter Four, I am going to take on the big, giant, insane world of social media, branding, marketing, blogging, direct selling, and client-maintenance. Most artists cringe when I bring these painful, but necessary lessons up. It's a brave, new world. And cutting off your ear to get a little attention isn't going to work (unless you upload it onto YouTube and share an Insta with a hashtag, that is). Wait. What? Didn't understand any of that? No worries, you will after you've read Chapter Four. I've got you covered.

Finally, the Conclusion will wrap up some loose ends and then point you to some final action steps.

The entire point of this book is to help you, inspire you, and get you to where you were destined to be—where the passion that lives inside of you is taking you. My passion has taken me so far in this life, and I know, with a little help, it can take you to where you want to go too.

You're on your way, let me help you get there.

First Steps

What's Your Passion? What makes you excited? What is it that you do, create, or imagine that makes you happy? Spend some time here thinking about what excites you or what you're most curious about. *Write about it here:*

Now I want you to visualize yourself creating art. What do you see? Where are you working on? What do you look like? How do you feel? What is the feeling you're trying to create in this space? ***Describe it here:***

Where do you see yourself in a year? In five years? In ten? I want you to envision this in the most inspired and bold way. Don't hold back. Don't think about obstacles right now. I don't want you thinking about your day job. I want you to **DREAM BIG.** ***Describe your future self here:***

If you'd like, draw it:

"We all have 10,000 bad drawings in us. The sooner we get them out the better."

—Walt Stanchfield

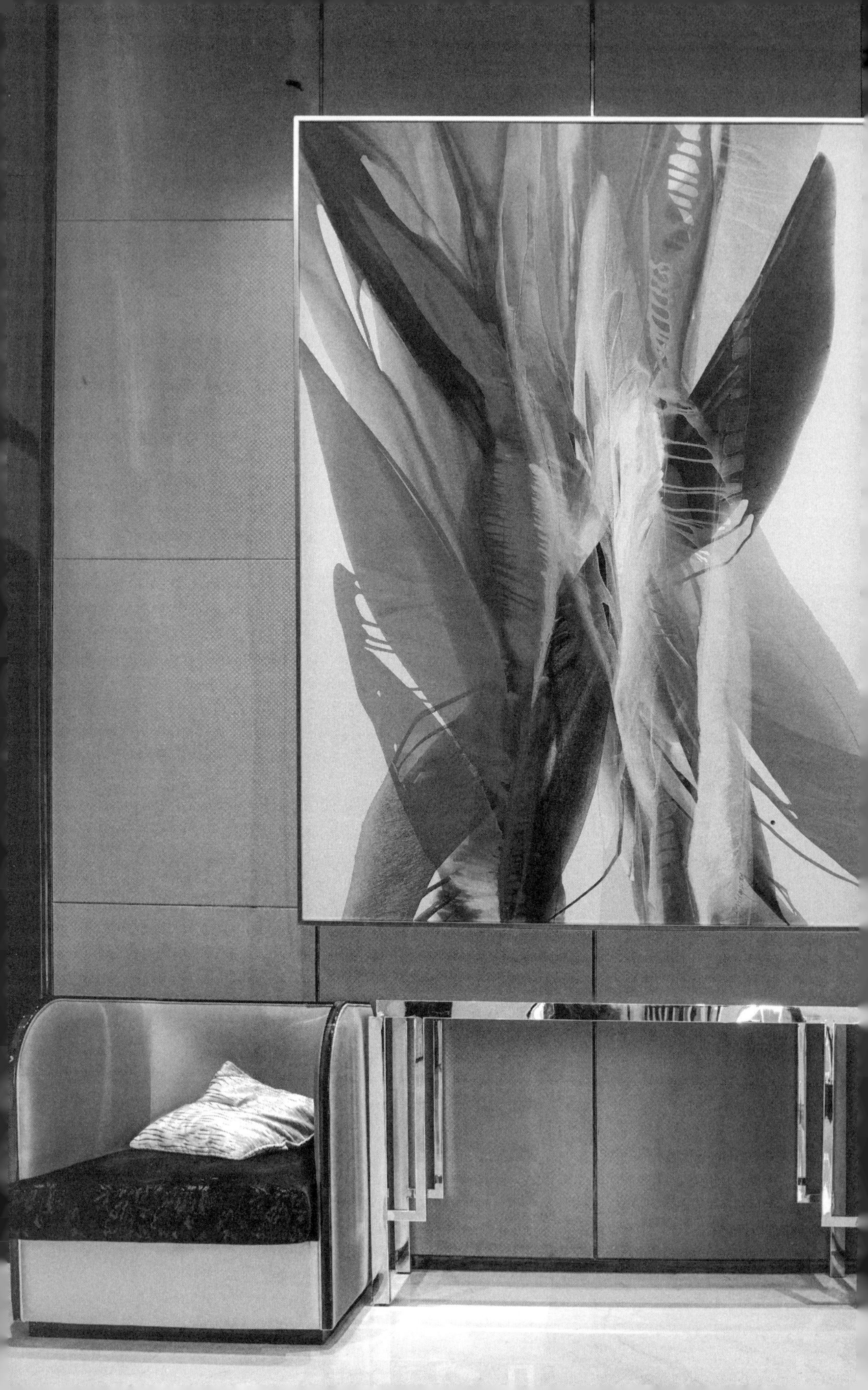

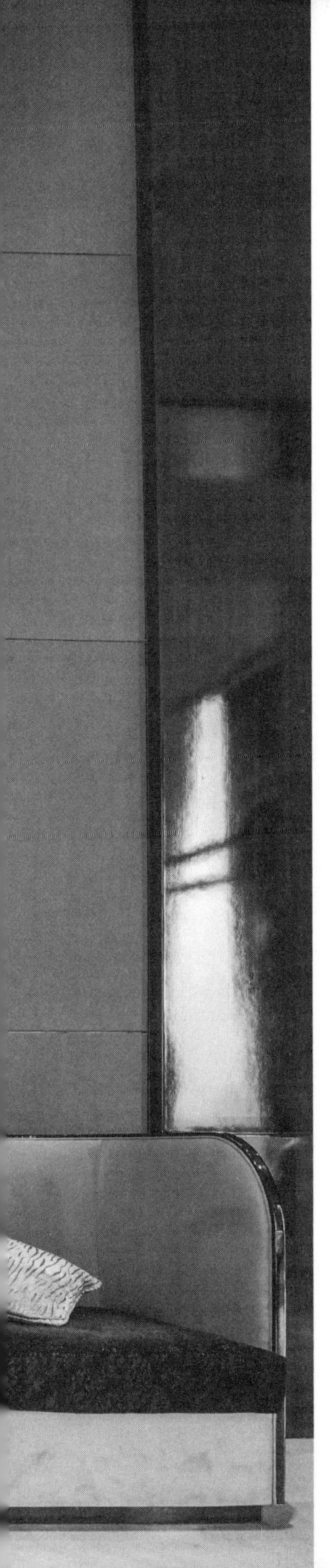

*“The **scariest** moment is* ALWAYS *just before you start.”*

— Stephen King

Artist: Bette Ridgeway

chapter one

SO YOU'RE AN ARTIST

“DON’T ASK YOURSELF WHAT THE WORLD NEEDS; ASK YOURSELF WHAT MAKES YOU COME ALIVE. AND THEN GO AND DO THAT. BECAUSE WHAT THE WORLD NEEDS IS PEOPLE WHO HAVE COME ALIVE.”

— Howard Thurman

What's Your Dream

At the end of the introduction, I asked you to think about your ideal life. I wanted you to visualize it. I wanted you to see it. I wanted you to feel it.

Now, I need you to believe it. I need you to believe it's totally possible and within reach—if you're willing to do the work, take the necessary steps, and move toward the life you've imagined for yourself.

I need you first, and foremost, to believe that your dreams, your passion, your desires are no less valuable or more important than anyone else's. You need to believe that you were created to create—to bring something amazing and miraculous into this world. That is your purpose. That is your destiny. You already know what it is, because you're passionate about it. Those incredibly exhilarating feelings you get when you think about doing what you want to do—that's your passion, that's your reason for being here on the planet Earth.

Now that you feel it in your bones, I need you to shift your mindset to a positive one.

Repeat after me: *I can do it. I can do it. I can do it.* **I can and will.**

Yes, other people are ahead of you. Newsflash: There will always be someone better than you, ahead of you, richer than you, more successful, more famous. And guess what? That means someone is also behind you, poorer than you, less successful, less well known.

You need to reframe any of your current thinking you have around being an artist, especially notions that are negative, hopeless, or down-right false into something positive. Let me guess, over the years you've been told a few of the following bits of advice from well-meaning people:

There's no money in art.

Better have lots of back up plans.

Enjoy being broke, hungry, and miserable.

All artists suffer for their art.

People who sell their work to anyone other than big name galleries are sellouts.

If you want to create art, you need a wealthy donor.

If you want to be successful, you have to work constantly and give up any hope of a real life.

Get comfortable waiting tables for a living.

Am I on to something? Have you been told similar things? Here, get it all out, write down all the nonsense you've been told about being an artist, go ahead. It's just between you and me:

Wow, that's a lot of negative energy out there. Feel better? Probably not. Just writing those things brings me down. So where do we go from here?

We need to move beyond all the lies we've been told when it comes to art. It's my firm belief—no, more than belief—I *know* this, because I have experienced it and witnessed it for myself time and time again: What you believe will become reality. If you have negative thoughts, you'll attract negative outcomes. If you have positive thoughts, you'll have positive outcomes. So you're right if you say you need to suffer, be poor, and never sell in your lifetime in order to be a "true artist," that's exactly what you'll do. But, you'll also be right if you start thinking in a different way:

> *There's lots of money in art. Demand is high for authentic and beautiful work.*
>
> *There is a place for me and my art in this world.*
>
> *It's okay if I have a day job to support my passion. My passion sustains me. Fuels me.*
>
> *I don't have to be miserable, broke, or hungry to be con sidered a "real artist."*
>
> *I don't need to suffer daily for my art. Life has its own way of bringing enough suffering. I don't need to make it any worse with my attitude toward my work.*

I think I'd like to sell my work—to anyone who appreciates it—not just big-name galleries. Because, I believe what I do adds value to the world, and if someone out there wants it, then who am I to prevent that?

Having wealthy supporters is a wonderful thing, and good for people who have them, but it's not necessary for me to create every day.

If I truly want to be successful, I need to have balance in my life—there is space and time—for all that I hope to achieve.

I don't have to settle for anything less than the life I hope to achieve, but that being said, I am willing to do what needs to be done in the meantime, even if that means waiting tables.

Okay now your turn. I don't want you to be Pollyanna. I want you to be real here. Honest. I want you to think about some of the negative thoughts you have (look at your list above) and now I want you to think about them in a positive way. I assure you, when you have positive thoughts you'll have positive feelings, and with positive feelings, you can take positive actions.

What action do you want to take?

There. *Now do you feel better?* I certainly do. Reframing the negative has always brought me peace and serenity. And it's definitely brought me success. I've also seen it work wonders on the artists I work with daily. Now that you have a positive mindset, you're ready to roll up your sleeves and get to work.

Do You Have What It Takes?

"Energy and persistence conquer all things."

—Benjamin Franklin

This isn't a trick question. I think there is a definite mindset that determines if one is prepared to be an artist, which in reality, is no different than an entrepreneur. I believe the same skills that are required to take risks and run a profitable business are the same for an artist. If you're reading this book, you've most likely defined yourself as an artist already. You're comfortable with, or getting comfortable with the idea of, telling people you create for a living. If this is the case, then you're well on your way. Now I want you to start thinking of yourself as an entrepreneur too. **All artists are entrepreneurs.** In fact, there are similar traits that I've seen in the most successful artists and entrepreneurs.

They both seem to be:

1. **Big Thinkers.** They have the ability and audacity to think big.
2. **Fearless.** They know that the path to greatness comes with obstacles, and they're not afraid to go after them, or take a road not taken before.
3. **Risk-takers.** They're comfortable leaving the safety of dry land to set sail on unchartered waters. They know that the rewards of discovery far outweigh the risk of not doing anything at all.
4. **Adaptable.** They aren't afraid of change.
5. **Resilient.** They accept failure as a part of the process and aren't thwarted by obstacles.

6. **Offbeat.** They aren't afraid to be different. Assimilating into a crowd is not their thing.
7. **Lifelong Learners.** They're not afraid to ask for help or seek advice from a mentor. They enjoy learning, taking classes, shadowing others, and don't pretend to have all the answers.
8. **Resourceful.** They don't accept that having little to no money is an excuse. They figure out ways to survive and thrive, often leveraging their skills and talents to make ends meet.
9. **Persistent.** They persevere no matter what. No is just a word. It doesn't stop them from doing the work that needs to be done.
10. **Committed.** They are fully invested in their work. They make a commitment to their clients or their employees or themselves, and they never break it. They don't procrastinate or put off what needs to be done. They show up and do the work.
11. **Strong.** They have the fortitude to keep going despite being tired and to work through any difficulty.
12. **Problem-Solvers**. They both seem to be able to think things through and make adjustments as necessary. Throwing their arms up and saying, "It can't be done," is not in the artist's or entrepreneur's repertoire.
13. **Passionate.** They don't do anything in life without enthusiasm, especially what they love.
14. **Energetic.** They are constantly seeking fuel for their creative fires. They seek out energetic people, culture, music, art, and environments that recharge and sustain them.
15. **Grateful.** They are well aware that their talents are God-given and their skills are unique and therefore a necessity in this world. They believe whole-heartedly in giving back.

If you find yourself nodding and saying, *Yes, that's me! I am most of those things!* Then you're well on your way. However, if you found yourself saying things, like: *I am not fearless. I am a bundle of nerves! Or, I hate failure! I can't handle rejection! Or I hate change. Why can't things just stay the same!* Well, there is hope for you too. We all have our "issues." Each and every one of us struggles—whether it's with rejection, procrastination, organization, or even validating our own self-worth, is beside the point. I don't expect you to say yes to every single one of those qualities of artists and entrepreneurs. Heck, I have my own challenges. One of the things I struggle with every day is self-doubt. *Am I doing enough? Am I giving enough? Am I doing the best I can?* I think all artists struggle with self-doubt. I think we're all our own worst critics. No one can say anything more horrible or vicious to me than what I've already thought and said about myself. It's crazy! I know it, and yet, I do it. I do it because it's natural. I do it because I am an artist and an entrepreneur. We, as a group, are preternaturally disposed to want to be better, strive for more, and to do our best. It's also the thing that propels me forward, moves me toward my best self. I know I can't be all things to all people every day of the year—it's physically and statistically impossible. It's okay to have self-doubt, but you have to channel it in productive ways. You can't let it paralyze you or your work. I have seen artists with thousands of paintings in their body of work. *Thousands.* Is every one of

"Be yourself — not your idea of what you think somebody else's idea of yourself should be."
—Henry David Thoreau

their pieces amazing? Absolutely not. They might have just one or two outstanding or noteworthy pieces. Does that make them failures? Less than artists? Absolutely not! In order to get to those one or two extraordinary pieces, the artist had to paint 1,000 pieces. It all adds up. The good days and the bad days add up. It's cumulative. You aren't going to be fearless every day. But, all you need are a few moments of fearlessness to break away from unhealthy patterns or behaviors, and you're well on your way. You may not be a risk-taker by nature, but it only takes one risk—showing a painting to someone for the first time, submitting artwork to an exhibition or a gallery owner, or making a call to a mentor—to prove that you are one after all. You may be a procrastinator, but with a little scheduling and built-in, fail-safe maneuvers, you might just become one of the most committed artists at work today. Our weaknesses are where our greatest opportunities for growth and potential await us. (I will go into more depth about process in Chapter Two, but it's the mindset I want you to be aware of right now.)

"Enthusiasm is one of the most powerful engines of success. When you do a thing, do it with all your might. Put your whole soul into it. Stamp it with your own personality. Be active, be energetic and faithful, and you will accomplish your object. Nothing great was ever achieved without enthusiasm."
—Ralph Waldo Emerson

Now I want you to think about the above list of qualities that are essential in every artist and entrepreneur. I want you to complete each sentence below. All you have to do is think of one time when you exemplified the trait. (If you can think of more, write about those times too). Now sure, I know, doing something ONE time does not make you an expert, but I want you to recognize aspects of your personality that you may have not valued before or given their due respect. You may have gone your entire life thinking, "I'm not a big thinker. I am a details person." But, try saying, "I am a big thinker because this one time I thought of…." And see what happens. Getting yourself to think of examples will lead to more examples and will eventually rewire your brain and help you rethink some outdated ideas you may have of yourself.

I am a big thinker, because this one time I…

I am fearless, because this one time I….

I am a risk-taker, because this one-time I...

I am adaptable, because this one time I…

I am resilient, because this one time I…

I am offbeat, because this one time I…

I am a lifelong learner, because this one time I…

I am resourceful, because this one time I…

I am persistent, because this one time I…

I am committed, because this one time I….

I am strong, because this one time I….

I am a problem-solver, because this one time I….

I am passionate, because this one time I….

I am energetic, because this one time I…

I am grateful, because this one time I…

Now look at this list and read it over a couple of times. Where there any traits you struggled to find an example? If so, where do you feel you have opportunities to grow?
Write them here:

Now look at the previous list of opportunities to grow. I want you to write down at least one thing you can do, if not today, in the coming weeks to help you grow. (For example, if you see you lack commitment, perhaps suggest setting a timer for twenty minutes to work each day this week. If you lack gratitude, reach out to someone who might need some encouragement or help.) Make your suggestions doable and manageable. Don't set yourself up for more failure and self-recrimination.

Write your suggestion for self-improvement here:

Taking the Leap of Faith

"Why do you stay in prison when the door is so wide open?"

—Rumi

Once you've made the decision to call yourself an artist, you have to start living like one. That means you have to, gulp, start creating art regularly and consistently. One of the most prosperous artists I know shows up to his studio at the same time every day, stays all day, and quits at the same time each night. He has developed a habit and a schedule that works for him. He takes his work just as seriously as he takes his clients. Many people have the perception that an artist's life is "easy," but most working artists know that it is anything but. Artists have to get out of bed and work just like the rest of the population. Sure they love what they do, but its work. Make no mistake. And, sometimes it's work that doesn't pay—for years.

I also know artists who maintain full-time jobs—with insurance, benefits, and regular hours—raise children, take care of their aging parents, and they take their art no less seriously than those engaged with it full-time. It may mean setting the alarm for 4 or 5 a.m., and working for two hours before having to shower and get ready for work. Or it may mean, coming straight home from work and working for two hours. It also means sacrifice. As I said before, you can't be all things to all people all day every day. Some things have to go. It may be television shows, it may be reading for pleasure, it may be visiting with a group of friends regularly, for a time. You have to make the decision what is the most important thing in your life and what is the least. Prioritizing is essential. Just for the sake of it, I'd like you to list the activities you normally do in a day. Fill it out as precisely as you can. Include when you wake, eat, fritter away time on social media, work, etc. I want you to be absolutely honest with yourself. No one else is going to read this. No one is judging you.

Assess your time and how you're spending it right now:

5 a.m. ____

6 a.m. ____

7 a.m. ____

8 a.m. ____

9 a.m. ____

10 a.m. ____

11 a.m. ____

12 p.m. ____

1 p.m. ____

2 p.m. ____

3 p.m. ____

4 p.m. ____

5 p.m. ______________________________

6 p.m. ______________________________

7 p.m. ______________________________

8 p.m. ______________________________

9 p.m. ______________________________

10 p.m. ______________________________

11 p.m. ______________________________

12 a.m. ______________________________

Now that you've done that, I'd like you to go over that list with a marker and delete what you don't need to be doing. I want you to be merciless, as if your life (your art) is depending on it. Is there an hour, just one hour, where you can start? When you're finished, write down a time of day (and duration, one hour, two) that you're willing to commit to working for the next thirty days:

Now list the thing you will give up in order to ensure that the time commitment is met.

Write it here:

Promise yourself a reward for sticking to the schedule for 30 days straight. (Examples might be: An hour of reality television, a fancy coffee, a new journal, or paintbrush).

Write the reward here:

A Word about Gratitude—The Most Essential Quality of Every Artist and Entrepreneur

"Acknowledging the good that you already have in your life is the foundation for all abundance."

—Eckhart Tolle

I know I mentioned earlier in the introduction that in 2008, my company suffered a massive setback during the recession. I took some huge risks, but I did something else that I didn't mention earlier. During that time, I decided that it was time to refocus my energy and use my time to begin to give back. I had learned so much and I felt I had so much to share and give. I was also feeling the need, a deep calling, to reach out and help others. As it always does in life, a strange series of fortunate accidents, led me to cross paths with someone who would need my help at the time. During an event I was hosting, I was introduced to Joules Evans, a breast cancer survivor who subsequently introduced me to a beautiful young woman named Vanessa Tiemeier, who was afflicted with terminal breast cancer. They needed help with finding a venue and a partner to support something I had never heard of—the Scar Project. Well, little did I know that our conversation that night would turn into a life-changing friendship and the opportunity to participate in an amazing project that celebrates and honors the incredible journey faced by young women who suffer from breast cancer.

"One person with passion is better than forty people merely interested."
—E. M. Forster

Over the next several months, I worked with Joules and Vanessa and my friend Pam Irvin to bring the Scar Project here to Cincinnati, and even hosted the exhibition in our gallery.

We invited the amazingly talented photographer David Jay to showcase his work. David, who is internationally known for his portraiture, was personally touched by breast cancer, when his good friend was diagnosed at thirty-two years old. He went on to photograph the raw beauty, strength, emotion, and the character of women facing the journey. The result was breathtaking. What he was able to show was not just the effects of the disease on these women, but the scars and pain that unite us all. We are all, truly, in this together.

It breaks my heart to write the next sentence. I can't even do it without crying, but Vanessa passed away a three years ago. She fought so courageously while she was here, and she touched so many lives, mine included. She brought art and beauty and life and love and truth to so many people when they needed it most by bringing the Scar Project to Cincinnati. She definitely

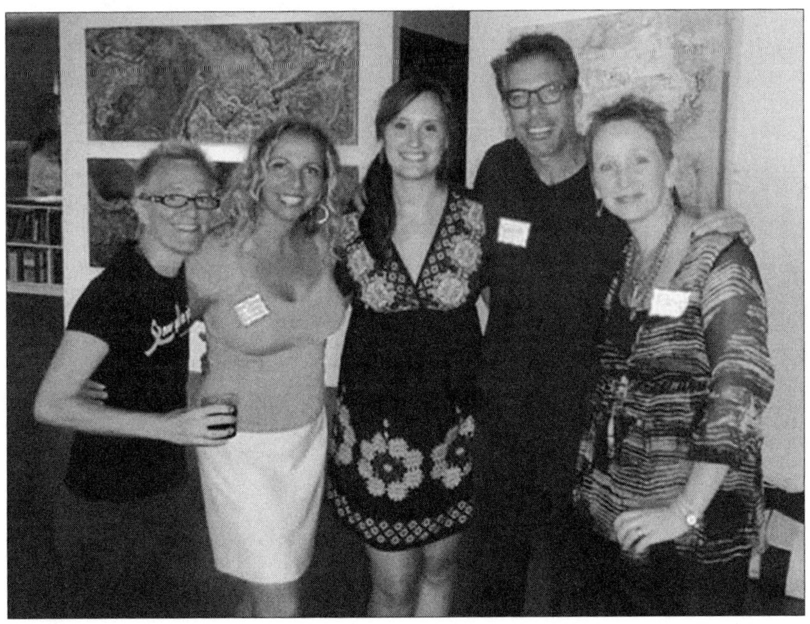

The Scar Project committee: Joules Evans, myself, Vanessa Tiemeier, David Jay and Pam Irvin

impacted my life. She changed the lives of every person who walked through our gallery and was moved by David Jay's portraits of courageous women baring their scars. She gave when she didn't have to. She was an inspiration to me. She showed me that until my dying breath, I too, should give and be grateful for this life, for my health, for my opportunities, my gifts.

We should all show gratitude. We should show it unabashedly. And, we should communicate our gratitude regularly. I try to do it every day, but I also try to go the extra mile whenever I can. I am a gift-giver and write many personal thank you notes. That's how I like to show gratitude. But, that's just one way to show appreciation. I get so much joy from surprising people with well-thought out and personalized gifts and notes. But, there are other ways to give and show gratitude. Volunteering your time, for example, is a good way to give back. One way I give back on a daily basis is I like to point out positive attributes in the people I work with. I don't think it's an accident that I have such a high-performing, loyal, and dedicated team in my gallery. I believe gratitude and appreciation are the secret ingredient. The more I compliment them, the more confident, self-assured, and capable they become. The more I recognize their talents and hard-work, the more they're willing to give. If you want to get more out of your work, your life, your clients, your family, yourself even: You must give, and give often. But, most importantly you should give with joy and love.

"I have no special talents. I am only passionately curious."
—Albert Einstein

Brian Goodman

© Brian Goodman

"Once in a while you get shown the light in the strangest of places if you look at it right."
— Robert Hunter

When I think of an artist's artist, I can think of no one better to introduce you to than Brian Goodman. I discovered his work three years ago when he submitted his work to *Blink Art Resource,* a publication we produce each year featuring artists' work and distribute to galleries and interior designers. I was mesmerized by what he captured, and then after meeting him and getting to know him, I knew it's no accident that he's become such a success in the art world. At first glance, one might say because he's relatively new to the fine art scene, he was an overnight success. But, Brian is anything but.

Brian has been an artist his entire life. He began practicing the art of photography at nine years old. Back then, he was using a Kodak Hawkeye Instamatic that his father, Dick Goodman, gave him. He used it to capture moments and landscapes while on vacation with his family in Yosemite, the Grand Canyon, Yellowstone, and throughout the Pacific Northwest. His father was his first "collector" and framed and hung his prized pictures in his childhood home. His mother and father's pride and enthusiasm encouraged Brian to pursue photography in college, where he studied fine art photography and photojournalism.

After college, Brian moved away from fine art and photojournalism and began to take on commercial assignments. He opened his first commercial studio in 1987 in the converted garage in his backyard before moving into a larger space in a local industrial park. In 1992, he was recruited by Mamiya America and Leaf Systems to demonstrate the premier of the Leaf Digital Camera Back at the acclaimed international photographic trade show, Photokina, in Cologne, Germany, subsequently becoming a regular beta tester and demonstrator for Leaf, Mamiya America, and Sinar-Bron at future Photokina and other trade shows, as well as in studio. Within the next few years, Brian became one of the first professional adapters of digital technology for commercial photography, with his studio, Public Works Productions, being the first fully-integrated digital commercial studio on the West Coast. Brian and his wife, Shira, purchased their own 6,000 square foot studio building in 1999, never thinking they could ever fill the vast space. But over the next thirty years, Brian's business easily grew into the studio space, as he served major clients from Westwood One Companies, Apple Computers, University of California Los Angeles, Kaiser Permanente, Disney Records, Nissan USA, Toyota USA, El Al Israel Airlines, Neutrogena, L.A. Eyeworks, Classic Custom Vacations, United Signature Foods, Pacific Asia Museum, Brighton Collectibles and others. He worked seven days a week, managing his business and his employees, as he continued learning his craft and building his reputation in the industry. Eventually, his company would become the leader in the field of digital commercial photography.

But during this time, Brian never abandoned his first love—fine art photography. He applied all that he had learned from his commercial photography experience and began to experiment with his personal photographs. Always fascinated with the visual interplay between light color and texture, Brian captured evocative photos that expressed the raw emotion of the scene, the subtlety and complexity of movement, and the dance and playfulness of light. In a word: ***MAGIC.***

But, how did Brian make the leap? How could he give up a profitable business (in other words, steady income) and become a full time fine art photographer? He said the decision was made for him—in more ways than one. He had done it all, seen it all, and accomplished all he wanted to professionally. On the one hand, he was ready to make the change. On the other he knew it was a risk. But, he followed the signs. When one of his clients who provided his company with the majority of his business decided to "go in a different direction," Brian knew this was the time to seize his moment. It was now or never. Without a major client to answer to, Brian could start planning his exit from the commercial photography world and concentrate on being the fine art photographer he had always wanted to be.

Now, one would think that the transition from commercial photographer to fine art photographer would have been easy, but, nothing is ever as easy as it seems. While the commercial gig helped hone Brian's skills as a photographer and businessman, there were aspects of the fine art world he wasn't prepared for. "In the commercial world people have a definite need to market their goods, whatever they may be. The company needs to market and sell the product. So they come to me to photograph something for that market," Brian says. "But, fine art is different. It's not something that everyone thinks they need. Most buyers have some sort of disposable income. If they see something they like, they'll purchase it."

In other words, your market is not predetermined or defined. Buying art is also unquantifiable and somewhat spontaneous in its very nature. As Brian points out, "I find that buying art is an 'in the moment' sort of thing. Say you're on vacation and you see something that catches your eye, and you want a memory or it matches your house—you'll buy it then." Being at the whim of the buyer or the collector is a new experience for Brian, but the learning curve has been swift and has leaned toward success. He's learned that getting his work out there and giving it as much exposure as possible only helps. He adds, "My experience at art shows has been that people don't buy as much as I first expected. They come to look and to appreciate. But, I also realize that's just the first step in making the contact." Brian advises getting your work in galleries, being online, using social media, using resources like *Blink Art*, and giving collectors and buyers more opportunities to view or have "contact" with the work. As he points out, "There are a lot of artists doing wonderful work. But, it's not getting noticed. A colleague of mine recommended Blink as an easy way to get something out there in front of people, and it definitely opens doors for me. You have to be out where people can see you. They don't know what they want until they see it. So you have to be in as many places as possible."

Brian's transition from the commercial world to the fine art world is now complete. In 2016, he and his wife moved from their home in California to Port Townsend, Washington, with a full view of the majestic Olympic Mountains. Surrounded by local artists and annual festivals, Brian hopes the environment will encourage and inspire him as well as avail himself to more exposure. His studio is once again in his backyard, but this time in a 1,500 square foot barn, converted into a fully-equipped professional studio. He also has plans to build a gallery on his property in the near future where he will showcase his own work, as well as the work of local artists.

When I asked him what his advice was to other artists seeking to replicate his success story, he simply said, "Love what you're doing. That desire and that love will get you up every morning. And if you're good at what you do, you're going to produce beautiful work, and people are going to want it."

To learn more about Brian and his art, visit www.briangoodmanphotography.com.

© Brian Goodman

Action Steps

1. **Take one risk.** If you're not accustomed to risk, start small. Make a call. Buy a canvas. Tell someone you are an artist. If you're a risk-taker by nature, go big. Maybe it's time to submit that portfolio? Quit your day job? Only you know if it's the right time.

2. **Seek out a mentor.** Offer someone coffee or lunch to pick their brain about their process, or simply follow a blog of a favorite or influential artist.

3. **Commit yourself to a deadline.** Whether it's an exhibition or day when you'd like to have your work reviewed, write down the date and work toward it. Remember, you have only yourself to answer to.

4. **Find a meaningful and personal way to give back.** Allot a certain amount of your working week dedicated to helping someone else, whether it's another struggling artist or a neighbor in need. It doesn't matter who you help, it's that you do help. It's that you think for a moment how blessed you are, and remind yourself of how extraordinary your own gifts and talents are, and how useful they are to others. Do not overthink it, there are people in need everywhere. Start close to home. Do what you can, where you can, for however long you can.

Further Reading on Living Life as Artist and Entrepreneur

Big Magic: Creative Living Beyond Fear by Elizabeth Gilbert

Do the Work: Overcome Resistance and Get Out of Your Own Way by Steven Pressfield

How to Be an Artist Without Losing Your Mind, Your Shirt, or Your Creative Compass by JoAnneh Nagler

The Artist's Way: A Spiritual Path to Higher Creativity by Julia Cameron

Getting into the Vortex: Where the Law of Attraction Assembles All Relationships by Esther and Jerry Hicks

10% Happier: How I Tamed the Voice in My Head, Reduced Stress Without Losing My Edge, and Found Self-Help That Actually Works--A True Story by Dan Harris

Manifesting 1, 2, 3... and You Don't Need #3: How Thought Works and the Simple Tools to Create the Desires of Your Lifetime by Ken Elliott

Charities and Projects to Investigate

The Scar Project: www.thescarproject.org

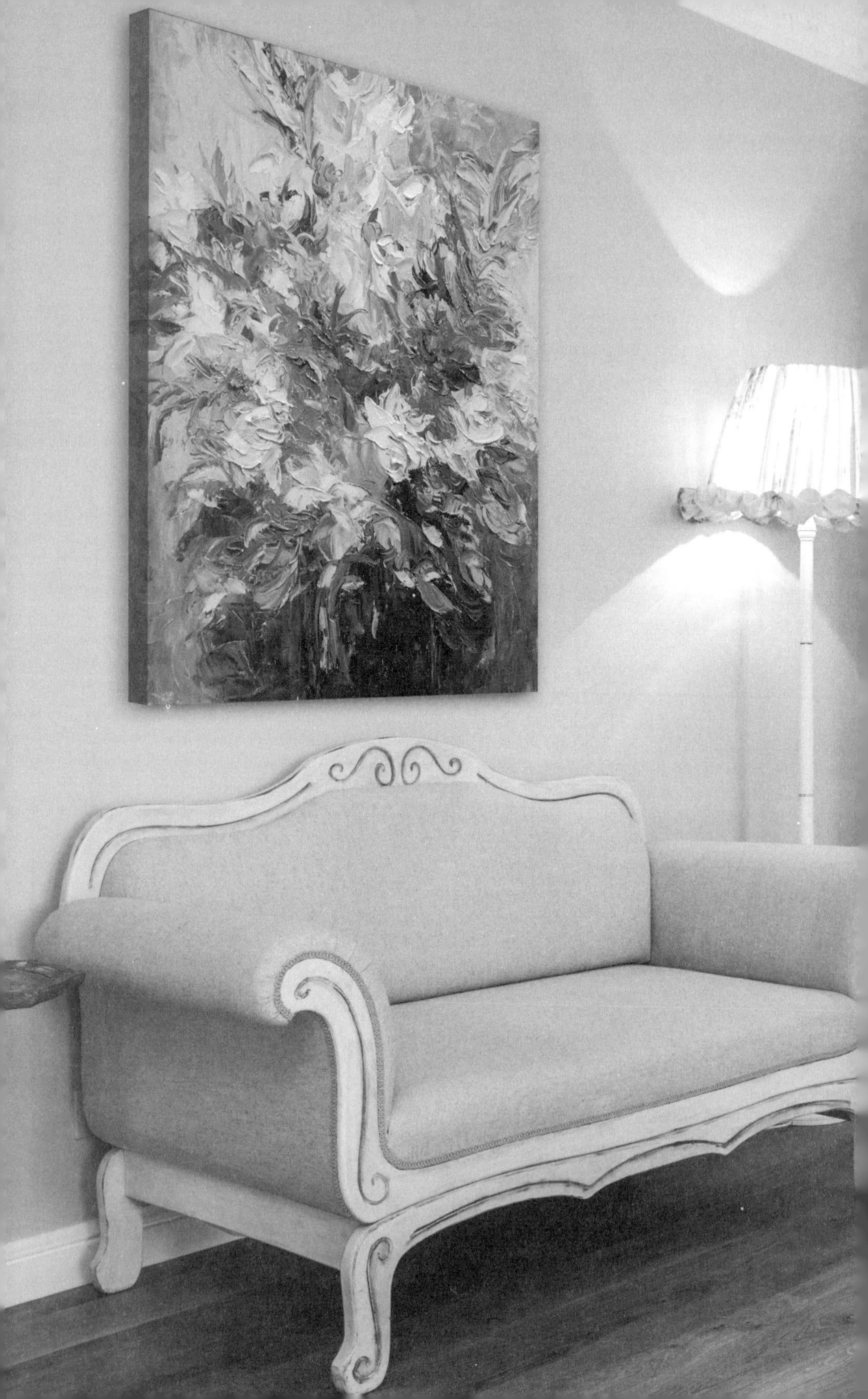

"Inspiration comes and goes, ***creativity*** *is the result of practice."*

— Phil Cousineau

Artist: Karen Rolfes

chapter two

YOU'RE A WORKING ARTIST, NOW WHAT?

"TO PRACTICE ANY ART, NO MATTER HOW WELL OR BADLY, IS A WAY TO MAKE YOUR SOUL GROW. SO DO IT."

— Kurt Vonnegut

The Most Important Secret

"Positive thinking is more than just a tagline. It changes the way we behave. And I firmly believe that when I am positive, it not only makes me better, but it also makes those around me better."

—Harvey Mackay

Over the years I have had the distinct pleasure to work with hundreds of professional artists. I have seen many succeed and I have watched many struggle. As exhilarating as it is to watch artists' careers soar, it's equally heart-breaking to witness talented artists lose faith, hope, or inspiration and eventually give up altogether. But, perhaps the most difficult thing to witness is when an artist, frustrated by their lackluster sales or their perceived lack of time or inspiration, grow embittered and begin to hurl condescending comments toward more profitable artists. Here is just some of the things I've heard over the years:

"They're just lucky!"

"They're hacks! My work is far superior!"

"They're sell outs. I could paint that too, if I wanted to make more money. But, I have 'standards.'" (Said with an air of pretention and a nose held high!)

"I would create that much if I had the time they did!"

"I would be able to do that if I had the income they did!"

Ah, unfortunately the list goes on. I wish I could say I haven't heard these things. And more than that I wish I could say that the people who thought these things made a complete turnaround, saw the error of their ways, and started to produce and sell art.

But, alas, no. That's not how this works. *That's not how any of this works.* Here's what I do know that works. First of all, you have to have the "right" attitude. Yes, I am going out on a very shaky limb here to earn your trust as a reader, and now saying without a doubt, there is a right and a wrong attitude when it comes to approaching your work as an artist. Before I even venture on to talking about process—I need to make this point absolutely clear:

> Without the proper mindset, that of course being a positive one, it doesn't matter what process or work or plan or art you do, you'll never succeed.

What? Did I just say that you won't succeed with a bad attitude?

YES. YES, I DID.

Here's what I believe, no, what I ***KNOW***, after witnessing successful artists earn a living selling their art for the past twenty-five years. This is the most important secret you will ever hear, and if you learn or remember nothing else, is above all you need a completely positive mindset to succeed. If you think it, you can do it. Yes, that's a tagline heard 'round the world. Yes, that's the same tagline you'll hear in business schools, and age-old, time-tested self-help books. But, it's an absolute fact.

Here are some other facts:

> If you look for negative outcomes, you'll find them.
>
> If you look for excuses, you'll find them.
>
> If you look for things to criticize—in yourself and others—you'll find them.
>
> If you think every single artist besides you is successful or profitable, you'll be right.
>
> Now, if you switch this up—and, yes, look on the bright side, the outcomes are much different.
>
> If you look for positive outcomes, you'll find them.
>
> If you make no excuses—at all (that means no more saying, "I wish I had more time, more money, more support")—and you're willing to hold yourself 100 percent accountable for your own failure or success, then you'll find the time, the money, and the support.
>
> If you look for things to compliment—in yourself and others—you'll find them.
>
> If you think everyone else is successful or profitable, and so that means you can be too—you'll be right.

This is not easy. This takes a lot of unlearning on your part. As children we're taught to be humble. We're taught not to toot our own horn. However, some of us have taken that all a bit too far, and have become so self-deprecating, it's downright self-destructive. As artists, we are meant to create. We were created in God's image. God was a creator. So we're all creators. Do you think God made you to create negativity, horrible art, and meant for you to suffer endlessly? I don't think so. We are meant to fully embrace and accept ourselves. We are meant to create what's inside us and pour that out and share that with the world. We can't do that if we're telling ourselves lies—that we're no good, we'll never make any money, and that everyone else who does is just a bunch of lucky, no-talented hacks.

"Talent is cheaper than table salt. What separates the talented individual from the successful one is a lot of hard work."
—Stephen King

Coming from a place of lack never helps anyone. We live in an abundant universe with good things flowing constantly. We can all tap into this flow of good and positive energy. There is enough for everyone. Someone else's success doesn't take away your success. Your success doesn't take someone else's success away. Own your own right to be happy, to be successful, to be inspired, to create, and the rest will flow. Below are some of my own tips to help you get to a more positive and uplifted mindset. It's not going to happen overnight. And like it is with your art, it's going to take practice—and mindfulness. You'll have to be vigilant and constantly aware of the thoughts—negative and positive—that you're having. The key is to nip the negative thoughts in the bud and replace them with positive ones as soon as possible (and as often as possible).

Litsa's Not-So-Top-Secret Steps to Think More Positively

1. **Speak kindly—to yourself.** This is fundamental. No more self-doubt, no more vicious thoughts, no more "woe is me" or "why do they have all the fun, get all the money, fame, etc., and not me." Give yourself some positive affirmations. Write them on Post-Its and stick them to your bathroom mirror in your studio. Talk to yourself. Out loud. Often. Say things like: "I am a beautiful, creative soul." Or, "I create beautiful work." Or, "I am a profitable and successful artist." (It doesn't matter that you haven't sold a painting. Convince yourself it's possible. Because, it is. Your thoughts attract outcomes. *Remember that.* Make sure every thought you have is attracting the outcome you desire.)

2. **Avoid negative or toxic behavior and people.** If you're the most negative person in your life, then my friend, you have some work to do with step 1. However, most of us aren't negative "by nature." We have to be taught and/or encouraged. And frankly there are some people who LOVE a good a drama. They feed off of it. They love a sob-story. They love to stoke the embers of rage. They love to revel in the pity party. STAY AWAY. We all have them, those negative-vibe types, who creep in, even on our best day. If you're related to these people, try to gently steer the conversation from the negative. Or just come out and say: "This conversation is becoming too

> **"You must be prepared to work always without applause."**
>
> —Ernest Hemingway

negative. This is not helpful." Then ask how he or she might "reframe" the conversation or problem to be more positive or to find a viable solution. However, if you work with or know chronically negative or unhappy people, keep your conversations short. Remember you're in control of what you put into your mind and body. Don't let others dampen your spirit.

3. **Adopt or practice a belief system or faith.** Now I am not saying you have to join a religion if you're not a part of one (or even believe in God, if you're an atheist). But, you have to adopt a value or belief system in life that will help you feel like you are part of something bigger than yourself. Then ask yourself: Are your beliefs making you a better person? If your beliefs are currently holding you back, keeping you from helping others, reaching out, or even being kind and generous in mind and spirit, then you may have some deep assessing to do.

4. **Think success.** As I said before, what you think, you will do and become. The most successful and happy people I know are optimistic people. They always believe, whether they have $5 dollars in their bank account or $5,000,000, that they're wealthy and have all that they need. They never act like the victim of circumstance either. They just do the work without complaint.

5. **Increase your expectations.** Yes, you read that correctly. In a world that is always reminding us to "manage our expectations" to avoid disappointment, I want you to do the exact opposite. I want to you aspire to greatness. I want you to

expect great things are about to happen at any moment. I want you to believe your life is just beginning. That good things are about to flow in an abundance of ways. Does this mean you won't have bad days? No. Does this mean you won't have disappointments? No. But, it does mean, you're at least open to the flow of positive energy and expectations. What you put out, you will get in return.

6. **Say no less, and yes more!** This is where all that talk of risk comes in. Yes, you need to take some risks. You need to say yes to experiences. Stop saying things like "I don't like… (insert whatever it is you usually say when you say "no" to things). "I don't like crowds." "I don't like all that fresh air." "I don't like that type of music." Instead, try saying, "It might be fun if I go." Or, "I might get inspired and learn something new." "I might meet someone!" Sure enough, if you have these thoughts, you'll most likely have those experiences too.

"I am seeking. I am striving. I am in it with all my heart."

—Vincent van Gogh

7. **Dream big.** Do not put yourself or your life in a box. So many people arrange their lives so they don't have to incur pain, suffering, or disappointment. They manage their expectations. They stay close to home. They criticize other people who do things differently than them. This is all to make oneself feel safe, secure, and in some cases, superior. It's also the best way to ruin one's shot at living the best, most incredible life ever. If you want big success, a big life, or just a life that you can call your own and feel fulfilled, then dream big. Dream and envision what you want your life to be like.

Doing the Work of Positive Living

I'd love for you to start thinking about this life—this life that is totally possible. In order to do so, we have to do a few things.

First things first: Make a list of possible positive affirmations that you can start saying and repeating daily. (Some examples are: "I can do it." "I can create anything I put my mind to." "I have all that I need." "I am happy." "I am healthy." "I love my life.") Think of the feeling you want to have—contentment, fulfillment, security, happiness, joy, bliss, or success—then work your way backward to the thought. What thought will make you feel most successful? What thought will make you feel most alive, most healthy? *Then write these thoughts here or on Post-it notes and place them where you can see them.*

Make a list of your "negativity buddies." (Don't worry, no one is going to see this.) Are you contributing to this behavior? Are you enabling it? Are you being enabled by someone to be negative? Think of ways you can either reframe conversations with this person (or persons) or avoid them altogether without causing any unnecessary harm.

In the words of the late George Michael, "You gotta have faith." Spend some time here thinking about your faith or value system. What do you believe? Are these beliefs holding you back or pushing your forward?

Let's imagine your success. What does success mean to you? What does being a "successful artist" look like to you? *Describe it in detail here:*

Let's talk about your expectations. Where have you limited your expectations in life? Lauren Graham, in her book, *Talking as Fast as I Can* has a great quote about expectations. She said, "…starting off with very low standards is a surefire way to ensure they'll be met." Talk about a time in life when your low standards and low expectations were met? How'd that make you feel? Remember the old adage, "You get what you settle for"? *What if you settled for more?*

What do you usually say "no" to? Are there any things you think you might be able to say "Yes" to this year? *Write about them here.*

Dream big. Go ahead. Sky's the limit. Write about your wildest dreams here—without fearing disappointment, managing expectations, or employing any other self-limiting behavior.

Self-Care and the Artist's Life

"Success is not for the chosen few...but for the few that choose it."

—Sandra Yancy

Show me a successful person and I'll show you someone who is serious about their personal development. As I've been saying, your journey as an artist, especially a successful one, begins by focusing inwardly. We've been talking about making small internal changes and shifts, so that before long, those changes will manifest themselves outwardly with big results.

We've talked about mindset—the importance of positivity, self-reliance, and taking personal responsibility for one's own behavior and success—now I'd like to focus on process and activities that help accomplish and maintain a positive and successful mindset.

I don't think it's an accident or a coincidence that some of the best and most successful artists I know also happen to be healthy and balanced individuals. They take care of themselves and their business and don't fall back on tired excuses, such as "I don't have time for self-care, health, or exercise." Nor do they believe that being self-destructive (especially by being decadent with drugs, alcohol, and food) means they're more dedicated to their life as an artist.

Almost all of the most successful and dedicated artists I have come to know live balanced lives. Over the years, I've gleaned many tips from them myself. And I know for a fact, because I practice these tips, that they indeed improve one's life. Below are some recommendations I have for living a more balanced, healthy, and productive life as an artist.

Litsa's 10 Tips for Higher Performance

1. **Exercise.** I can't emphasize the importance of exercise enough. Most people think, what do I need to be fit for? I paint or sculpt! I am not a marathoner or a professional athlete! I am not saying you have to join a CrossFit gym and schedule your life around your workouts, but what I am saying is you absolutely need to make exercise a non-negotiable part of your daily routine. Whether you prefer walking, running, yoga, dance, aerobic classes, swimming, spin classes, or going to work out on a machine at the gym, it doesn't matter. As long as you do something, anything. Exercise gets the blood flowing in your body. It charges the brain, and naturally cleanses your body from toxins. Countless studies show how exercise is key in fending off anxiety and depression. Depression and anxiety is the death knell of the creative person. By keeping the mind healthy, you'll notice sharpened concentration and more accessible creative visions. Many artists, in fact, recommend going on "artist's walks." It's during the meditative trance of walking, deep breathing, and mind-emptying, that many artists receive creative visions or ideas. I encourage every artist to make walking or exercise an absolute priority every day. Granted, I know it's tempting to roll out of bed and head straight to the computer or studio, but by making time for exercise, you're making time for your art. Don't think of it as a distraction or diversion, consider it a necessary and vital part of the creative

"From 30,000 feet, creating looks like art. From ground level, it's a to-do list."

—Ben Arment

process. And, I know if you say, "I just don't have the time!" I am here to say: Everyone has the same twenty-four hours in the day, and yes, you too can find a few minutes to exercise. In fact, back when my girls were small, I scheduled time each week with a local Pilates instructor. I was working full-time, starting my business, and raising babies, and I made time for fitness. *(Helpful tip: If you find it difficult or intimidating, find a friend who you can walk with or who will keep you accountable. Or set an alarm and a timer, and exercise for a specific time each day.)*

"Write it. Shoot it. Publish it. Crochet it, sauté it, whatever — MAKE IT."
—Joss Whedon

2. **Eat well.** I can't emphasize this enough. (Maybe because I am Greek, I have an edge on this.) But, the Mediterranean diet is no joke. By eating healthy, whole, non-processed foods, rich in Omega-3 fatty acids, dark green leafy vegetables, fresh fish, meats, and oils, as well as fruits, I've managed to maintain my health and weight. Moderation is key too. It's tempting to want to reward yourself with sweets or alcohol, for a long day's work, but consider your treat a healthy, nourishing meal. By eating healthy, you'll have more energy to create. You'll feel better about yourself, and you'll enjoy more healthy days than sick ones throughout the year—all the better to help with your work!

3. **Create a beautiful, inspiring environment to do work.** Again, I am biased here, but I absolutely believe that where you work is crucial to your ability to produce and create. By making your space beautiful, open, tidy, and inspiring, you're creating a space that invites creativity. Now, some people like a cluttered space (and, yes, studies show that

some mess or clutter enhances creatives abilities), but there is a difference between organized and functional clutter and filth. If your space is tired, dirty, cluttered and uninspiring, you're not going to want to show up for work each day. However, if your space makes you feel excited, alive, and energetic, then it is doing exactly what it should do as a space. Some artists believe that their workspace is "sacred" and advise protecting the space from negative energy or people who may bring negative energy into the space. The famed artist, Agnes Martin, once made this recommendation about creating and preserving one's studio:

> ***You must clean and arrange your studio in a way that will forward a quiet state of mind. This cautious care of atmosphere is really needed to show respect for the work. Respect for art work and everything connected with it, one's own and that of everyone else, must be maintained and forwarded. No disrespect, carelessness or ego [and] selfishness must be allowed to interfere if it can be prevented. Indifference and antagonism are easily detected — you should take such people out immediately. Just turning the paintings to the wall is not enough. You yourself should not go to your studio in an indifferent or fighting mood.***

It's not enough that the space is maintained and beautiful, but that the **people and energy** you invite into it as well. Be careful of the negative energy that people bring into the space. Be mindful of every item you have in your studio. Does it distract, depress, or disturb? Or does it inspire, invigorate, or stimulate? Only you know the answer to that. *(Helpful tip: Spend some time working on your work space today. Spend a couple of hours arranging it in an inspiring and work-friendly way.)*

4. **Rest.** I don't need to elaborate here too much. One of the biggest ways to lose your concentration is by not getting enough sleep. You must maintain a consistent sleep schedule. Ariana Huffington's new organization, Thrive Global, was inspired by her realization that she had suffered from burnout and was not allowing her body to sleep or rest. She now has a website dedicated totally to helping people rest, sleep, and avoid burnout. In this work, work, work, work world we live in, it's easy to neglect rest periods. However, we were designed to have a built-in rest period in our day. If we don't use it, we get sick, feel unbalanced, and eventually our ability to create suffers. Sleep. Rest. Listen to your body. Don't push through exhaustion. It's unnecessary and can be costly. *(Helpful tip: Try to maintain a bedtime for a couple of weeks. Set an alarm and set reset your body, so that you have a consistent sleep/rest routine.)*

5. **Avoid procrastination.** One of the leading causes of artistic failure is procrastination or what some people call resistance. Steven Pressfield, an expert in procrastination and a writer, wrote several books that discuss the serious problem of procrastination in depth. (When you have a chance pick up, *The War of Art, Turning Pro,* and *Do the Work*). He knows how serious and difficult it is to overcome procrastination. It is easier said than done to stop procrastinating. Every artist knows it's a real threat to one's creative process. And it can become habit-forming. Putting off the work that needs to be done can become a way of life, and before you know it the work never gets done. I am not saying it's easy. But, I am saying, that you must stop. And the best deterrent to procrastination is establishing a routine and a schedule.

By setting an exact time to start and end work—each day and doing it consistently every day—you will overcome the resistance to work. It will become an automatic process. If this is intimidating start with one hour. Then two. Most creatives max-out after two or three hours. People who write, may only last an hour or two. Depending on the amount of creative energy exerted in your work, your time to create may vary. Creativity is exhausting. Like giving birth, creativity requires creating something out of nothing. It's forceful and it can be draining. By working too long one day, you may burn out and may not want to return the next day or the next. Then you fall out of habit and before you know it a week or two may pass. By setting a realistic time schedule each day to work within, you'll avoid burnout and ultimately procrastination. *(Helpful tip: Write the time you'll start working the next morning on a Post-It on your mirror the night before. At that time, show up to your studio or office. Then set a timer for one hour. Do that for 30 days straight. Before you know it, you'll have created a consistent practice.)*

"Can anything be sadder than work left unfinished? Yes, work never begun."
—Christina Rossetti

6. **Get organized.** Invest in a day planner or an online software calendar. Plan your month in advance, then break it down by weeks, and days. Then each morning make a small to-do list. Adding too many things in a day may leave you feeling overwhelmed and discouraged, and you may even avoid the list-making process all together. Simply list 3 absolute-must-dos each day, and schedule those things into your day before the day even starts. That way—you actually

do them, because you've scheduled them and made time for them. Also, by scheduling time to do things like work, exercise, eat healthfully, if someone comes to you and asks you to do something, you can respectfully decline, because you have something "scheduled." By making yourself and your career a priority—and scheduled in black and white—you'll be less likely to let others interfere with your time or success.

7. **Take yourself on an Artist Date.** The great author of the famed *The Artist's Way,* Julia Cameron recommends taking weekly "artist dates." And I'd like to take it one step further. Regularly find places that inspire you and instruct you, and spend time there. Whether it's a gallery, art museum, park, funky boutique, or local coffee shop, you can find inspiration everywhere. Soak up your surroundings and see what they can teach you. At least once a year, plan a trip somewhere you've never been. If money is an issue, it doesn't have to be an exotic location or long vacation. It can be a day trip or a weekend getaway. The key is to switch up your surroundings, get out of your studio, and explore the world around you. Even play hookie! If you find yourself finished with your work early, take off and do something fun. Treat yourself. Also, consider rewarding yourself with a special trip after a job well done. By giving yourself rewards and something to look forward to, you'll be more likely to complete the project. *(Helpful tip: Pick a place you would like to visit that you've never been before. Set a goal or a finish-by date, and then set up a trip to reward yourself.)*

"I don't wait for moods. You accomplish nothing if you do that. Your mind must know it has got to get down to work."
—Pearl S. Buck

8. **Get inspired, while staying informed.** I cannot recommend attending conferences, workshops, and seminars enough. I believe you should schedule yourself for AT LEAST ONE conference, seminar or workshop a year. Whether it's to enhance your business acumen, your artistic technique or expand your network, these events are invaluable. Costs may vary, and some could be cost prohibitive depending on what stage you are in your career. But, you need to stay informed about your market, your process, and what's going on in the world you're working in. A conference I like to attend annually is Artexpo New York. I also recommend joining me at my company's annual Success Summit. (For more information, visit ADCfineart.com.) Find one that is close by and attend for a day, if you can't afford to travel a long distance for one. *(Helpful tip: Schedule some time this week to research conferences. Is there something you want to know more about? Look for online classes or seminars to sign up for.)*

"Success usually comes to those who are too busy to be looking for it."
—Henry David Thoreau

9. **Read books.** This is probably the least expensive, yet most powerful way to get and stay inspired. As the great Zig Ziglar said, "People often say that motivation doesn't last. Well, neither does bathing—that's why we recommend it daily." Books are a great way to stay inspired. All you need is a library card, and you have access to the greatest minds and mentors in the world. By scheduling time to read each day, you'll be amazed how much you can read in one year. All it takes is twenty-minutes a day. If you just read for twenty-minutes each day, you can finish a book in a month. If

you read for an hour each day, you can increase that number to three or four books a month. I also joined a group of like-minded women who meet monthly to discuss our books. We call ourselves the Master Mind Group. Just as Napoleon Hill recommended forming a Master Mind group nearly eighty years ago, in his continued best-selling book *Think and Grow Rich*, we meet each month to discuss books that encourage and inspire us to be better leaders, business women, and humans. *(Helpful tip: Find and build your own Master Mind group of like-minded individuals hungry for knowledge and inspiration. Schedule a monthly meeting. Take turns picking books that will inspire and interest you.)*

"It is good to have an end to journey towards, but it is the journey that matters in the end."
—Ursula LeGuin

10. **Be social.** When we enjoy strong social support, we can accomplish impressive feats of resilience and even extend our lives. Researchers have found that social support has as much effect on life expectancy as smoking, high blood pressure, obesity and physical activity. In other words, don't ignore your friendships or your family. By building and maintaining strong social and emotional bonds you'll remember why you do what you do. You'll find your work more fulfilling and you'll focus on what really matters. *(Helpful tip: Schedule coffee breaks with friends throughout the week to bolster your social connections. Make time for your family and loved ones too. It's easy to get overwhelmed when deadlines press or when you're locked in to a creative endeavor. As Stephen King once wrote, "Art is a support system for life, not the other way around." In other words, you need your family and friends.)*

Chin Yuen

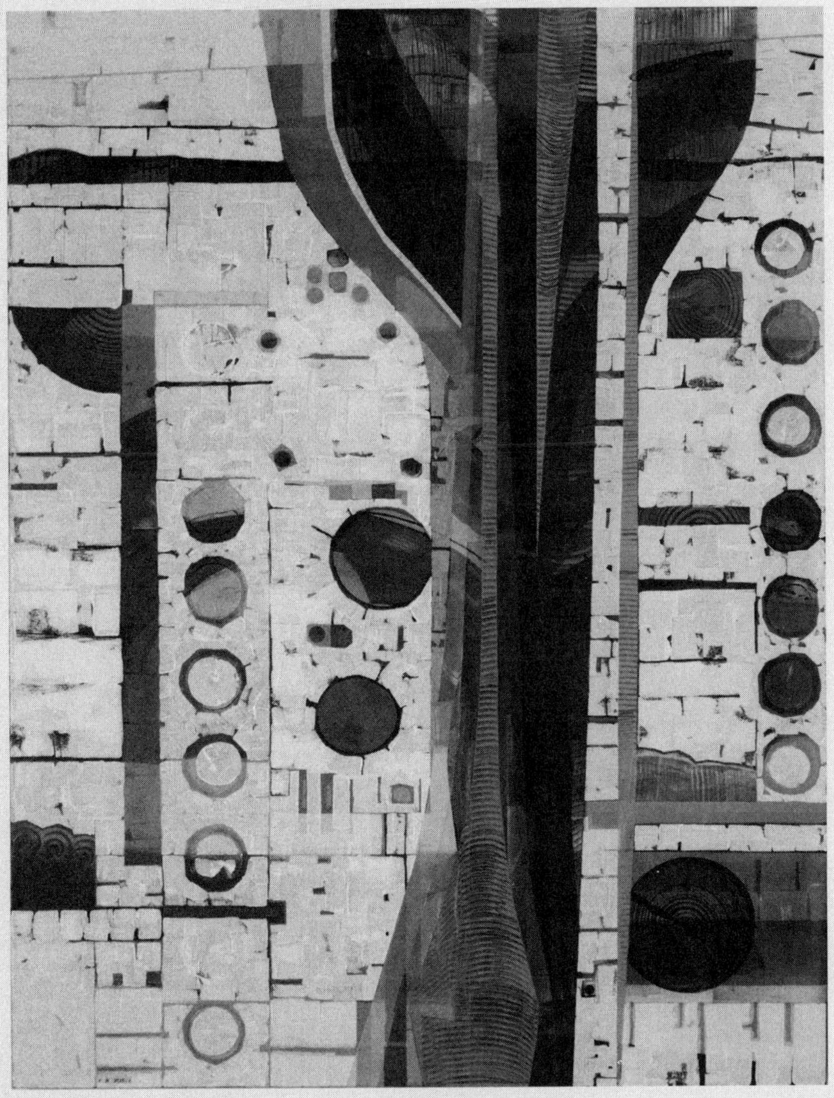

© Chin Yuen

The Importance of Self-Care

When I think of a balanced, healthy, and successful artist, I think of the international award-winning Malaysian-born, Canadian painter Chin Yuen. Chin is truly a "student of the world." She studied in Singapore and England before moving to Canada to further her education. Chin received a Bachelor of Fine Arts from the prestigious Emily Carr University of Art and Design (Vancouver) and a Master of Arts from the University of Victoria. After graduation, she traveled extensively and worked in Italy and Japan before returning home to Canada. Chin continues to travel for both work and pleasure. She finds inspiration everywhere, as she says, "from pop culture to decaying wood." The consummate professional, working artist, her work has appeared on the cover of books, in residential homes, hotels, healthcare facilities, and corporate clients. Her arresting body of work, which feature colorful dynamic abstract paintings, is one of my top sellers.

But, Chin is more than an artist. She's an entrepreneur, albeit a reluctant one. "Like most artists, I wish I could do less business and more painting. However, in order to be financially viable, I need to embrace it as part of the process," she says.

Chin learned early on that to be a successful artist, she needed to incorporate a business-like attitude to her process. Some artists, especially those starting out, might find her process incredibly informative. She says, "a typical day for me starts on the computer, where I deal with emails, social media, business inquiries or sales, and household affairs. I usually need to know that I have at least two to three hours to paint before I enter the studio; because once I am there, I hunker down and paint without interruption." Chin knows the importance of protecting her time in the studio, so she schedules that time and paints without worrying about the emails, phone calls, or business aspects of being an artist.

As I recommended previously, Chin too, knows the value of a break and giving one time to regenerate one's creative energy. She explains that when a painting is on its way she'll paint intensely for a few days (a few hours of intense and uninterrupted hours at a time) and then when it is done she'll reward herself with a short break before starting a new painting. "It is physically demanding," she admits and knows that she needs to give her body and mind time to rest and recuperate. In order to stay fit and healthy, Chin aims to swim three times a week to stay mentally and physically fit.

Chin also knows how vital relationships and giving back are to her creative process. "Since painting is an inward activity, I try to find balance in teaching and sharing with others. I also like challenging myself to learn new techniques and meeting other artists by joining workshops."

This year, Chin will be spending a month in Berlin, Germany, as an artist-in-residence. As she points out, the reward of such a program is twofold: "This commitment will offer me two things I love: painting and experiencing another culture." A life-long learner and a dedicated student of life, Chin seeks out opportunities to constantly stay engaged and inspired.

Like me, she has her own tips for staying balanced and healthy as an artist, "My advice to artists is to be focused and organized. Know what you want and prioritize your life to achieve your goals. Don't shy away from the business side, because it might take a while before you are 'discovered' or represented by a gallery that sells your works."

To learn more about Chin and her art, visit www.chinyuenart.com

Action Steps

1. **Set your routine down in writing.** Buy a calendar or a planner. Establish a routine that you can commit to every day for the next thirty days.

2. **Read for twenty minutes.** If you've read this chapter, congratulations, your activity is done for today! Now be sure to schedule twenty minutes into each part of your day.

3. **Go for a brisk walk.** If you're not accustomed to physical activity, don't push yourself too hard. Start with twenty minutes. If you are physically active, still get up and go for a mental-health walk for twenty minutes—no music, no friends, no distractions. See where your mind (and your feet) take you.

4. **Phone a friend.** Reach out and talk to someone if you're feeling especially adventurous, invite that person to your favorite coffee shop.

5. **Pick a reward for yourself for sticking to a routine for a month.** Getting started is half the battle. But as Mary Poppins put it, "A job well begun is half-done." You're almost there. Now set a reward for yourself for starting and completing a month of your new routine.

My reward for sticking to my routine is . . .

Further Reading on Living Life as Artist

The Secret by Rhonda Byrne

Turning Pro: Tap Your Inner Power and Create Your Life's Work by Steven Pressfield

Vein of Gold: A Journey to Your Creative Heart by Julia Cameron

Design the Life You Love: A Step-By-Step Guide to Building a Meaningful Future by Ayse Birsel

Design Your Day: Be More Productive, Set Better Goals, and Live Life on Purpose by Claire Diaz-Ortiz

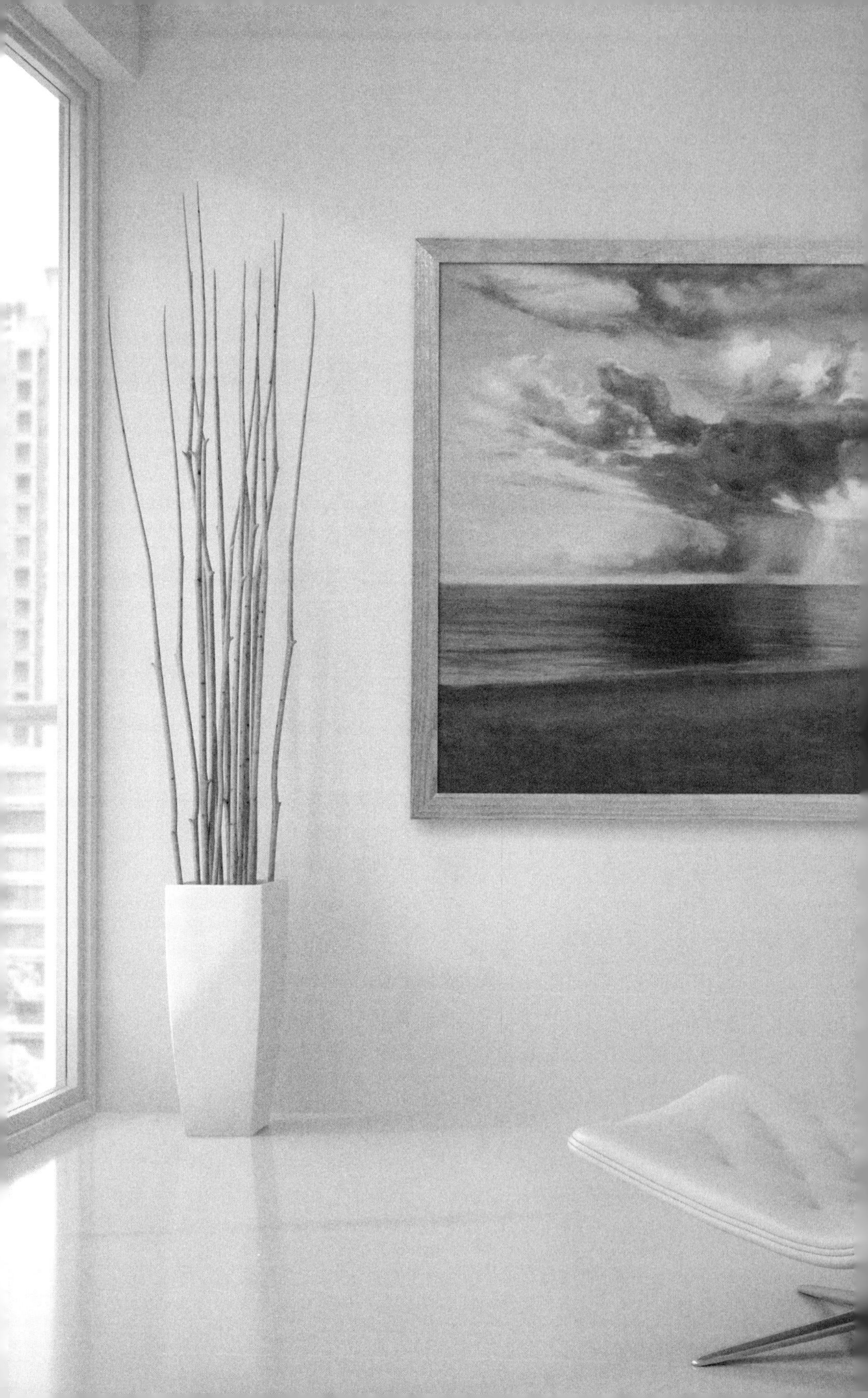

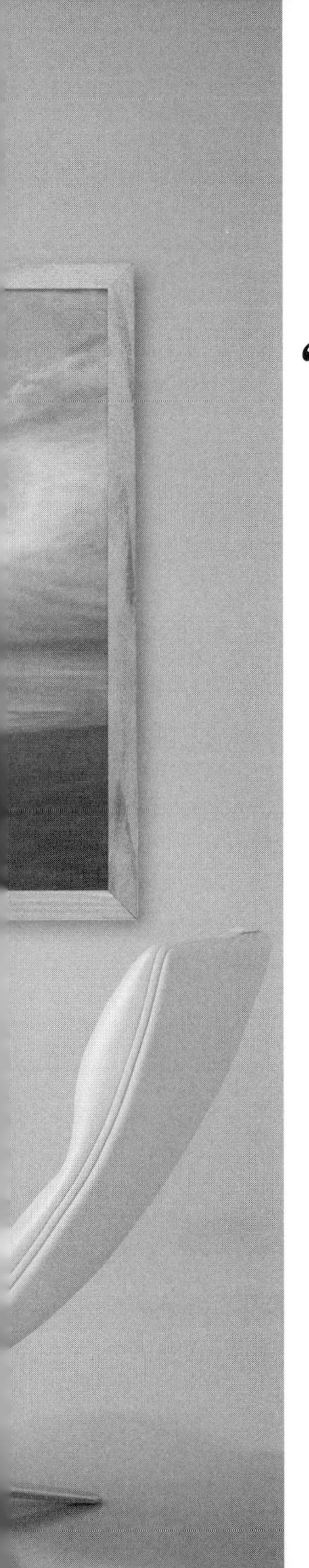

“Making money is art and working is art and **GOOD BUSINESS** *is the* ***best art.****”*

— Andy Warhol

Artist: Josie Gearhart

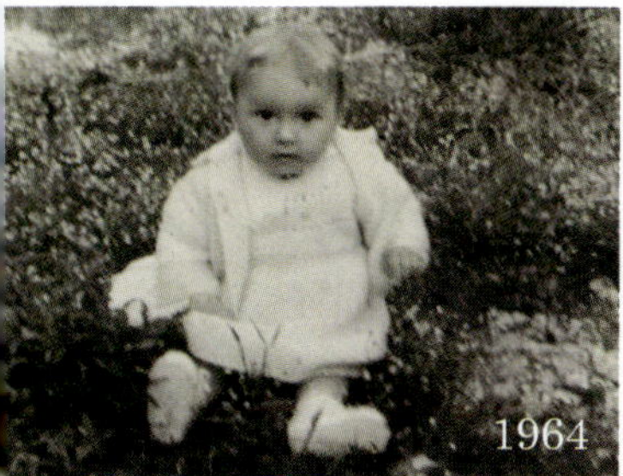
1964

Where It All Began

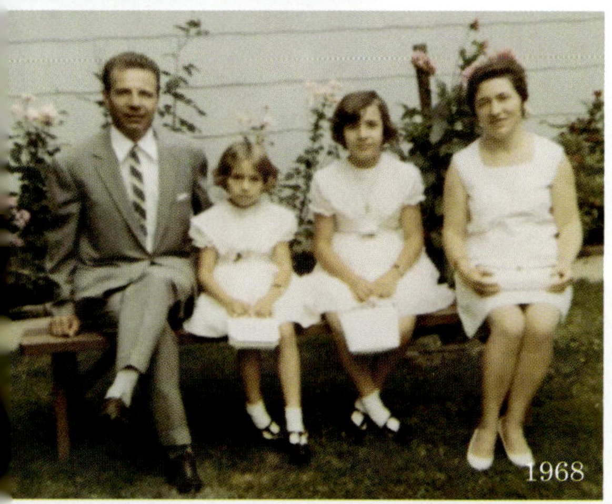
1968

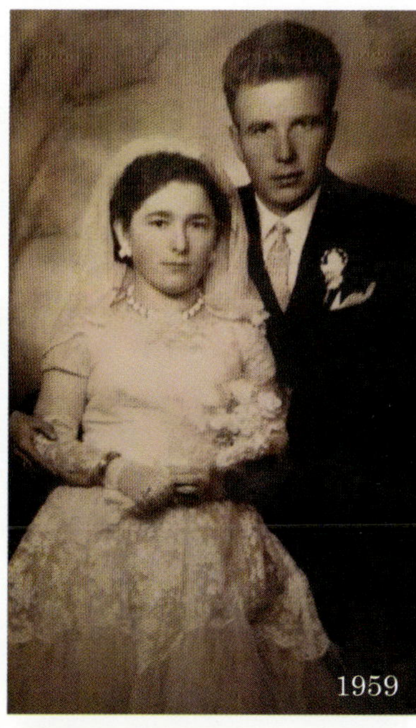
1959

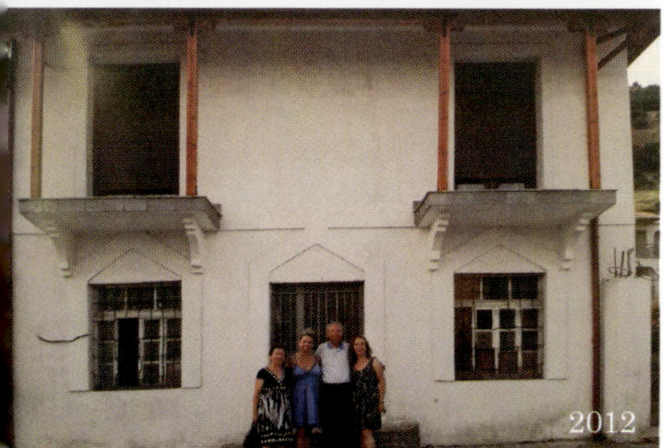
2012

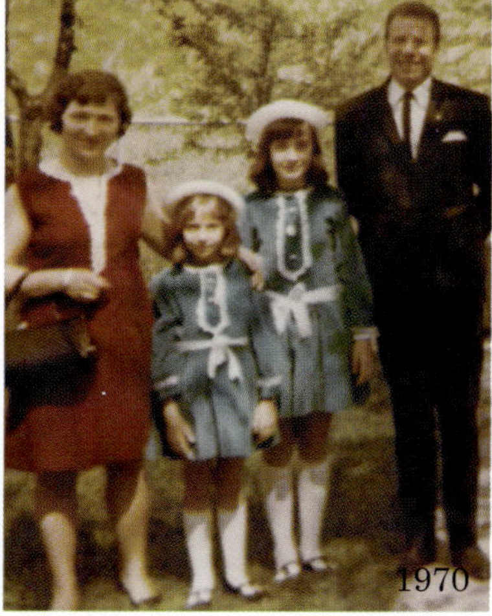
1970

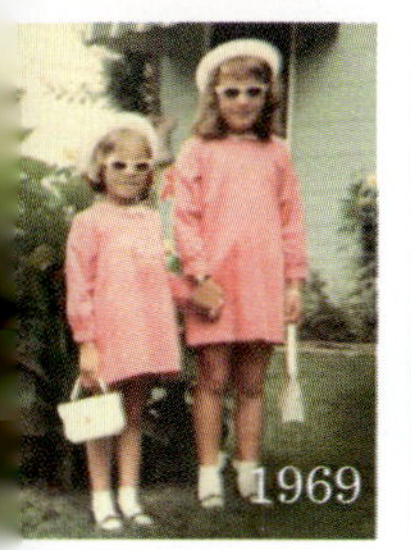
1969

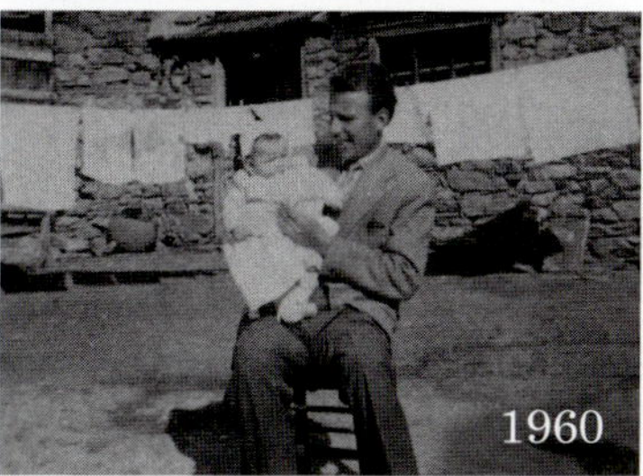
1960

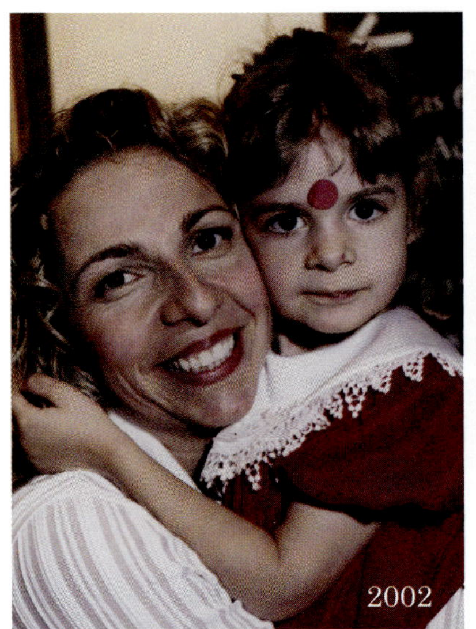

2002

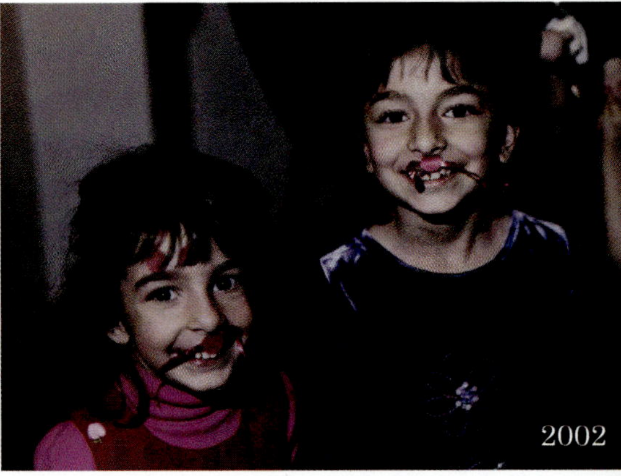

2002

My World

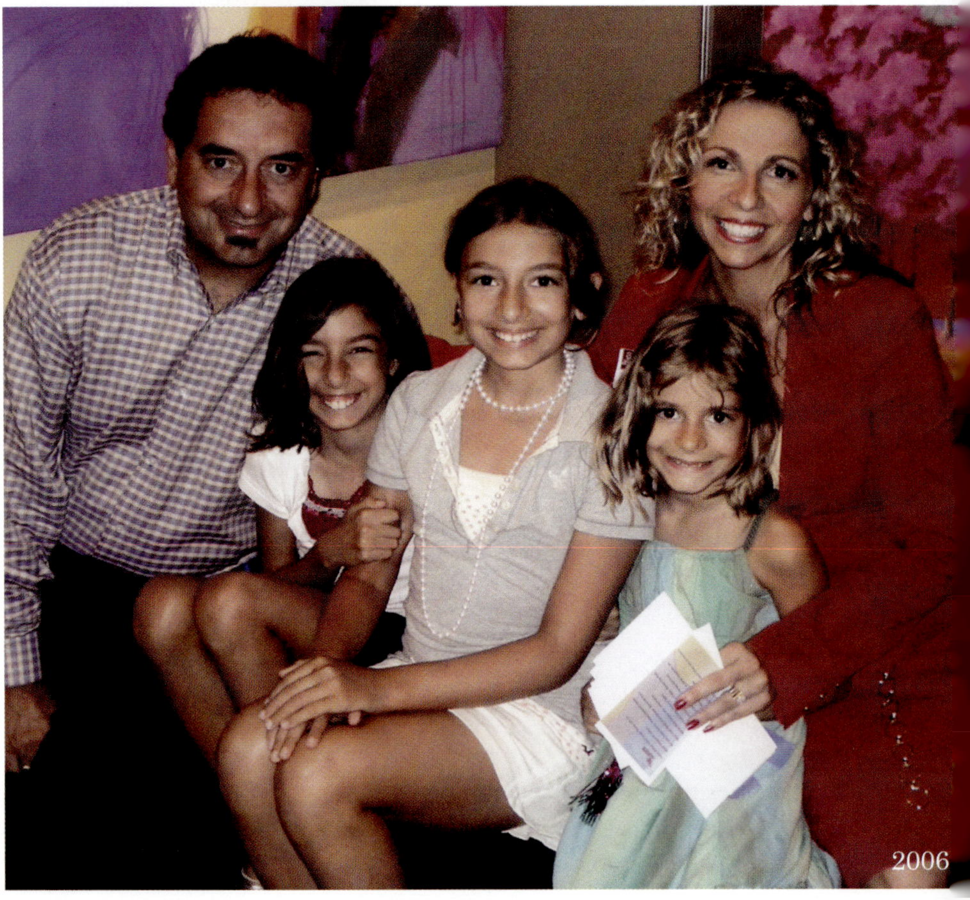

2006

Early Days

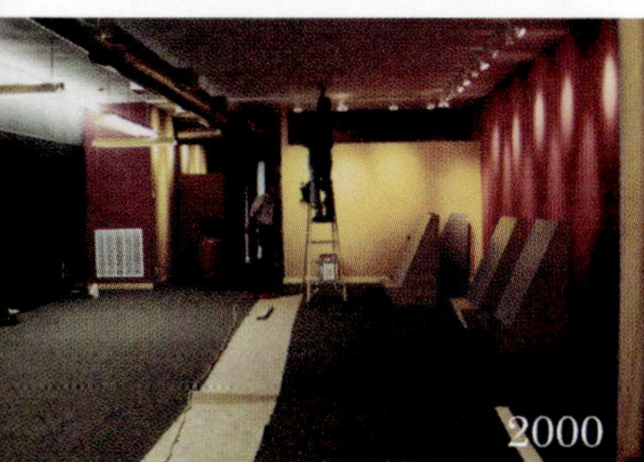
2000

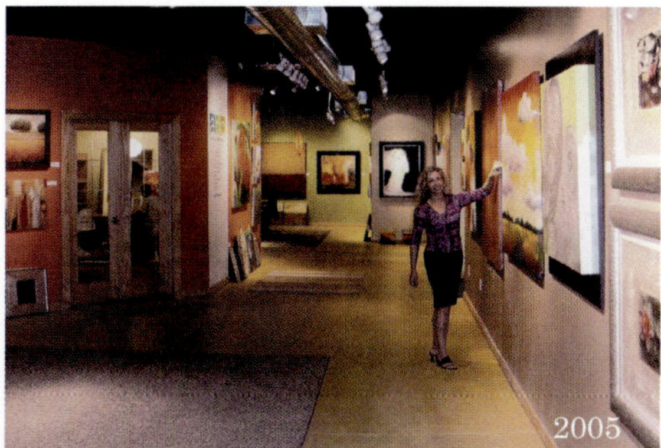
2005

1996

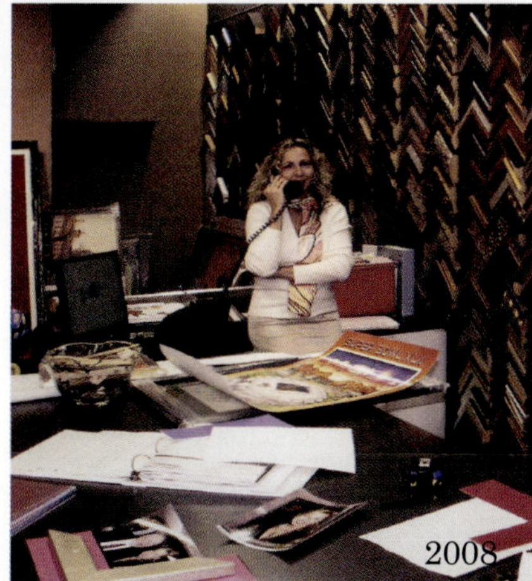
2008

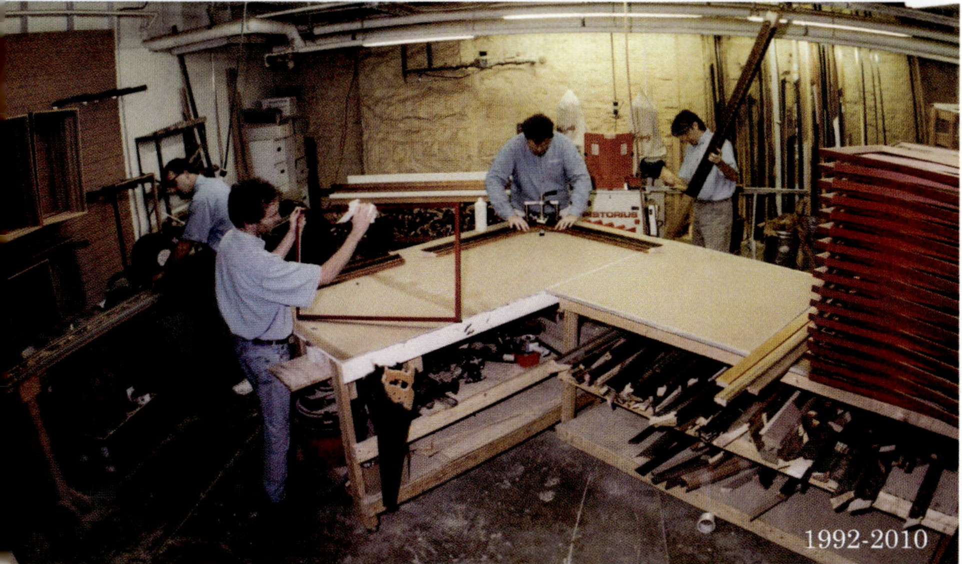
1992-2010

Growing Pains Pay Off

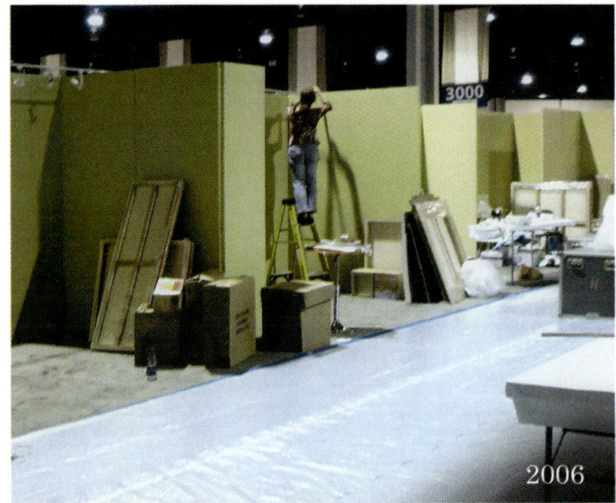

2006

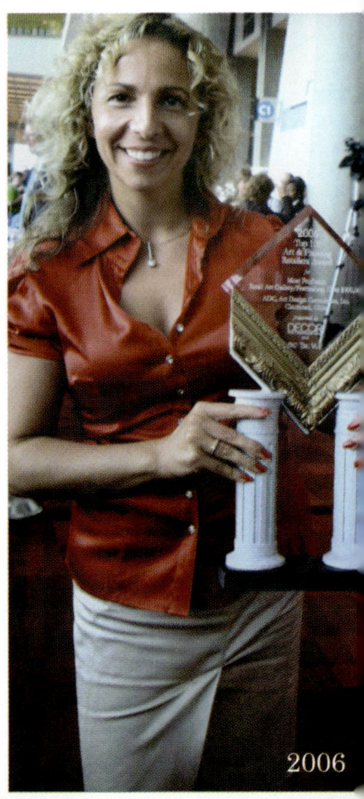
2006

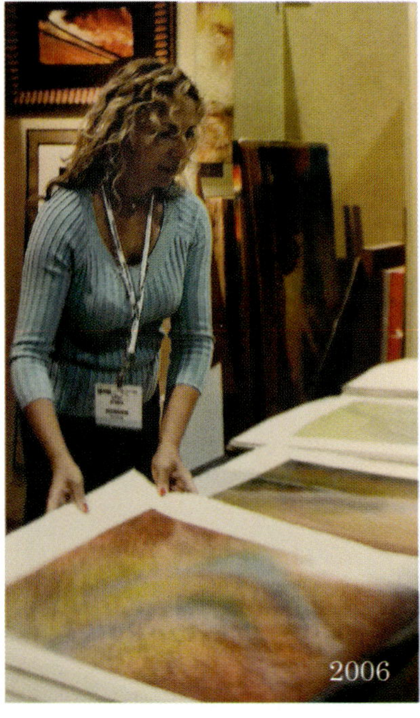
2006

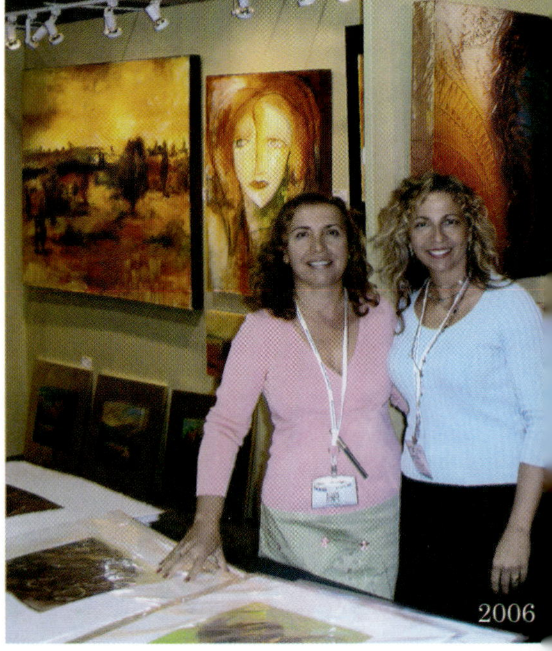
2006

Before & After

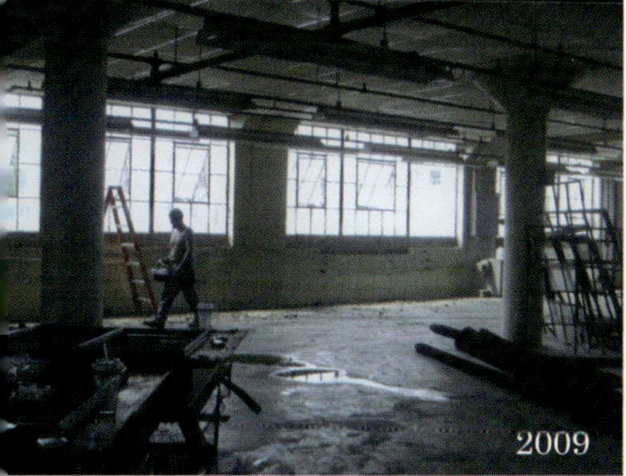

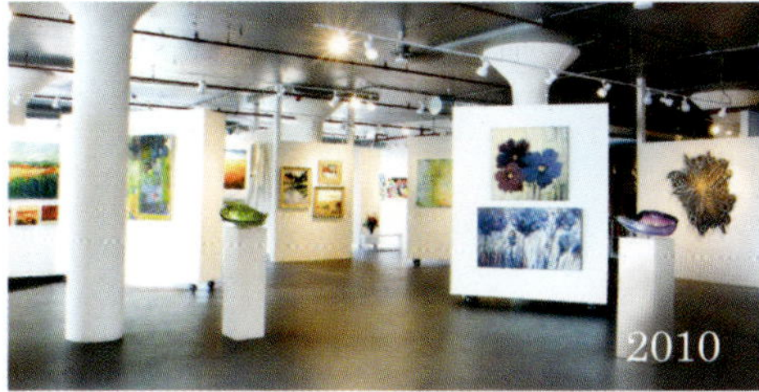

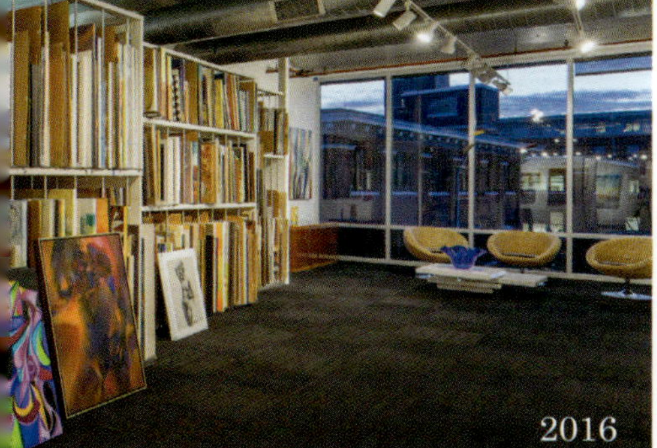

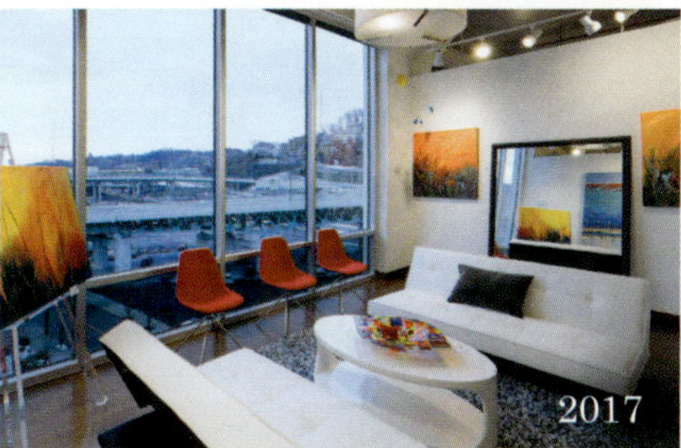

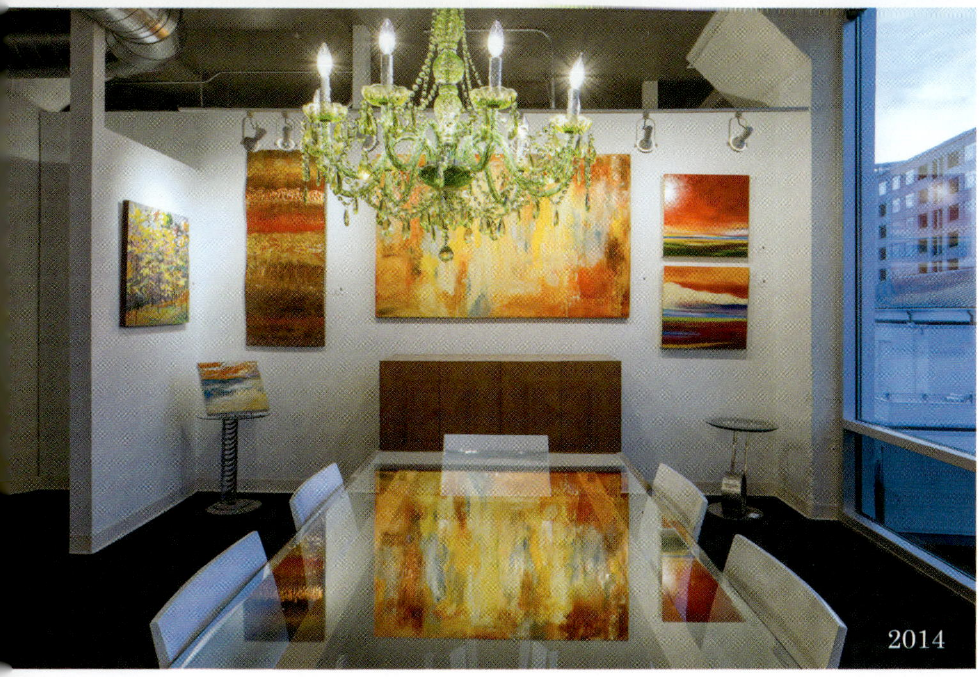

2014

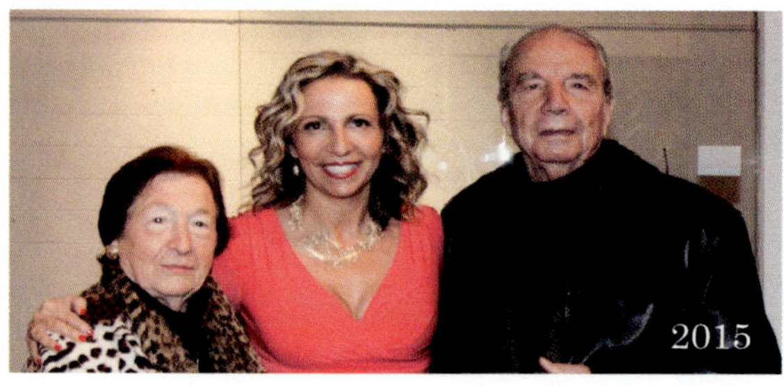
2015

So Grateful for My Family

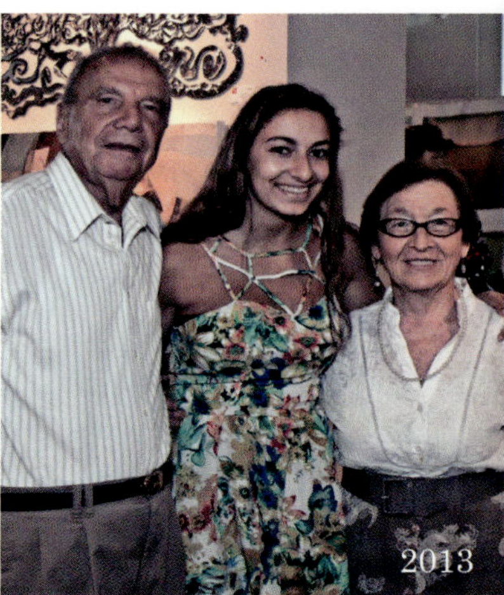
2013

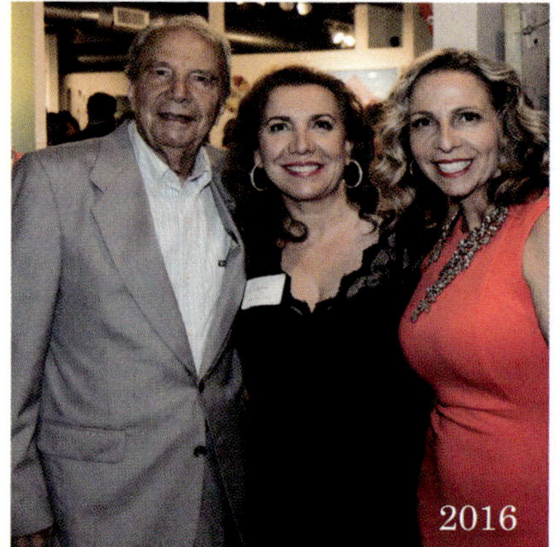
2016

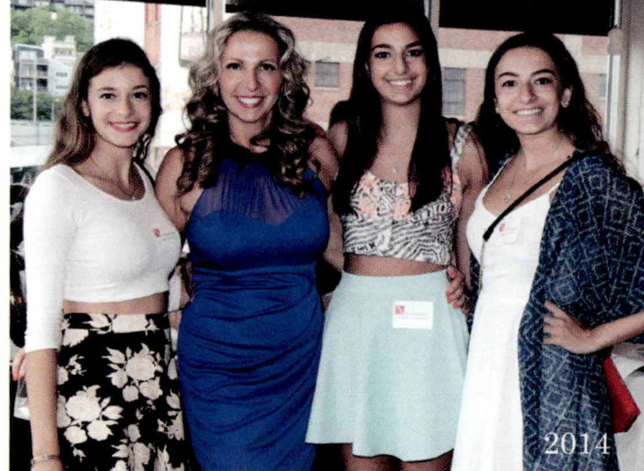
2014

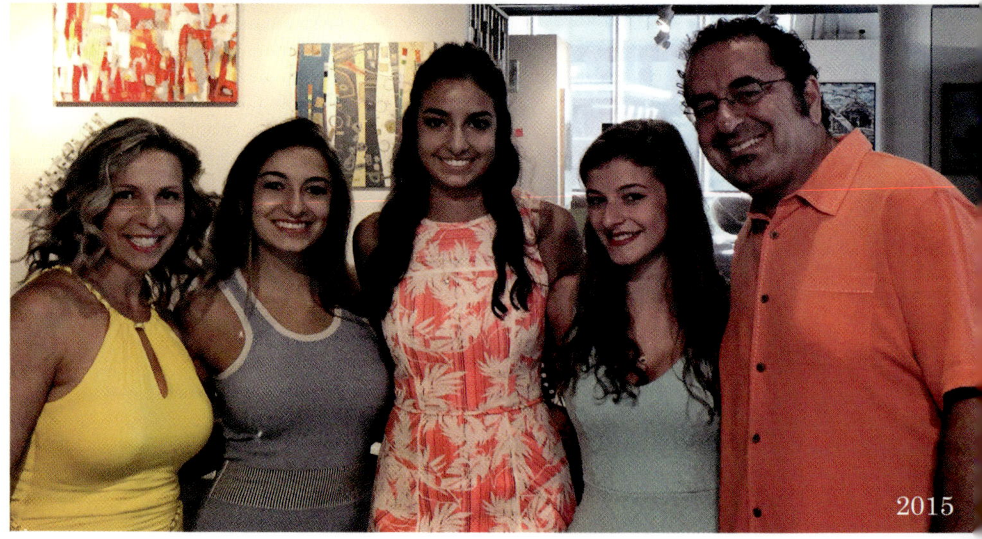
2015

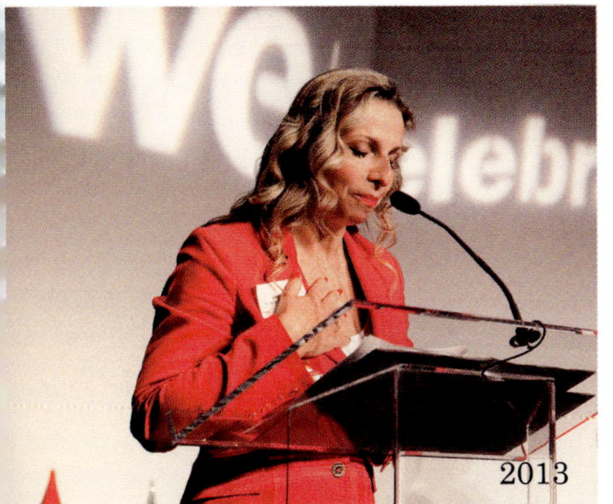

2013

Recognition for All Our Hard Work

I want to dedicate this award to my parents Petros + Sofia Poulos, who are here with us today. They taught me to follow my dreams and that it's OK to take risks, especially when it helps you and everyone you love.
They did that in 1967 when they left their small farming village in Greece with two small children in tow for the land of opportunity - America. They wanted a better life for their family and they succeeded. I'm living my dream of a rewarding career because of my parents' decision a risk. It changed the course of my life.

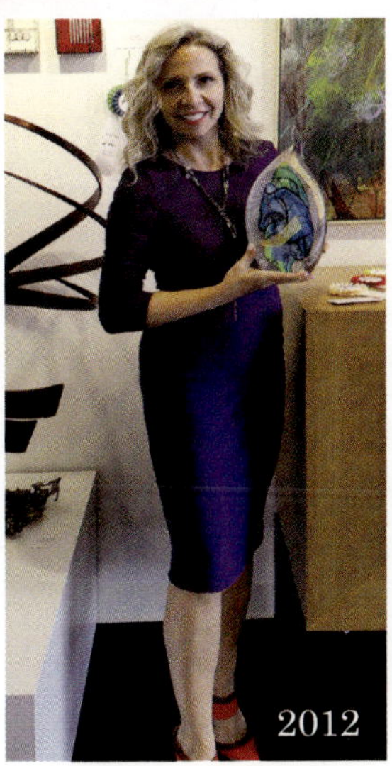

2012

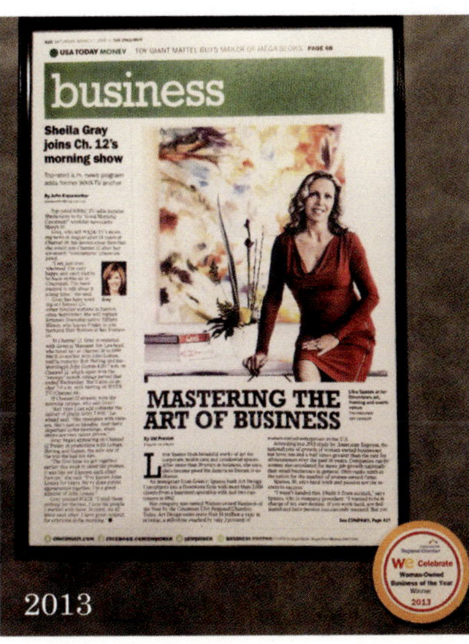

USA TODAY MONEY TOY GIANT MATTEL BUYS MAKER OF MEGA BLOKS

business

Sheila Gray joins Ch. 12's morning show

MASTERING THE ART OF BUSINESS

2013

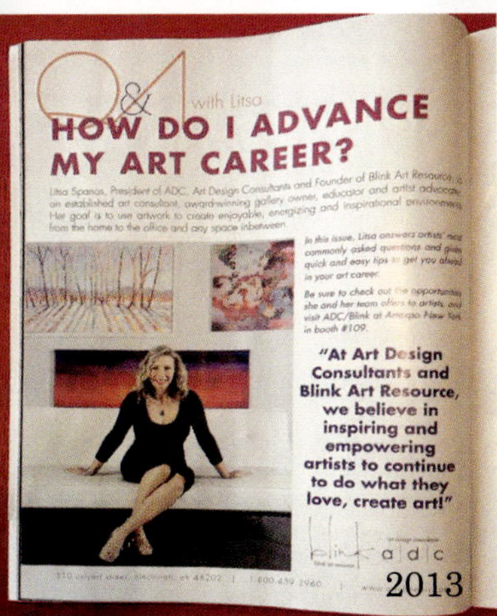

Q&A with Litsa

HOW DO I ADVANCE MY ART CAREER?

Litsa Spanos, President of ADC, Art Design Consultants and Founder of Blink Art Resource, is an established art consultant, award-winning gallery owner, educator and artist advocate. Her goal is to use artwork to create enjoyable, energizing and inspirational environments from the home to the office and any space inbetween.

In this issue, Litsa answers artists' most commonly asked questions and gives quick and easy tips to get you ahead in your art career.

Be sure to check out the opportunities she and her team offers to artists, and visit ADC/Blink at Artexpo New York in booth #109.

"At Art Design Consultants and Blink Art Resource, we believe in inspiring and empowering artists to continue to do what they love, create art!"

blink a|d|c

2013

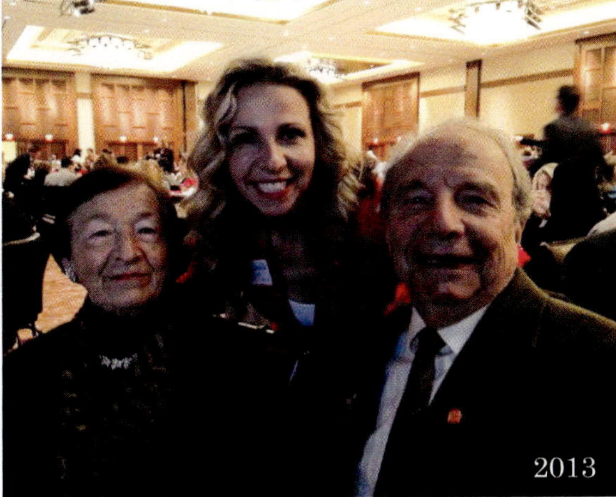

2013

ACA - The Academy Awards for Artists

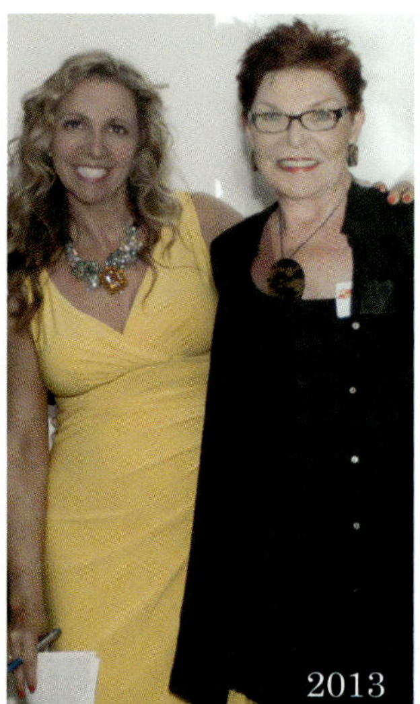
2013

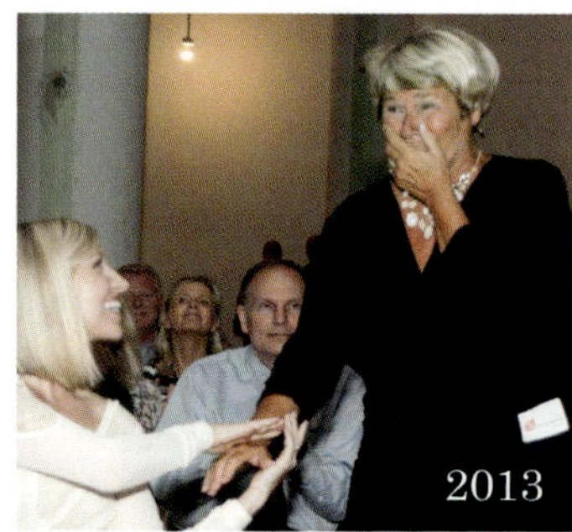
2013

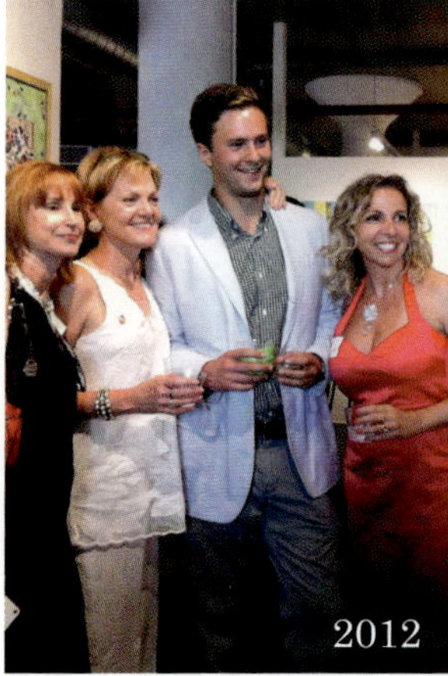
2012

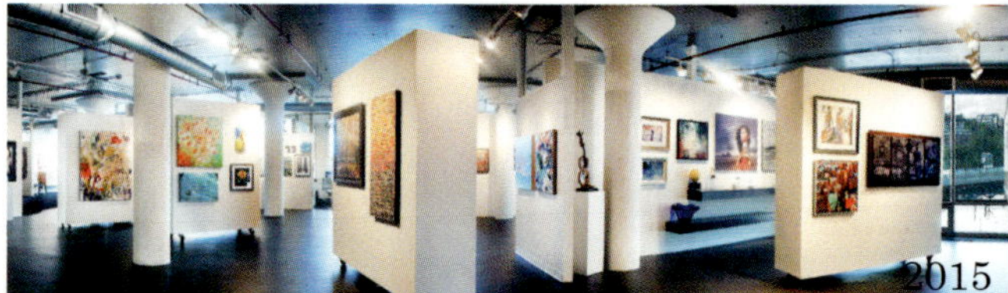
2015

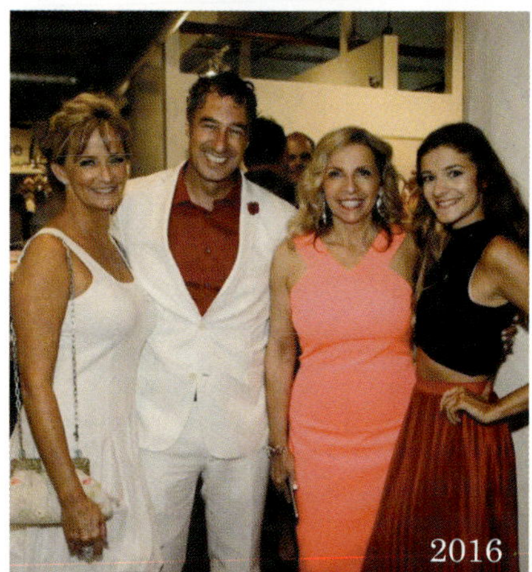
2016

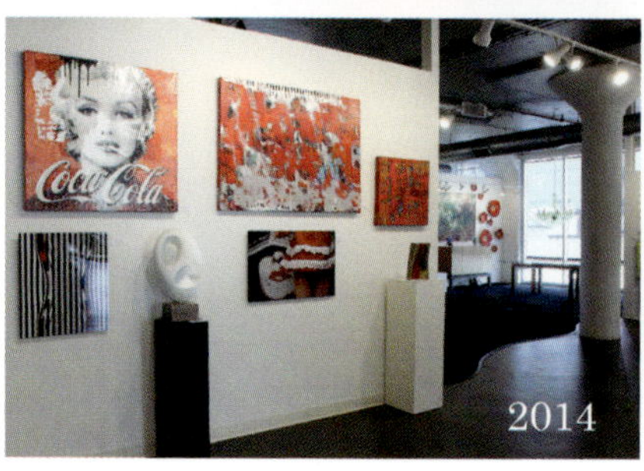

2014

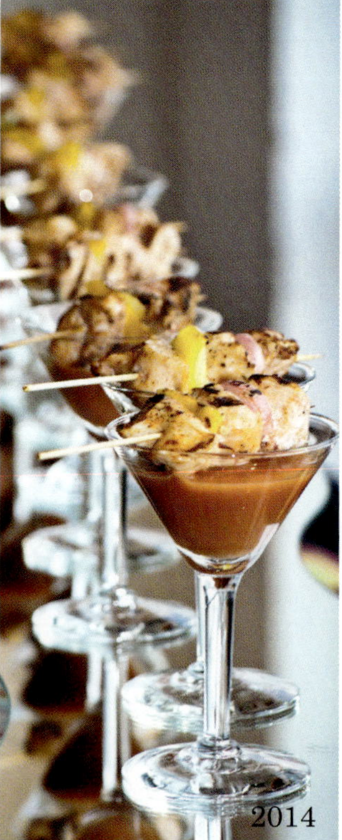
2014

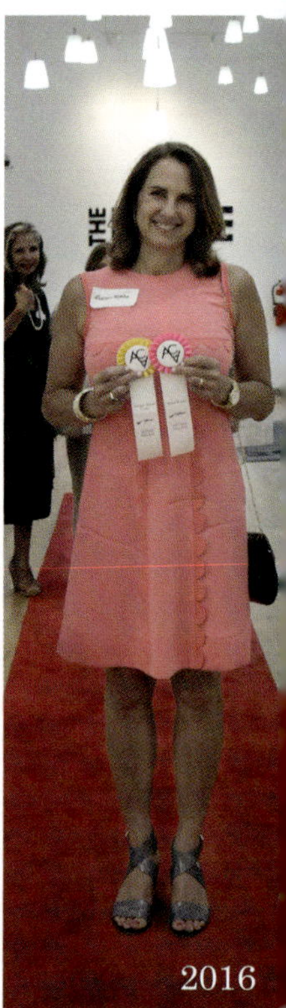
2016

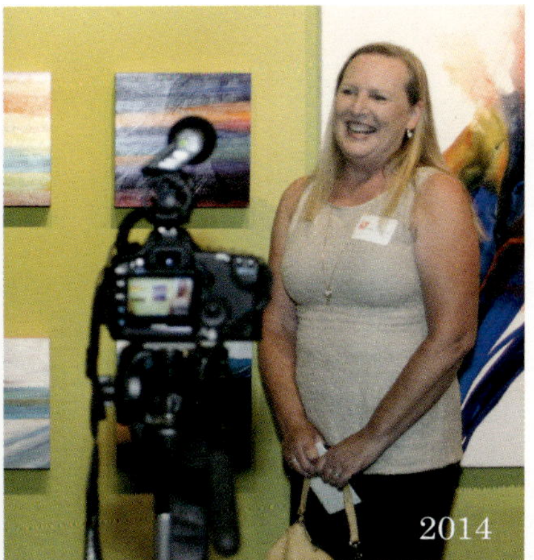
2014

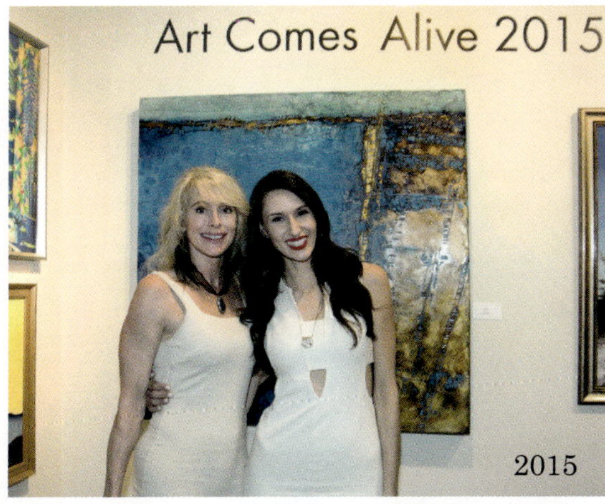
Art Comes Alive 2015
2015

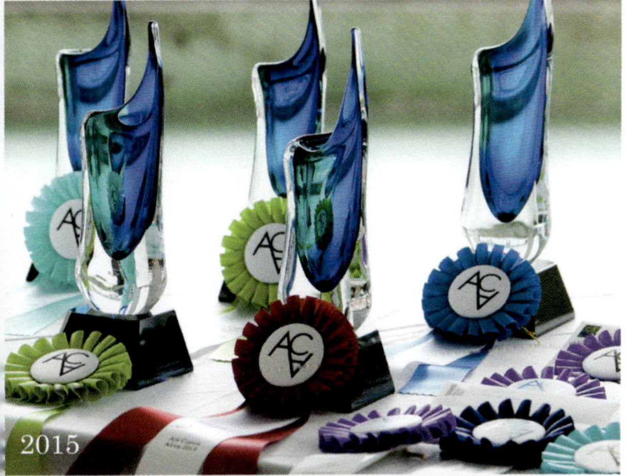
2015

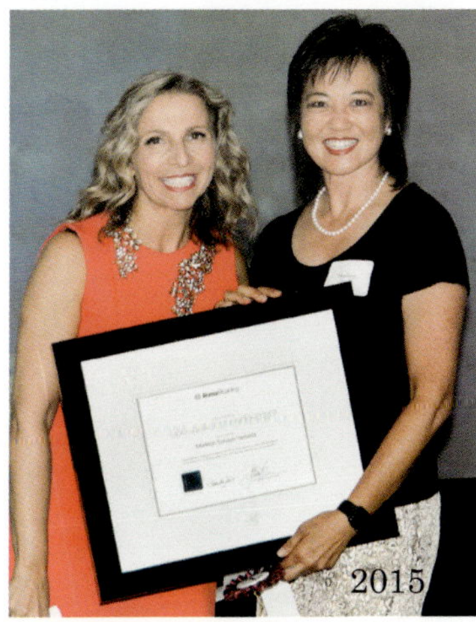
2015

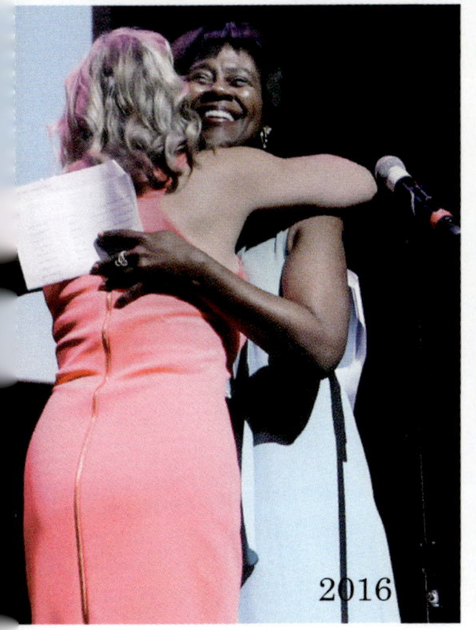
2016

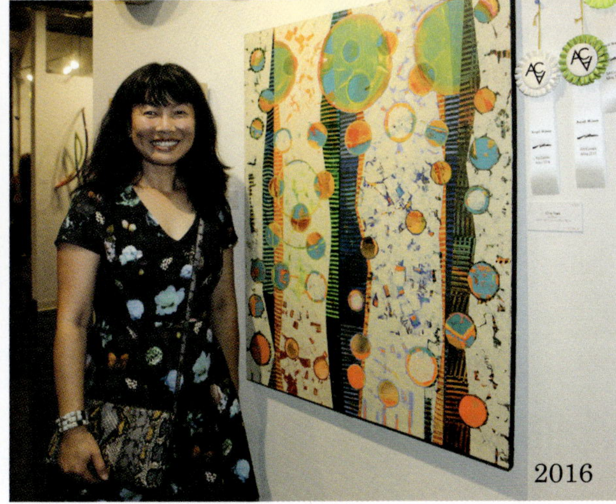
2016

Blink Art - Connecting Artists to Collectors

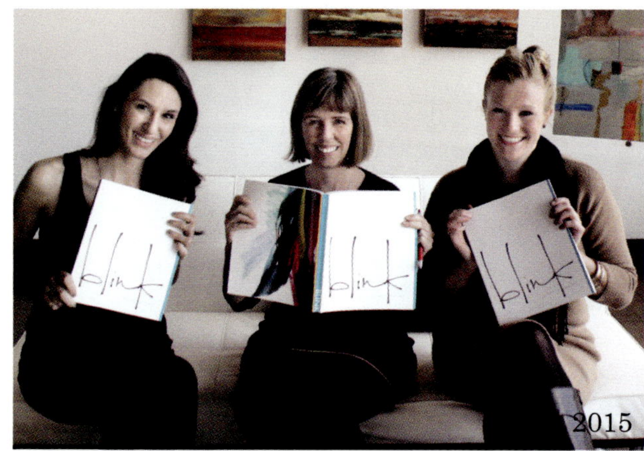

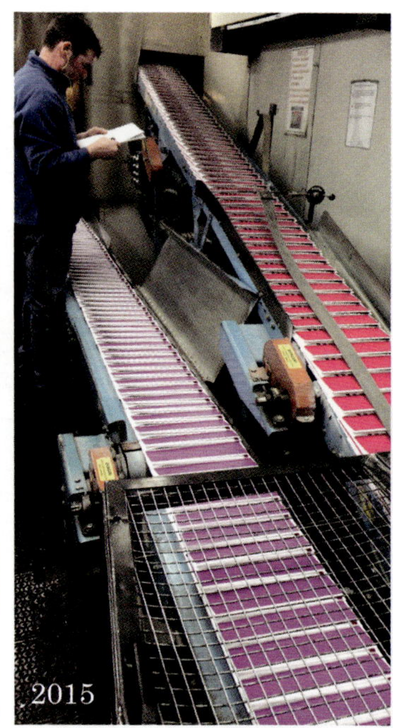

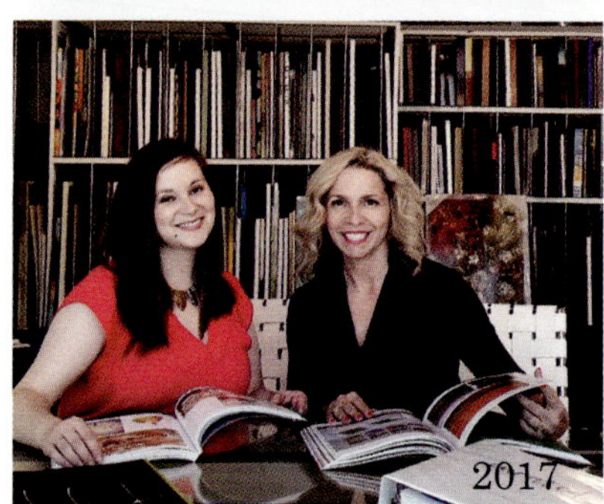

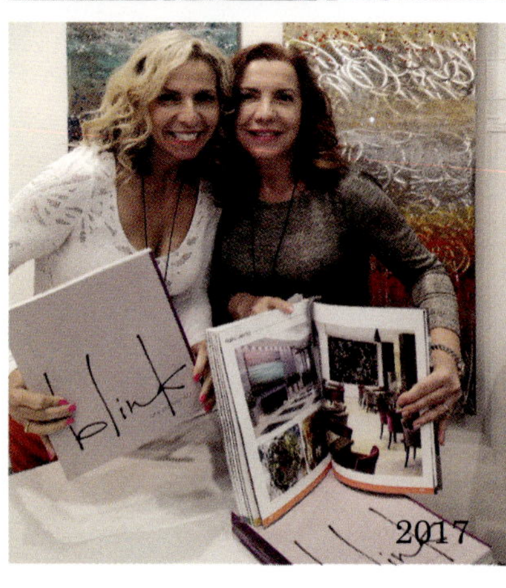

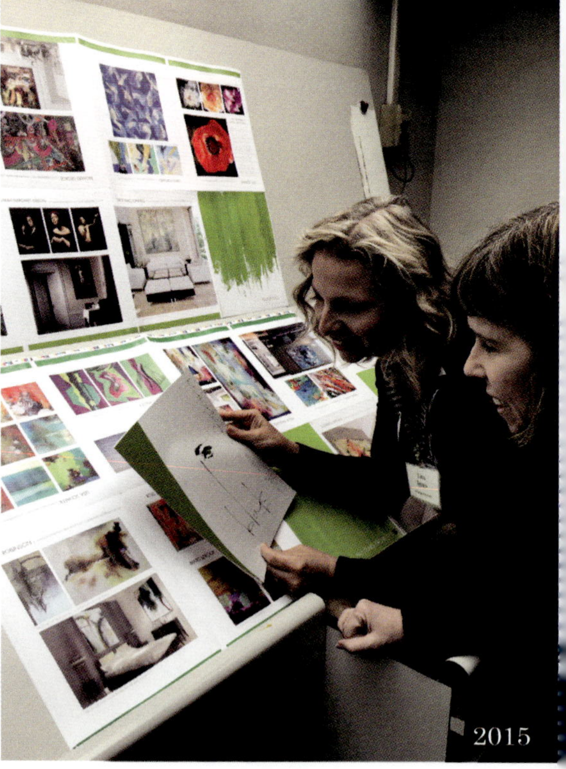

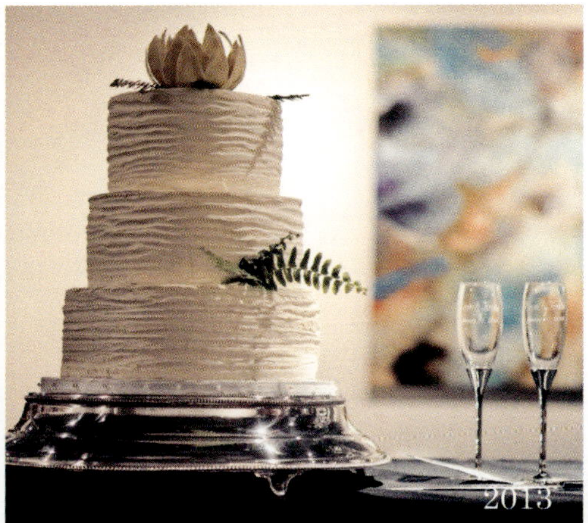
2013

The Gallery in the Sky

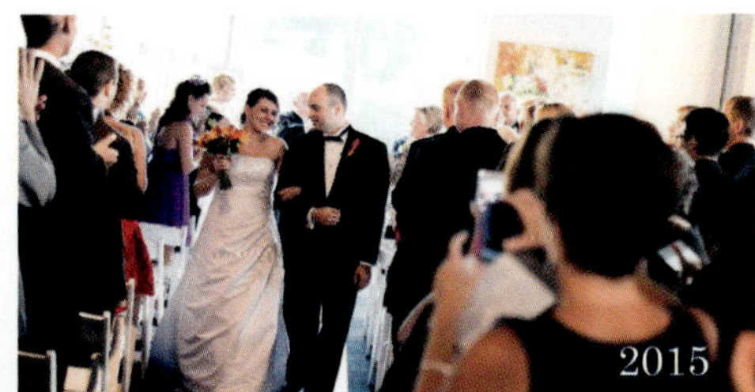
2015

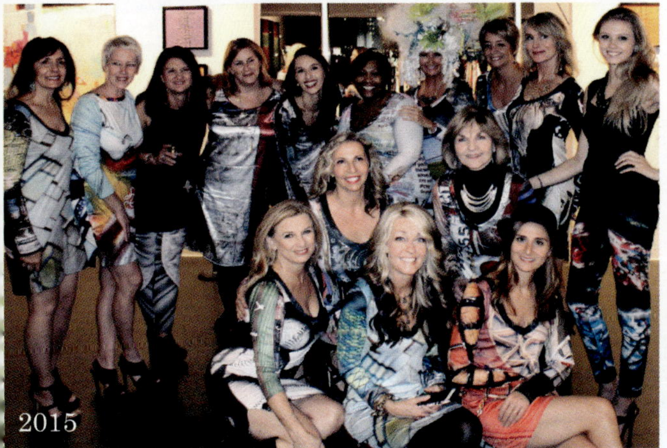
2015

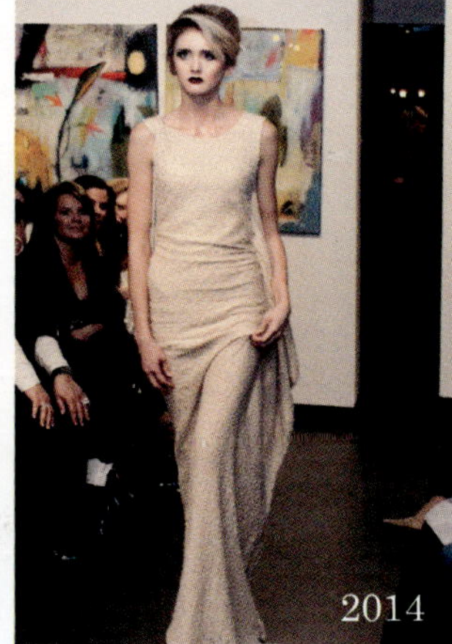
2014

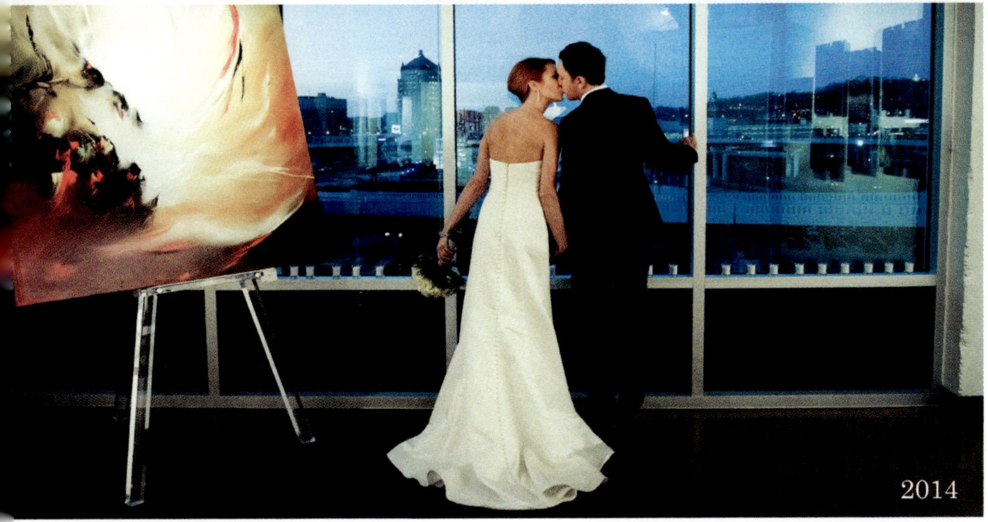
2014

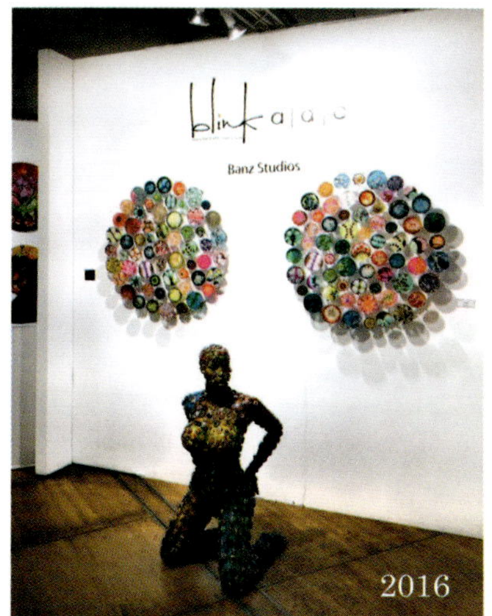

2016

Taking Our Artists Where They Have Never Been

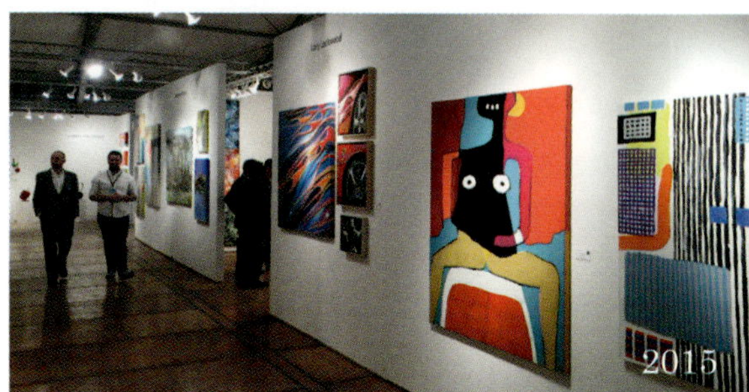

2015

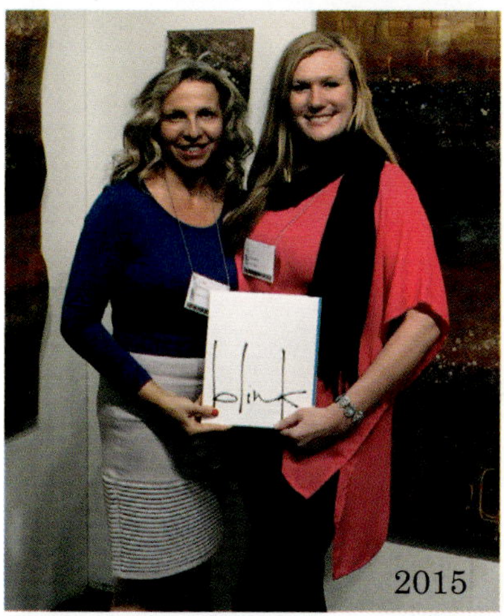

2015

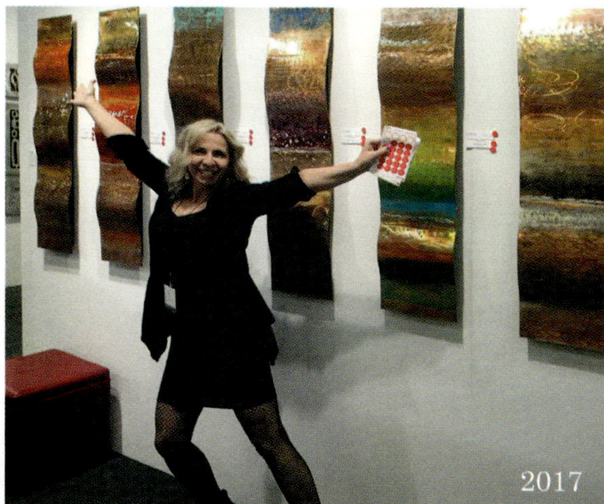

2017

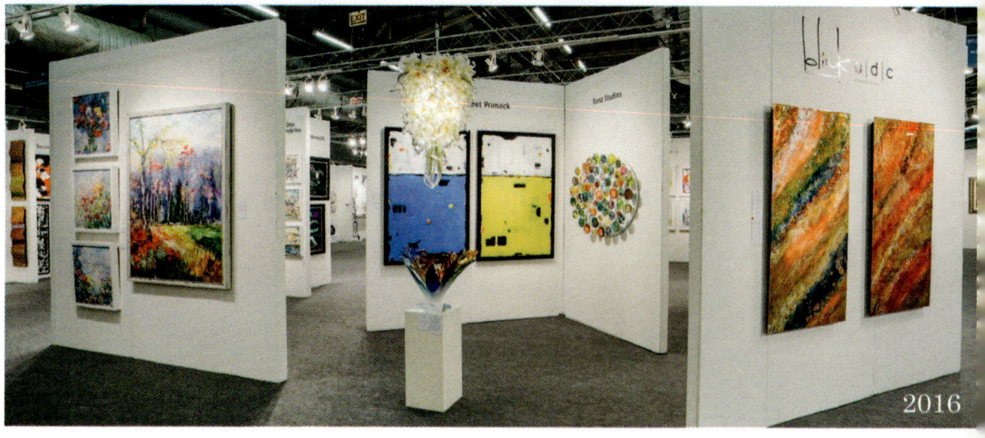

2016

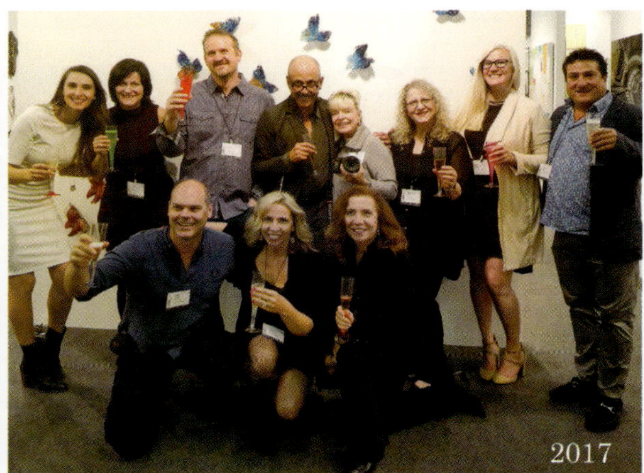
2017

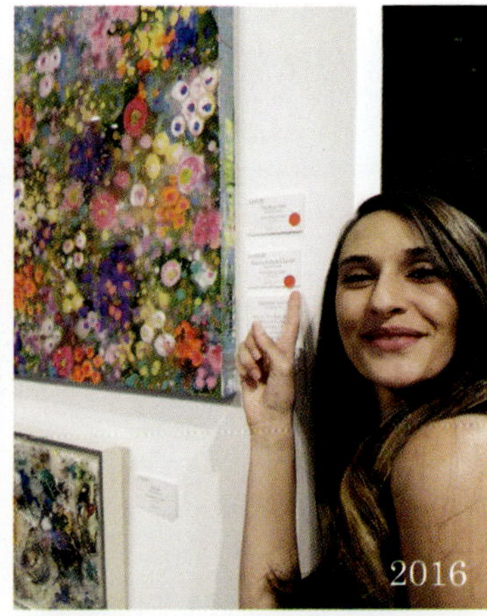
2016

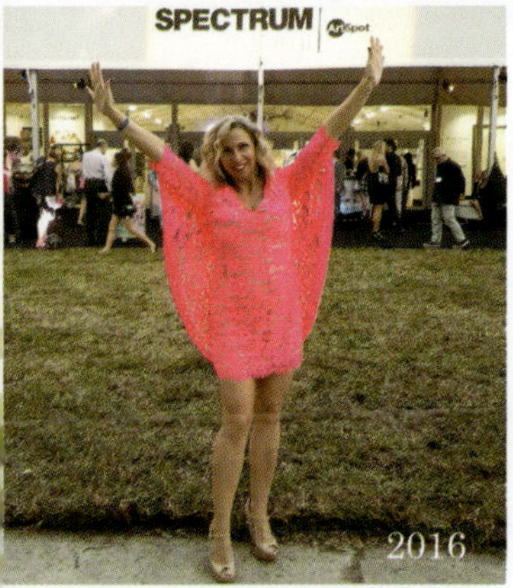

2016

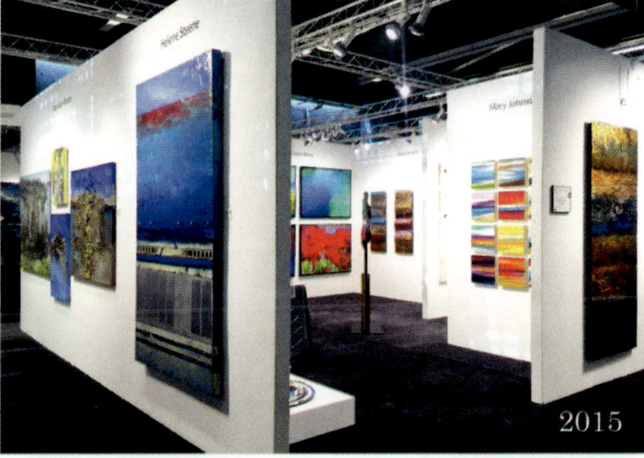

2015

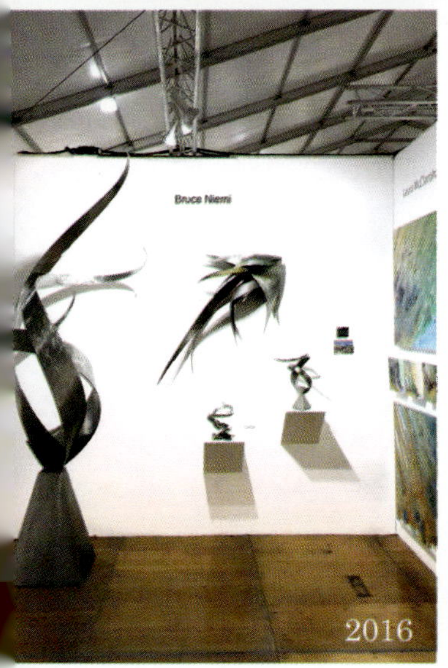

2016

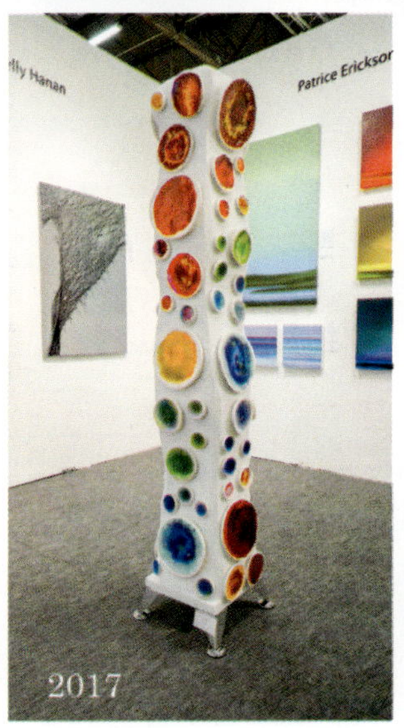
2017

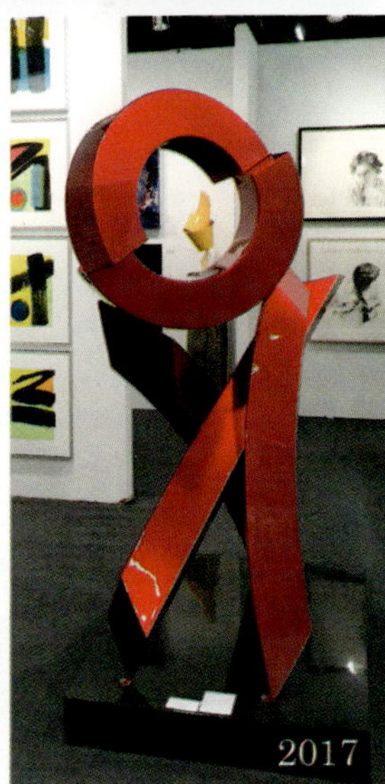
2017

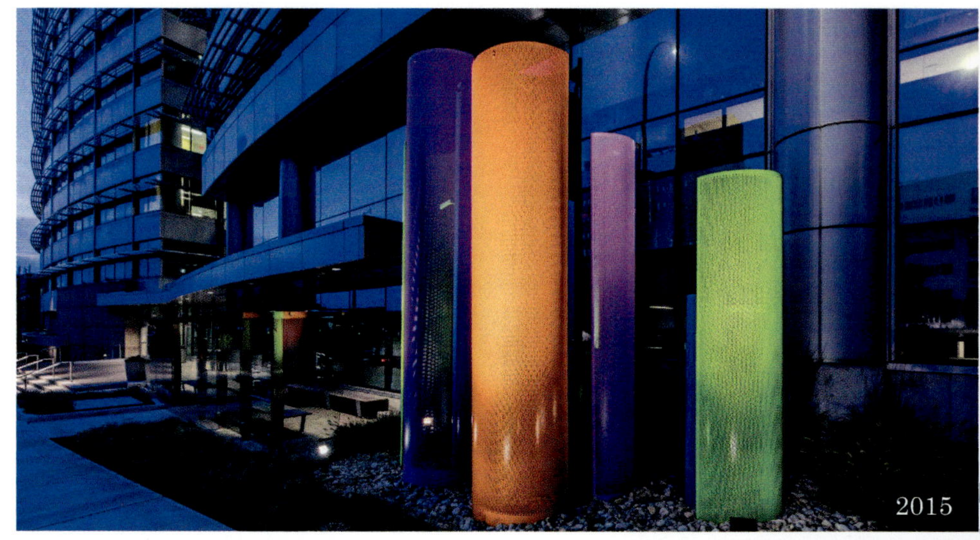

WOW-Worthy Projects

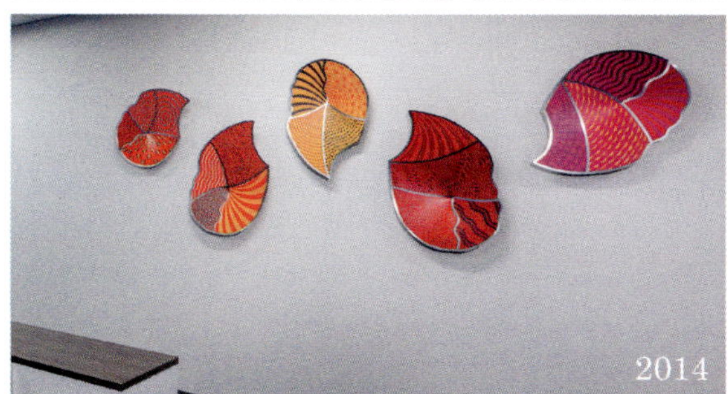

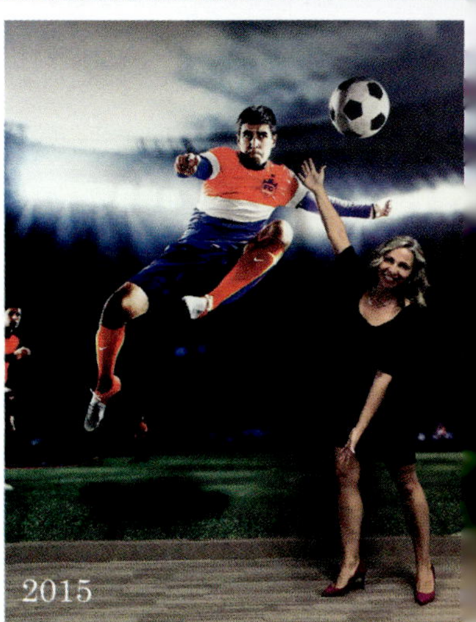

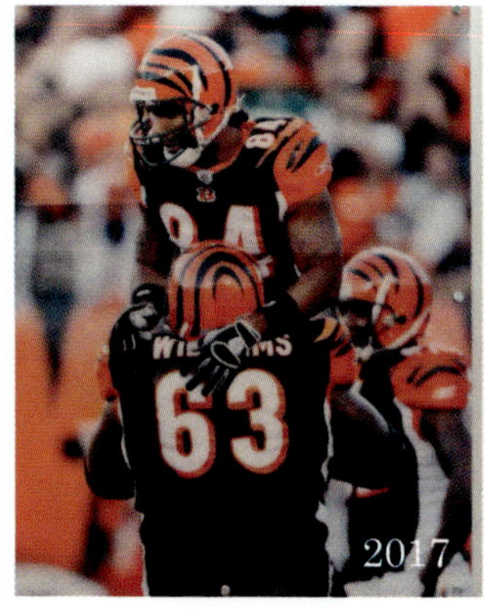

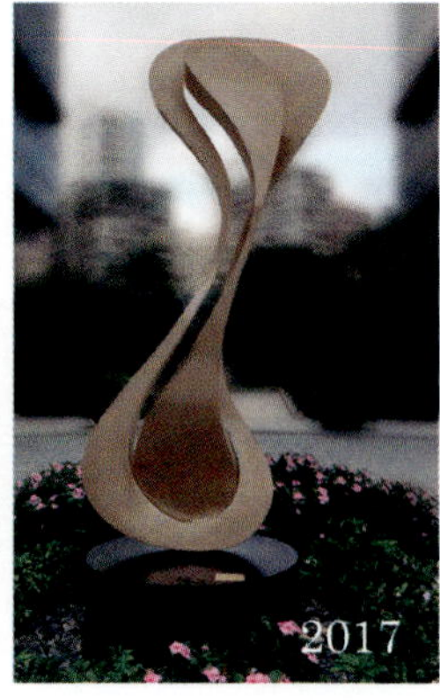

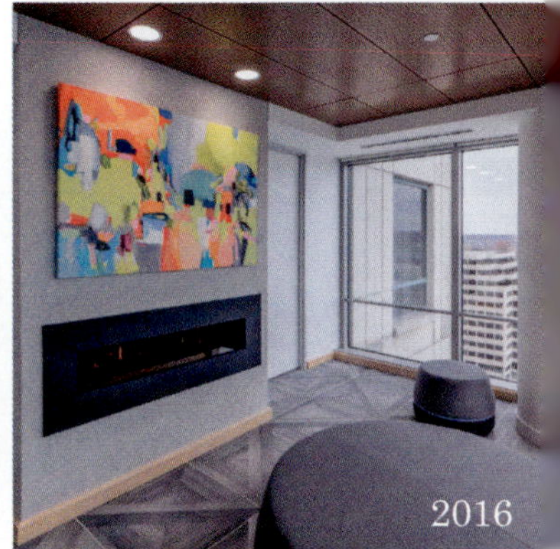

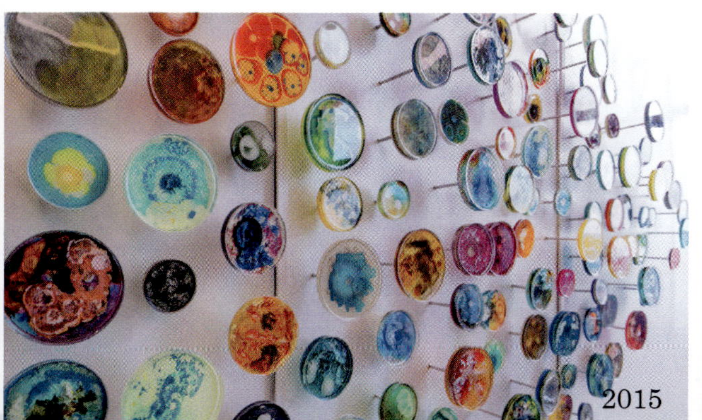
2015

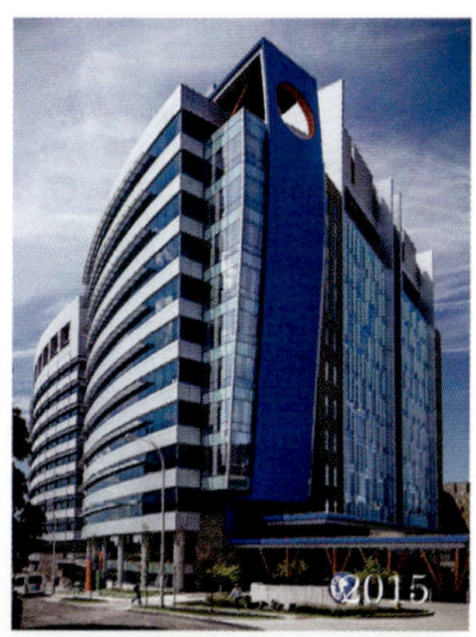
2015

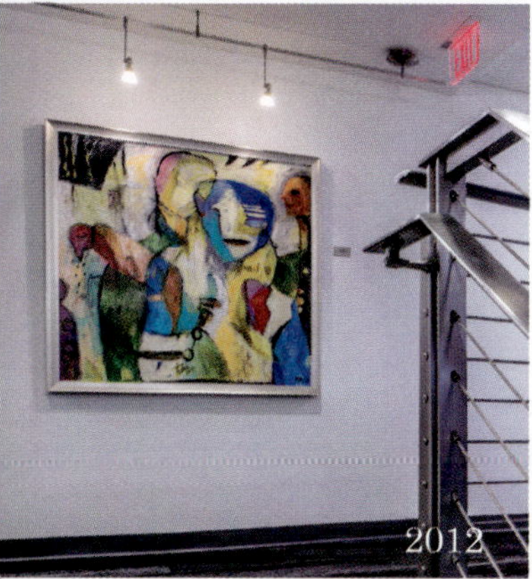
2012

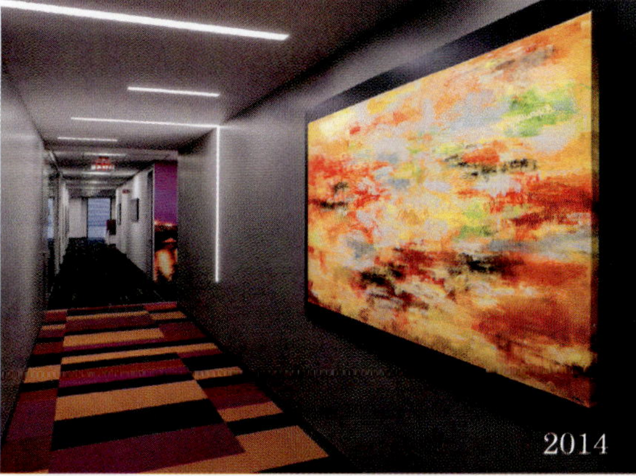
2014

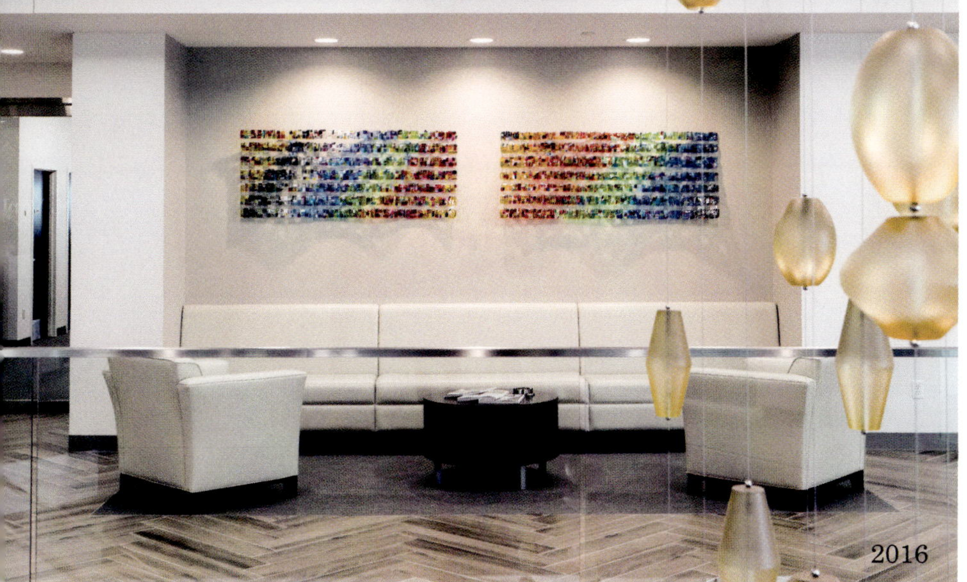
2016

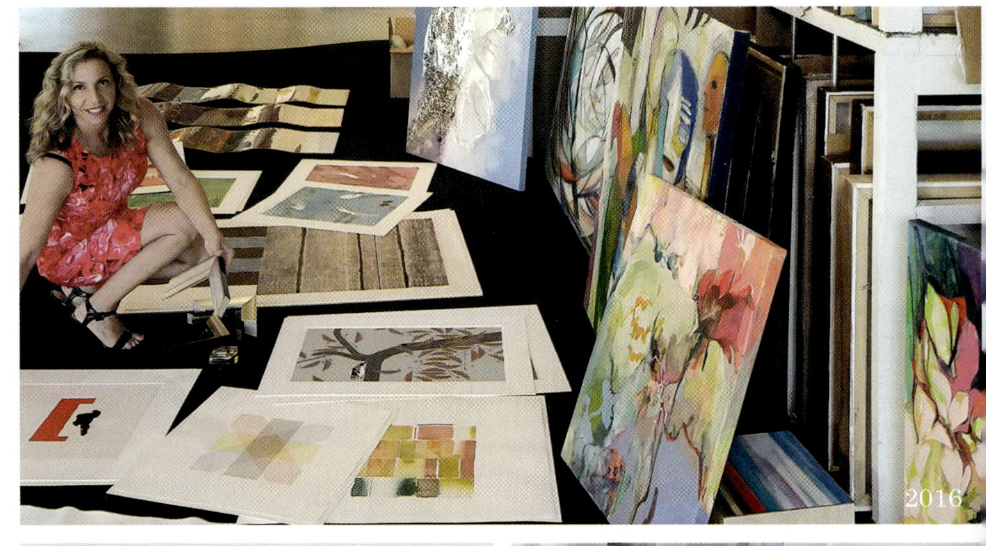
2016

All in a Day's Work

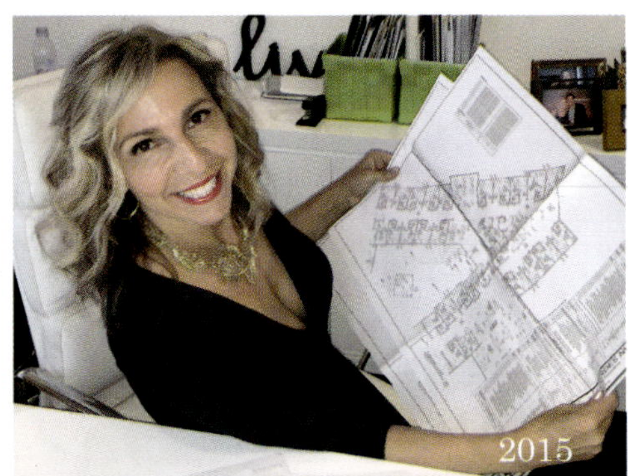
2015

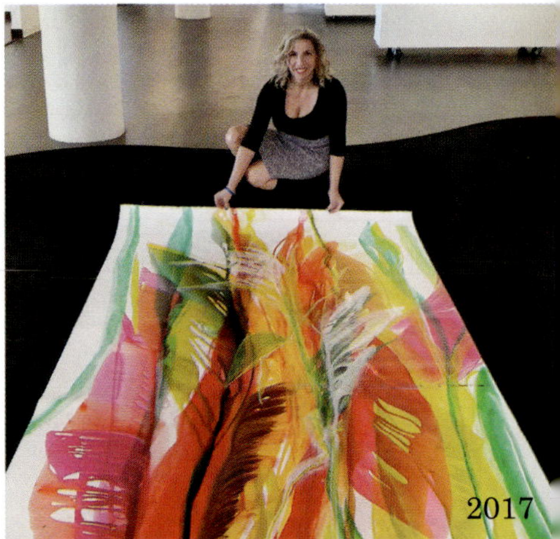
2017

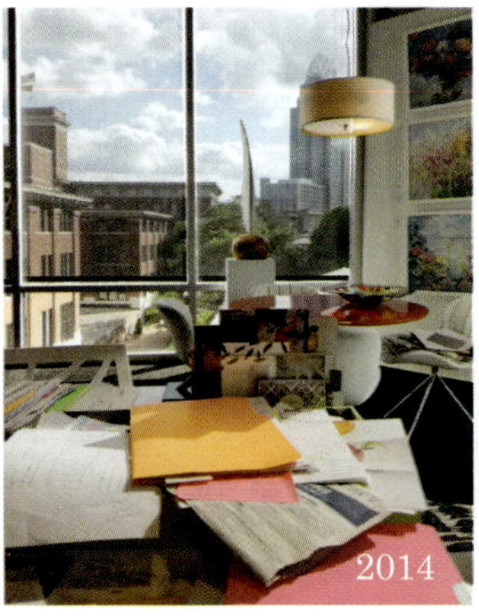
2014

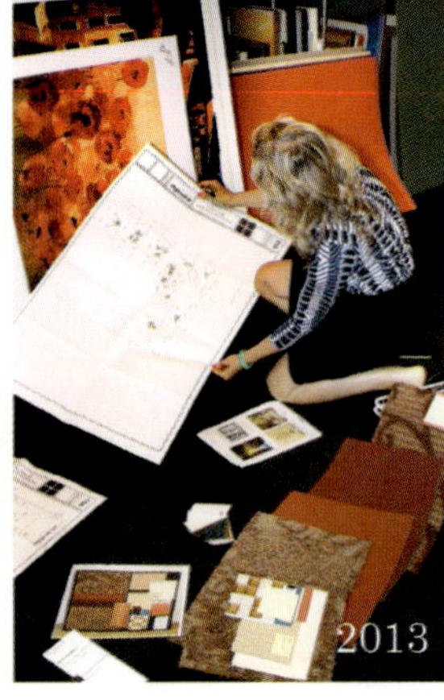
2013

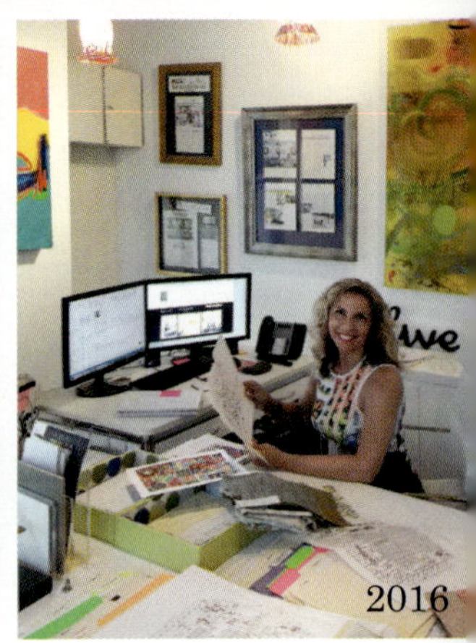
2016

chapter three

SO HOW DO I MAKE MONEY?

"The most common money-related mistake artists make is a reluctance to invest in their own careers."

— Caroll Michels

Separating Yourself from Your Art

You Are Not Your Work

The most common questions I get asked as a gallerist from artists relate to the price of their work. Perhaps there is no question more common than this:

So how much am I worth?

Let me stop you right there. Before I even begin to talk about pricing, selling, and promoting your work, I need you to understand this fundamental thing: *You are not your art work.* Let me repeat this: You are not your art work. When you say things like "How much am I worth?" you're attaching a dollar amount to yourself and your talent. It is impossible to quantify your humanity or your talent. What I, as a gallerist, (and what collectors, buyers, clients, and appraisers) can do is, however, pay a price for your *art work.* It's difficult to do, but you must separate yourself—*your ego*—from the work you do. This is a lesson that artists not only need to learn, but most people in general could benefit from separating themselves and their self-worth from the work they produce. Your value comes not from the prices your work goes for, but from the work itself. The work you do, the life you lead, and the passion you put into your projects is priceless, regardless of what your art is going for in galleries. By looking at your work as something separate from you, several opportunities avail themselves to you. First, you're not going to go on a rollercoaster ride of sheer joy with each sale and then absolute desolation and self-recrimination when your work does not sell. You will be able to accept both circumstances as part of the "process," and as a result you will not make business decisions that are subject to your emotional state (more on this in a bit). Secondly, by separating yourself from your work, you'll be able to accept valuable criticism and expert advice from people who know the industry and what is selling. For example, when someone says a piece is worth about $100 in your particular region or market, you're not going to cry saying, "I am only worth $100! But, I went to an expensive MFA program! I have all these loans and rent to pay! Oh, I am worthless. I should just quit and liquidate all my pieces." No. That's not it at all. Nor should you get an inflated ego and sense of self if your work is selling for thousands of dollars. Your work might demand that. I've seen many successful artists overinflate their prices because their accolades, ego, and sense of entitlement have gone to their heads. There is nothing worse than watching an artist not sell their work, because it's priced too high for their market. All of this is to say, there is a right and a wrong way to price your work. There is a right and a wrong way to do business. It has nothing to do with luck—or how much you as an artist "is worth." It has everything to do with using common sense, ethical practices, and knowing and understanding how your particular market works.

"We artists are indestructible..."
—Pablo Picasso

Pricing Your Art

"From a small seed a mighty trunk may grow."
—Aeschylus

Remember how I told the story of my father working at Sterns and Foster earning a little over two dollars an hour? I need you to remember that when pricing your work. We all need to start somewhere. And NO ONE, I mean, NO ONE, starts off at the top. Everyone has to work. Has to fail. Like the Aeschylus quote above, I need you to think of your art career as something you need to tend and invest in, in order to watch it grow. The work you're doing now, the time you're putting into it every single day, is like planting and tending seeds in a garden. You know it will grow if you water it, come to it daily, and give it the sun and light it deserves and requires. You also know that if you do all this, at harvest time, an abundant garden awaits you. But, you need to give it time. And, you need to do the work in the meantime.

Original artwork, like all non-fungible commodities (houses, jewelry, etc.), varies in its worth. And like all investments, art can grow or decline over time. Every buyer, collector, or investor, is not only buying a piece that they can take home and admire every day, but they're taking a calculated risk and investing too. And like all investments, the values and markets are dependent on a number of economic conditions and factors. Remember when I told you about the day the market crashed in 2008? I wasn't the only gallerist affected. The entire art market suffered. Artists, galleries, investors, collectors, all were going through the same thing. Economic recessions and depressions not only affect the prices of art, but the demand—hence whether or not people can afford to buy the art. In fact, there are a number of variables that affect the price of art. What are they?

Factors to Consider When Pricing Art

1. **Your Experience/Talent/Accolades:** I can't express this enough. Good work demands a good amount of money. Period. How do you know your work is good? Well, you've submitted it for awards and contests and you've won. Maybe you've won fellowships, obtained grants, served as artist-in-residence programs, or perhaps your work has been included in a museum exhibit or a book anthology, has been published or mass produced, or been commended professionally or critically by peers and art critics. The more exposure you get, not to mention accolades and experience you build up, the more your work will be valued. The more time your work has spent in exhibitions, galleries, or has been in the public view the better. Through exposure you build an awareness and an audience, and awareness and an audience build a demand. And a demand in your market sets the price. How do you find this out? ***You need to do your homework.*** Once you find out where you fit in, you also need to consider the size of your artwork (more on the "price per square inch method" later), and the type of your work. For example, sculpture and large canvas paintings tend to cost more to make and the cost

"If people knew how hard I worked to get my mastery, it wouldn't seem so wonderful at all."
—Michelangelo

of materials is always a factor in pricing your work. (You never want to price a piece lower than the materials you spent to make the piece. That's just good business.) Then you need to research other artists who are similar to you in your region, your medium, your subject matter, and your amount of experience, and see what their work is selling at. With sites like ours AD-Cfineart.com, as well as Saatchi.com, Etsy.com, or Vango.com, and even artists' personal websites, it's easy to look at how other artists are pricing their work. If you're feeling particularly bold, you might want to reach out to a comparable artist in your region or genre who has been successful at selling their work and offer to buy them coffee. Find out more about them—their awards, submissions, work process, and pricing. By seeking out others, and then in turn, doing the same to others who seek you out for help, you will be able to build a rapport with other working artists and can more carefully assess where you fit in. You want to slowly, incrementally increase the price of your work. If you are working with a gallerist or consultants, let them advise you. They know the market better than anyone. They will be able to tell you what the market is willing to pay for certain types of art. Listen to them, and then price accordingly.

"Nothing is particularly hard if you divide it into small jobs."
—Henry Ford

2. **Consistency:** Besides setting the appropriate price for your market, the most important thing with pricing art is consistency. Whether online shops, your own website, your own studio, or in a gallery, everything, and I mean

everything, has to be priced equally. This is an absolute must. Why? Oh, I could tell you some stories. First of all, you never ever want to insult a buyer by sizing them up and pricing your work based on what you think he or she will pay. It's simply unethical. In fact, I recommend never showing your work to any buyer without pricing it first. This is an industry absolute. Just because you think someone has more money to spend does not mean you upcharge them. When I have clients who come to me with more money to spend, I don't change the prices of the paintings, I sell them more paintings! You never want to insult a buyer or make them feel like a fool. Nor do you want to damage your relationships with gallery owners, studios, or consultants who represent your work.

"Promotion and perception are synonymous twins of art marketing."
—Jack White

Many, many years ago I had a friend who was a gallerist who represented an artist and sold a considerable amount of work to her clients on the artist's behalf. She even sold one piece at around the two-thousand-dollar price at one point. Buyers were willing to pay this amount. One day shortly after making the $2000 sale, the gallerist found out her artist was liquidating all of her work—with comparable images, subjects, and sizes—*for a $100 apiece.* My friend immediately received a call from an angry client who felt duped by her. The buyer thought my friend had sold him an overpriced, devalued piece of art. She then had to explain that she hadn't changed the price or the value of the art work and that was the price originally set. It was the artist who devalued the work. Whatever the artist's reasoning or emotional state—maybe she was feeling down or needed money quickly (as I was talking before about emotional decisions that hinder you)—this was a bad business decision. By undercutting the gallery, she lost credibility and devalued her artwork. My friend could never sell her work in good faith to a client again and ended their relationship. Let this be a lesson: You can always charge more for your art, but you rarely want to be in the position where you have to devalue your own pieces. By setting and keeping a price, and then maintaining that price in your own studio, on your website, you're assisting the gallerist, buyers, and collectors, because your buyers will know what your art work is worth. If you want to keep a good relationship with a gallery owner, you don't want to sell your work at a lower rate or cut "deals" on the side. You need to think of your gallerist as a partner, who is representing you and your work to buyers and clients. They will serve you in the long run. Don't destroy relationships with your gallerists, consultants, or clients or your own reputation for a one-time sale.

3. **Your Overhead:** All businesses have overhead costs. Gallery space, utilities, office supplies, insurance, employees, exhibition fees, materials, healthcare are just some of mine. Every business person knows to consider overhead when pricing your work. If you're a sculptor who uses a particularly expensive kind of marble—you must factor the cost of that marble into the price of the work. You may also factor in a percentage of the cost of the tools, the space you use to create it, and then you have to think about your own hourly rate. You can use tools

like Glassdoor.com or Payscale.com to see what the average hourly rate a fine artist with your level of experience can charge an hour. Writers, for example, just starting out may charge $9 an hour, but more experienced ones can charge up to $75 an hour. The same goes for architects, surgeons, consultants. In every business there is a level of expertise that demands a certain pay scale. Again your expertise, accolades, and accomplishments factor into your hourly rate. According to Payscale.com, the hourly rate for a fine artist currently ranges between $9.00-$40.00 an hour, that's an average hourly range of $19.83 an hour. If you're a mid-career artist and spend ten hours working on a piece, that's a base pay of $190.83. If your materials cost over $300, then the lowest possible price you can wholesale your work for would be $490.83 (about $500 or $1,000 retail). The "price per square inch" model is also helpful. Once you establish your hourly rate, the percentage cost of your materials, you divide your work down into a "square inch" price. That way whether the size of your canvas is 12 x 12 or 120 x 120 the cost per square inch is the same. It keeps you from guessing whether you should charge $1,000 or $10,000 for a piece. Not only does it keep you from inflating your art's worth, but it keeps you from devaluing it as well. And again, it keeps you honest and consistent, which also helps enhance your credibility as an artist. Another thing to consider is the "retail" price of your work. What you just set was the "base" or "wholesale" amount. In order for gallerists or consultants to make a profit they will usually charge twice the amount (again, the gallerist has

"In art the best is good enough."
—Johann Wolfgang von Goethe

to cover his/her overhead, which is considerable, while still making a profit). So if you know the base price of a piece is $500, a gallery will sell that piece for $1,000 (and keep 50 percent of the profit). If you have similar pieces in size and subject matter on your website, you too should be charging $1,000 retail for similar pieces. Again, you never want to undercut a gallery or art consultants. They are there to help you market and sell your work and give you exposure. As a bonus, consider this, the work you sell at the retail price point (without a consultant or gallerist) goes directly in your pocket. Again, I repeat, lowering the value of your work only hurts you in the long run.

4. **Your Market and Audience:** If you haven't been a fine artist for a considerable amount of time, established exposure, credibility, or achieved accolades, you might find your market or audience is limited. You might need to "sow some seeds" in order to get your work some exposure (more on marketing and advertising awaits you in Chapter Four). You might want to start with a coffee house or a restaurant, an art show, or a contest. This is just an educated guess, but I doubt you're going to get a buyer for a $2,000 piece while they're ordering their half-caf-latte on their way to work. Look at what other artists are charging for their pieces in that coffee house. Similarly, if you are at an art show, don't be afraid to price your work accordingly. Do your research beforehand. Make sure you know what other artists are charging for their work. You don't want to be the lowest priced art work

"You don't want a buyer to feel that he's been foolish or cheated. So they all get the same price."
—Bill Hambrecht

(nor do you want to be the highest). Again, you want to be competitive. Let me assure you, people never buy art work because it's "cheap." They buy what they love and what they want to look at every day. If they're an investor, they're buying with the hopes that you'll succeed as an artist, and someday they or their progeny will reap the rewards of the investment. As a rule, I think buyers are suspicious of prices that are too low. Just as overpriced work can scare buyers away, so too can too low of a value. People are looking to *invest, not spend.* People are looking to be delighted, intrigued, and inspired by your work. Don't let them down.

Do Your Homework

Practical Exercises to Do Today to Help You Price Your Work

1. Using multiple sources—national websites, galleries, and studios, as well as local galleries, artists' websites, and studios—list at least ten artists who work in the same medium as you and next to their names write the average price of one of their pieces (that most resembles yours in size, detail, nuance, or concept).

Artist	Average Price of Work
1.	1.
2.	2.
3.	3.
4.	4.
5.	5.
6.	6.
7.	7.
8.	8.
9.	9.
10.	10.

2. Out of those ten artists, which ones have the same amount of experience or accolades? How much are they charging for their work?

3. Based on your career level and experience how much could you reasonably charge an hour for your time spent working? (Remember you can use Payscale.com). Then honestly assess how long it takes you (average) to do a piece? How much should you be earning per piece?

4. Consider your overhead per piece. What does this cost? (Do not over inflate this. Be honest.)

5. Add your overhead to your total hours worked multiplied by your average pay per hour? What is the base price of your piece? Now multiple this price by 2. Now you have your retail price.

6. Now measure the size of the piece in square inches. Divide the total number you came up with above by square inches. You just found out how much you could charge per square inch for your paintings. (For example. If you discovered your base price is $500 and your piece is 200 square inches, then your cost per square inch is $2.50. Now if you have a piece that is 1,000 square inches, you have a base price of $2,500 and a retail price of $5,000. Remember, if your work is being represented or sold, you'll get for a $2,500 for the piece, and the gallery will receive $2,500. If you sell it directly, you receive $5,000.)

7. How does this price compare to your contemporaries in your region? Too high? Too low?

8. This final exercise requires more introspection. Are you comfortable with this amount? How does it make you feel? Do you have work to do to get over your ego, whether it's a false sense of entitlement or a lack of your own self-worth? Have you made strides to separate your ego from the price of your art work?

Selling Your Art

"Making money is art and working is art and good business is the best art."

—Andy Warhol

Now that you've done your research and you know how to price your work (approximately, remember your gallery and consultant will ultimately advise you on what your market is paying for artwork in your medium), you're ready to get out there and sell. Yes, this is a cringe-worthy word to most artists. But, I want you to let go of any feelings that you (and your ego) have about selling art work. Remember, there is no shame in making a living doing what you love. In fact, it is the ideal life—to be paid to do what you love. Do not be shy about your desire to make money from what you create. Please, if I can advise one thing, don't be too pretentious about your work. This is art. It's not cold fusion. Each piece of your collection is not single-handedly saving the world. Let's be real here for a moment. And this is exactly what we are about to be when it comes to selling and presenting your artwork to potential buyers.

Getting Real About Selling Your Work in Six Easy Steps

1. **It's all about relationships.** The absolute best advice I can give anyone in business—not just artists—is to know your customers. Don't just spend time talking to them and telling them all about you and your work. LISTEN. Listen to what they want, what they like, what they're going through. Showing you care about them endears them to you. Give them ample opportunities—several—to get to

know you, too. (We'll talk about this at length in Chapter Four.) I can't emphasize enough the power of social media, blogging, and networking. And I am not just talking about putting "stuff out there," but I am talking about responding and engaging with your audience as well. Spend one-on-one time with buyers too. If a buyer emails you with a question, ask for their phone number. Pick up the phone and talk to them. I never think of myself as a sales person. Ever. I think of myself as someone who is "helping" others. People come to me seeking advice about artwork and how to beautify their space or make it more welcoming, healing, or inspiring. I see it as my job to listen to their needs and help them make the best choice. When artists come to me, I see it as my privilege and duty to advise and guide them as best as I can so they can continue to prosper in doing what they love. At the end of the day, I believe the strongest relationships are rewarded with sales. It's just a natural by-product of a real relationship that is mutually beneficial to both parties. *In sum: Build relationships, and you'll have an easier time selling.*

"The artist's object is to make things not as nature makes them, but as she would make them. "

—Raphael

2. **K.I.S.S.** ***(Keep it simple, Sch-weetheart)***. Do not, I repeat, do not use industry jargon. As I said before let go of your pretention and hifalutin airs. Clients who understand the industry will see right through you. You can't fool someone who knows better. And the more someone knows, the less likely they will need to hide behind jargon and false-pretenses. And those who don't understand, or who are new to the industry, will be confused and put off. You don't want your buyers to feel stupid, ill-informed, or un-

comfortable. Remember it's all about building an authentic relationship. The art world is small. And reputations precede you. You always want to present yourself in the most real, authentic, and caring way. If you must use technical terms, and you're with someone whom you know isn't familiar with them, take a minute to explain the terms. (However, again, know your audience. You don't want to patronize other artists or experts.) Tailor your words to the person with whom you are speaking. I always discuss art differently with other artists and designers than I do with corporate clients. *In sum: Always, be sure your client or buyer understands you.*

"The first requisite of success is the ability to apply your physical and mental energies to one problem without growing weary."
—Thomas Edison

3. **Qualify your client.** As I said in number one, getting to know your client and your client's needs are crucial to making sales. Not every buyer has the same budget or needs. Does the customer walking into your studio have collecting in mind or are they on a Pottery Barn budget? You need to ask important questions, and honest ones, to see what your customer wants and needs. Some questions illicit responses that are telling, without having to be too intrusive or rude. For example, you might ask: What does your home or office look like? What type of art do you currently own? Do you have a budget? These questions help to determine the customer's wants and needs. And getting these questions answered sooner rather than later, will ultimately save you time and energy. *In sum: Ask important questions up front.*

4. **Offer a variety.** As number one, two, and three point out, every buyer, customer, or client has a different set of

needs, a different budget, a different set of criteria for why they buy art. Until you have found your niche market, you need to experiment a bit. You need to offer a variety of price ranges, sizes, and subject matters. It's a way of "crowdsourcing"—by putting out as much as you can, you are giving your audience an ample amount to choose from. When you see what the majority of your audience is buying or interested in, you'll be able to use that data to help you create more of what sells. *In sum: Don't be afraid to experiment.*

5. **Keep it exciting.** Is your studio interesting and exciting? Offer your customers unexpected discoveries as they explore. Showcase pieces that you love. Consider the flow and create a space where people will want to linger. Get rid of any and all art that you haven't sold in years. You need to keep reinventing yourself and your space to attract new buyers, as well as offer your galleries new works to see. *In sum: Give buyers a reason to follow you and your artwork throughout your entire career. Don't get complacent.*

6. **Be grateful.** On no, here's that word *grateful* again. But, I can't emphasize how important this is. Show your gratitude for every sale. Handwrite a simple thank you card (and depending on how long you know the customer, a heartfelt note on personalized stationary) to the special client who just purchased one of your pieces or a gallery who is representing you. *In sum: Say thank you. It always goes a long way.*

But don't just take my word for it. Artist, galleries, and consultants, all have their own unique perspectives on selling their art work and making it in the art world today. I spoke to several and here's their take on what the secret is to their success and what they think artists like you can do too.

Lisa England Schuster

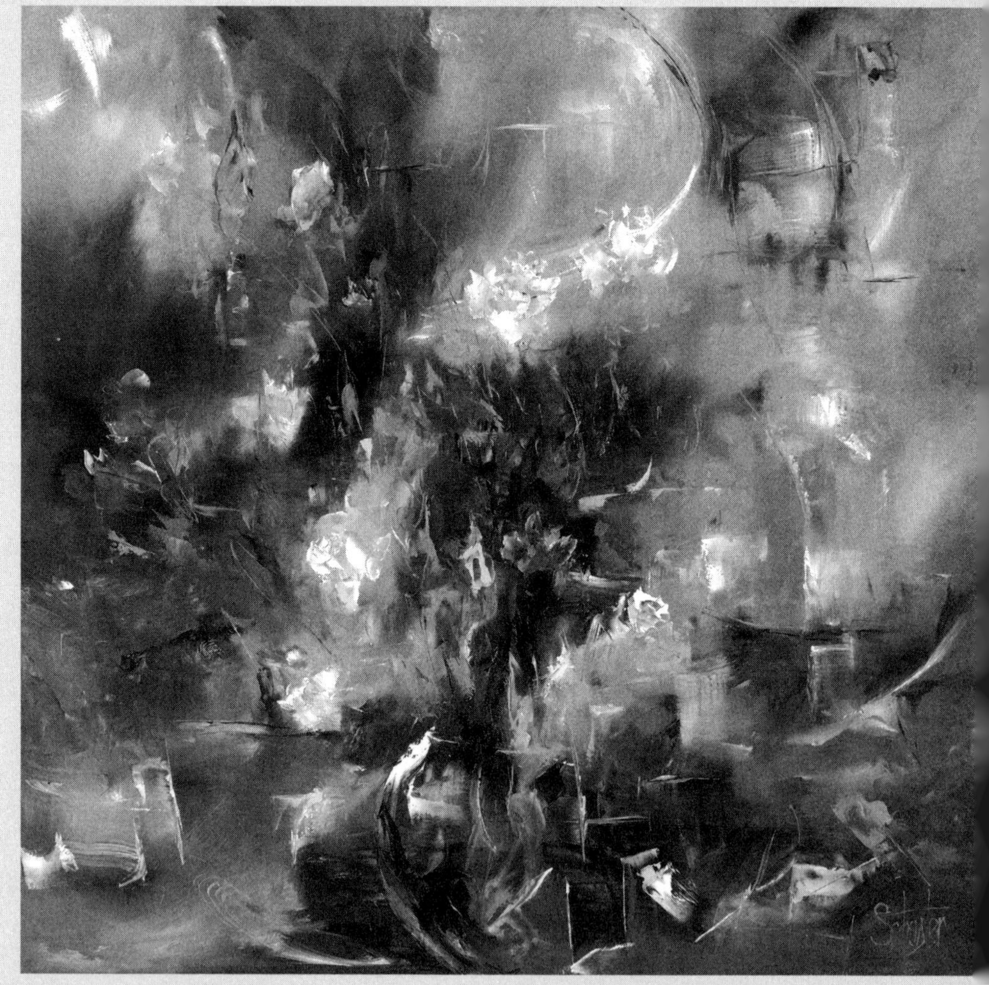

© Lisa England Schuster

Working with Designers and Galleries

Oh gosh, what can't I say about this incredibly talented artist? She has been an award-winning artist at our annual ACA Awards four times! She is one my top sellers, and over the years she's become a personal friend. I met her just five years ago through a friend who is an interior designer and was just blown away by her talent. (I couldn't get over the fact that Lisa didn't discover her talent as an artist until her thirties. And, boy, has she been making up for lost time ever since!) For the past twenty years she has painted hundreds of paintings spanning vast genres and mediums using countless techniques. What I love about Lisa is she is one of the most ethical and grounded artists I've ever worked with. She's been extremely successful in her career, and I think it comes down to the way she has approached the business side of her art. She knows what she's doing. And she understands how this business works and how an artist can thrive by working in it.

"Like most thriving relationships, a strong artist-designer relationship begins with initial mutual attraction," Lisa says about finding the right people to represent her work. And I couldn't agree more. Artists and gallerists have to have good chemistry. You need the person who is representing your work to be genuinely interested and passionate about your work. She adds, "The designers that look most alluring to artists are those who are genuinely busy; they have multiple designers on staff and continuous and multifarious projects. They are the ones repeatedly featured in local magazines and other media. Ideally, they will have a brick and mortar showroom as well as a polished online presence in which you can showcase some of your work."

Lisa also understands what we galleries or consultants need and she knows how to best accommodate them, so they, in turn can sell your work. She astutely notes, "From the gallerist's perspective, they are looking for art that enhances rather than competes with other art they offer. They must like your artistic style and see it and you as adaptable. The more visible you are, the more awards and features you have received, the easier it is for a designer or gallery to establish your legitimacy and value to their clients."

And we both agree on this: Communication is key. She says, "Once the relationship has been sparked it is all about communication and trust. Be physically and emotionally available. Answer your phone or email immediately. Remember they are usually under tight timelines and there are many other artists to choose from. Allow yourself to be vulnerable." She also has great advice for artists who still take criticism personally: "If they like 80 percent of a work but want to change the other 20 percent don't take it personally. It is a chance to grow, expand your box a bit, to flex your creativity. Be a good listener; take the time to get a real feel for the space and the designer's vision."

Lisa also knows the value of establishing trust between the artist and gallery or designer. She advises, "If you commit to a commission deadline, commit. Don't make promises you can't keep." And like me, she understands the value of consistent pricing. "Make your pricing structure and terms clear upfront. If you meet their clients, make it very clear that you will never sell directly to their client, that you will always keep them in the loop. And then honor that commitment."

Her final, and I think most important piece of advice, is to do your best as an artist to support and celebrate your relationship with a gallery or designer. She says, "Refer your clients to them. Reference them in any media attention that you receive. Like and share their Facebook, Instagram and Twitter posts. Support their charities. And never underestimate their artistic sensibilities. Although they don't have 'artist' on their cards, they usually are artists, just working in a different medium."

To learn more about Lisa and her art, visit www.lisaschusterart.com

Roy Saper

Saper Galleries

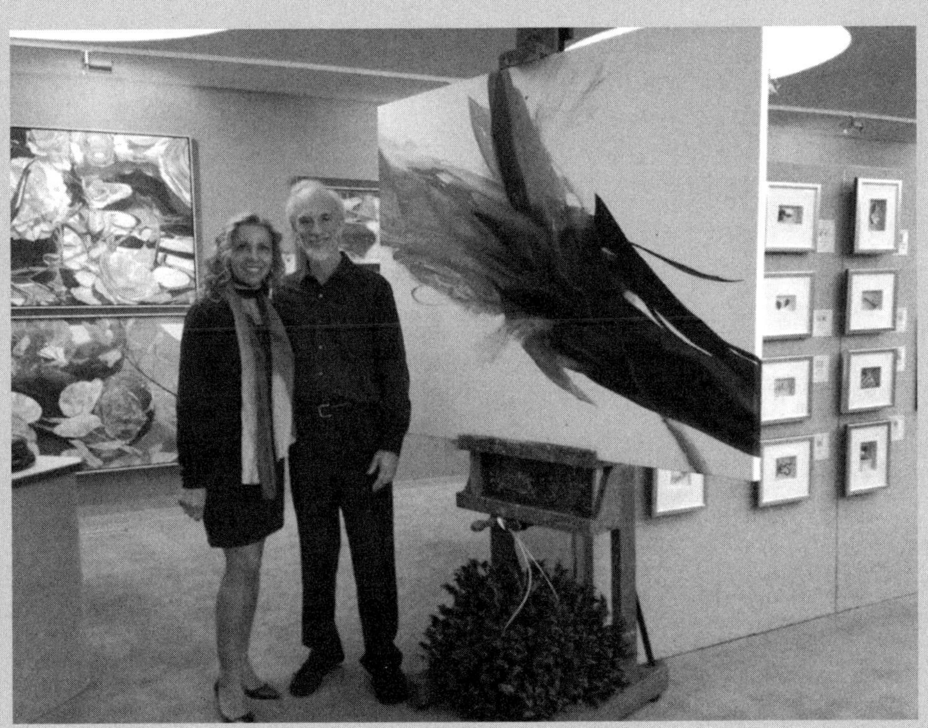

Working with Designers and Galleries

I met Roy Saper ten years ago under the delightful circumstance that we both won awards from *Décor Magazine*. He won for Best Art Exhibition, and I had won for Best Gallery. While we were in Atlanta to accept our awards, we immediately hit it off. And I've considered him a friend and admired colleague ever since.

Roy is not just a remarkable man, he's a distinguished and well-regarded gallery owner. He is so full of knowledge and down-to-earth, because he has experienced everything one can imagine in the art world. In fact, many seek him out for appraisals and for his expertise. When I asked him if he had any advice to offer artists seeking to submit their work to his gallery, he had so much information to share, I just had to pass it on. He certainly knows what it takes. So if you're an artist and you're serious about selling your work, my advice would be to listen to what Roy has to say.

Excellence is a word that that comes to mind, when I think of Roy. He has impeccable standards. If you're desperate and just looking to send a gallery "everything you've got," please don't. Roy recommends presenting galleries with only your best work. This takes some objectivity, and as I mentioned earlier, the ability to separate yourself and your ego from your work. You want your work to stand out—and that includes the framing. Roy adds, "If the artworks are framed, the framing should be outstanding too, and not look like the artist did it themselves or used a least-cost option. Badly presented or framed artwork will be a detriment to getting a gallery to accept it—or sell it."

And how do you know if it's excellent? It will take a trained eye. And that is something only time and experience will bring you. Roy warns, "If the artwork looks like student work, it won't pass muster at Saper Galleries. That means the artist successfully meeting their objective with phenomenal control, technical skill, and mastery of the medium." And there are plenty of artists who are able to achieve such objectives.

"We have some artists for whom we have sold more than 1,000 original works of art because they meet our quality requirements," Roy says.

Roy acknowledges, however, that art is a subjective business. And, he recognizes other galleries might find the quality of the work or subject matter of art that he rejected more suitable for their audience. "Not all artists are right for all galleries but presenting one's very best artwork increases one's chances of being accepted by a gallery," he reminds artists.

"Additionally, there should be a cohesive thread common to all of an artist's work," Roy advises. "Presenting a wide range of styles, subject matters, techniques, and media suggests the artist is still trying to figure out where to go—the artist is still searching, exploring, learning, testing." This is fine for an artist just starting out, but in order to work closely with a designer or a gallery, you, as an artist, want to refine your message and your medium. As Roy points out, "I want to see a body of work that represents the artist's style of the moment."

Like most galleries, Saper Galleries has submission guidelines and a consistent body of art work. Roy recommends all artists do their homework. Roy says, "An artist should connect with galleries that display artwork consistent with what the artist is doing, not a gallery that is totally different (in terms of medium, style, price range, or other measures)."

In order to get your work represented by a gallery, you have to contact his gallery via email. He recommends sending a direct link to high quality images that include details and the price. He adds, "Don't send anyone a link until you get high quality photos. Indicate also what other galleries are selling your work."

At the end of the day, Roy knows what every gallery owner knows, the very best sells. "Innovative, creative, unique, and quality work is what I like to see. If I believe we would have clients who would purchase what an artist has and it meets our requirements, you will receive checks from us."

To submit your work to Roy Saper Galleries, visit www.sapergalleries.com

Sylvia Rombis

Malton Gallery

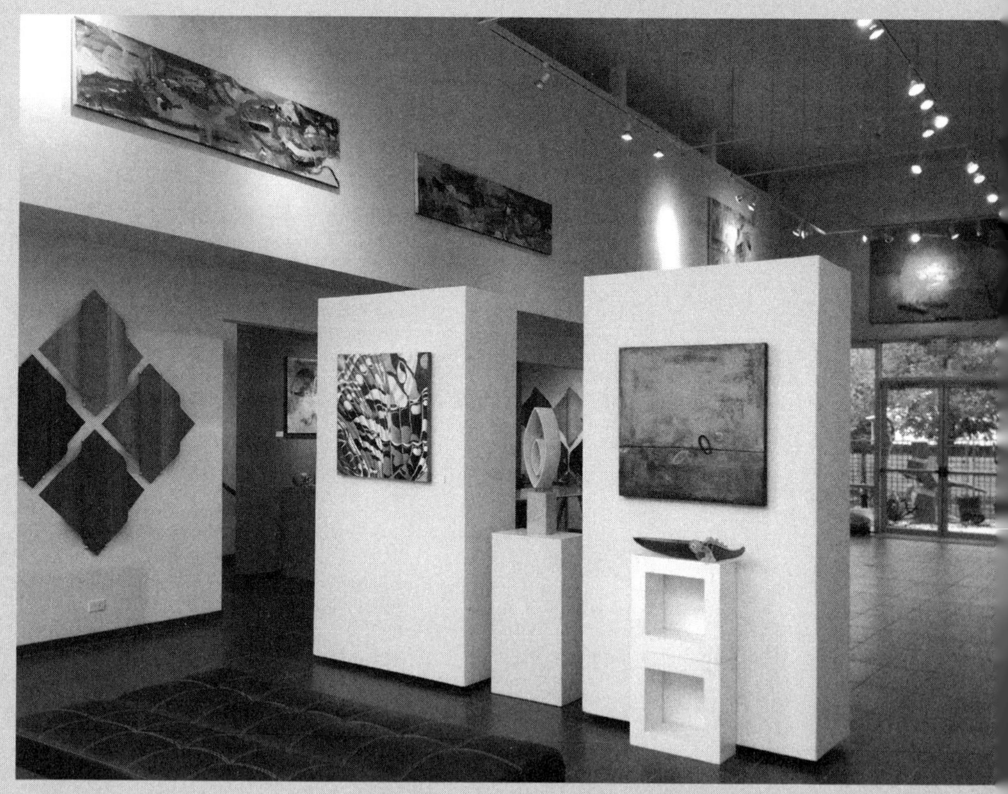

Submitting Work to Galleries

When I think of a gallery owner with a precise eye and an impeccable attention to detail, who knows exactly what her clients want, and what artists need to do to meet those clients' needs, I think of my one and only sister, Sylvia Rombis. As I mentioned in the Introduction, Sylvia is a true artist in her own right. (She got her start in the professional world designing evening wear and then moved on to fashion footwear.) She's also a phenomenal businesswoman. She received two Bachelor degrees in marketing and fashion design, and went on to earn her Masters in design. As a shoe designer, she was in charge of an product line worth $870 million. She traveled the world and took her products from the "fine art" stage—the prototype, which she designed—all the way through the engineering, production, and promotion of the product. During her successful career, she learned the importance of building and maintaining relationships, as well as understanding intimately the cost—both financial and emotional—of creating one's artwork.

Sylvia is a tireless worker and also the consummate mother. Several years ago, with two young children at home, Sylvia realized that the long hours on the road were not where she wanted to be. She realized her favorite part of work was designing and working on the prototype—the fine art stage—of her work. Like me, and our mother before us, Sylvia was and is drawn to beauty and creating something beautiful. When the opportunity to purchase the Malton Art Gallery came to her, she knew she had to take the risk. She also knew she could leverage her strengths as a business woman and her love of art and make the successful transition from corporate executive to art gallery owner. Over the years, she's curated a distinct contemporary gallery that caters to residential home owners and interior designers. She credits her success to one thing: "It's all about relationships. I do very little marketing or social media. I don't have to. I know every single one of my clients and treat them well. I give my clients extraordinary service. I am always there at every installation. When they thank me for my help finding a beautiful, one-of-a-kind piece, I ask them for only one thing: Referrals. And that's how I've built and maintained my business. There is nothing as valuable as your credibility and ethics. If people can trust you, they will want to work with you. And they will refer you."

And she looks for that credibility and ethics in her artists as well. "I work with professionals. I work with people who I can have a relationship with and who I can trust to bring their work into my clients' homes. Art is a personal thing. Our gallery currently has 1,200 pieces from 100 artists. I know every single one of my artists and their works. I also know which clients would love a particular piece of work. It's all about the right fit. My clients know I have their best interests in mind, and I know my artists know that too."

Her advice to getting work in her gallery? "Be professional. Don't waste a gallery owner's time. Any time they spend doing unnecessary things they're taking precious time away from their clients or other artists. Curate your best work and submit it—with the prices and details," she says. "Don't make a gallery owner click through a series of links to get the details. Be grateful and patient." She also recommends calling or making appointments to show work, "Don't just show up at a gallery. You wouldn't march past a personal assistant and barge into a CEO's meeting and demand that he reviews your resume. He would have to stop what he was doing. He would have to pull his time away from other people who deserve his time. It's ridiculous to think you would do that in the corporate world, and yet people do it in the art world all the time." She tells a story of a time a man brought his eight-year-old son and laid down a number of child's drawings on the floor of her gallery during business hours, when clients and customers were in the gallery. He demanded that Sylvia look and comment on his child's work. "It's crazy, but it happens. And he wasn't the only one. Many artists do it. And it just proves to me you're not ready as an artist and you haven't done your homework. If you want to be treated like a professional, you need to act like a professional. That means doing the work. That means researching a gallery and understanding how your work might fit in. It also means recognizing that a gallery owner is providing you a valuable service," she says. Many artists don't understand why gallerists want commissions. "I am the artist. I did all the work and you're just taking the money," she repeats and oft-heard remark from artists. "What I do isn't free. To keep the gallery open, heated, lit, insured, and beautiful to attract customers to the art isn't free. To hire assistants, framers, and installers isn't free. To promote the work and get it in the hands of clients isn't free. It also takes up a considerable amount of time. What I do means artists can focus on creating work. And artists, as professionals, have to understand that there is a cost for that," she says.

So how does an artist "wow" a gallery owner? Sylvia says, "First and foremost, they show me that they're professionals. They've defined themselves as an artist. They have a clear elevator speech—and it's clear they know who they are talking to. They treat gallery owners with respect and have selected their very best work, 5-6 pieces should suffice, to present in a concise and clear way. Any gallery owner would be happy to work with someone like this."

To submit your work to Sylvia, visit www.maltonartgallery.com

The Importance of Shows
How, When and Where to Show Your Work

Here's something else I've heard over the years:

"All galleries owners want to see that I'm a professional, that I have accolades, and that I have exhibited before, but how can I achieve these things if I can't get into a gallery?"

Ah yes, the age old conundrum, how does an artist earn credentials if they can't get their work in the door? There are plenty of ways to get exposure, earn valuable experience, receive feedback, and earn those prized credentials and accolades most gallery owners are looking for. Here are just a few suggestions:

1. **Open Studio Exhibitions:** Whether you rent a studio space in a larger studio or work out of your own home, you should promote and offer an "open studio" time to potential clients or buyers. At least once a month, host an event where you can show your work to potential buyers. Be sure to do your homework and practice acting like a professional artist—that means price your work before you show it, and only present those pieces you feel confident are your best work. Curate your "showroom" or "studio"—by featuring your selected paintings and have ready-available printouts with details for each piece that includes your contact information. Provide food, snacks, and wine. Advertise the event on social media. Set up an event on Facebook. Invite colleagues, friends, family members, neighbors, and recommend they bring friends. Send invitations to gallery owners in your area, with a teaser and a photo.

2. **Juried Competitions:** Juried Competitions are often organized by membership organizations of artists, and are advertised all over the Internet, in art magazines, journals, and universities. Juried art competitions are large-scale group exhibitions that offer the public the chance to see individual artist's work in particular styles (contemporary, modern, post-modern, classic, etc.), mediums (sculpture, photography, watercolor, oil, pastel, acrylic, etc.), or subjects (landscape, figurative, abstract, etc.). These shows give artists the unique opportunity to both meet potential buyers and be discovered by gallery owners who would like to represent their work. Additionally, it gives artists an opportunity to practice talking about their work and perfecting their "elevator pitch." (For more information, on how to craft an elevator pitch, **see page 178.**) Most shows are not free, and require an application fee, as well as the costs of sending the work to the exhibition site. Additional costs may be travel, lodging, food, and insurance. While the costs of being included in a jury may seem overwhelming, the benefits may far exceed the costs. If your work is selected or awarded you may have a chance to win a monetary prize or a contract (as well as an accolade to list on your resume and in your portfolio). You will also gain valuable feedback and criticism that may help your future work. You'll also establish connections and relationships with others in the industry. Each year, my gallery, ADC, Art Design Consultants, Inc., offers a juried competition, ART COMES ALIVE (ACA), an annual fine art contest and exhibition that awards the brightest and best artists working in North America, in a variety of categories. It's a great opportunity for artists to be acknowledged for their talents, gain exposure, and win purchase awards, and

gallery contracts. It's a unique chance for artist to get noticed by my clients, collectors, corporations, health care and hospitality industries, and interior designers, art galleries, and art dealers. (For submission guidelines and further details visit, ADCFineArt.com and click on the For Artists link.)

3. **Shows at Nonprofit Galleries:** Nonprofit galleries show the work of novice or undiscovered artists, who are trying to break in to the art world (or whose work might be deemed too edgy for the consumer market). The major difference between a typical gallery and a nonprofit gallery is the obvious: The nonprofit gallery doesn't depend on an artist's sales to stay in business. Rather, nonprofits depend on fundraising efforts, grants, or in some cases, established trusts. However, some nonprofits may request a small commission to help offset costs or expenses—the key is they do not profit at all from the commission. Nonprofit galleries do not "represent" artists or have contracts with artists. Nonprofits can afford to take more risks with the work they exhibit, because they are not purchasing and maintaining an inventory, and so they don't lose money if an artist's work doesn't sell. There are nonprofit galleries in most major cities, and all have submission guidelines, which you can find online. They also offer lots of opportunities to get involved in the arts community in the city and volunteer. Here's just a quick overview of some major city's nonprofit galleries. It's by no means comprehensive. If you live in remote location, try searching your town's name and nonprofit arts organization. You might be surprised to discover there is somewhere nearby you can submit your work.

NON-PROFIT ART GALLERIES

Atlanta	Eyedrum	www.eyedrum.org
Boston	Green Street Gallery	www.greenstreetgallery.org
Chicago	Hyde Park Art Center	www.hydeparkart.org
	Contemporary Art Workshop	www.contemporaryart workshop.org
Cincinnati	The Clifton Cultural Arts Center	www.cliftonculturalarts.org
	Weston Art Gallery	www.cincinnatiarts.org/ weston-art-gallery
Covington, Kentucky	The Carnegie Arts Center	www.thecarnegie.com
Columbus	ROY G BIV's	www.roygbivgallery.com
Los Angeles	Los Angeles Art Association	www.laaaorg.nationprotect.net
New York	Artist Space	www.artistsspace.org
	The Drawing Center	www.drawingcenter.org
	d.u.m.b.o Art Center	www.dumboartscenter.org
	NURTUREart	www.nurtureart.org
	White Columns	www.whitecolumns.org
Philadelphia	BASEKAMP	www.basekamp.com
	Crane Art Center Mission	www.cranearts.com
San Francisco	Galería de la Raza	www.galeriadelaraza.org
Seattle	SOIL	www.soilart.org

4. **Art Fairs, Conferences, and Tradeshows:** Regional, national, and thematic art shows and conferences are an ideal way to connect with galleries, private collectors, and interior designers. A quick search on the Internet will help you find one in your area. It's always best to start locally. Indoor and outdoor art fairs are popular throughout the U.S. and abroad. Locate the ones in your area and then follow their online submission guidelines or purchase the *Artist's and Graphic Designer's Market* annual publication that lists every possible venue to sell and show your work. Participating is a great way to get exposure, gauge the interest in your work, meet with buyers, and hear feedback in real time. There are also tradeshows and conferences to consider. These tend to be more expensive to exhibit your work, and you have to submit ahead of time—some tradeshows recommend planning six months to a year in advance. You may need that much time to coordinate the logistics—creating the work, selecting it, and preparing it for shipping and set up. You also have to consider your budget, and that includes advertising. Some tradeshows offer special advertising packages in their show guides, which gives you another platform to showcase your work before, during, and long after the show. *Before you arrive* to a conference or a tradeshow, you want to advertise yourself and let people know you will be there and generate interest in your work—this can be done through email, mailed invites, or on social media posts. One tradeshow ADC attends every year is Artexpo New York. For more details visit www.artexponewyork.com.

Some shows my team and I attend are:

Affordable Art Fair
www.affordableartfair.com/fairs/new-york

Ann Arbor Street Art Fair
www.artfair.org

Art Palm Springs (Palm Springs, California)
www.art-palmsprings.com

Art Market San Francisco
www.artmarketsf.com

Art Santa Fe
www.artsantafe.com

Art San Diego
www.art-sandiego.com

Expo Chicago
www.expochicago.com

FOTO SOLO
www.artexponewyork.com/foto-solo/

Old Town Art Fair (Chicago, Illinois)
www.oldtowntriangle.com

Palm Beach Modern + Contemporary
www.artpbfair.com

Spectrum Miami
www.spectrum-miami.com

Spectrum Indian Wells
www.spectrum-indianwells.com

Red Dot Miami
www.reddotmiami.com

Riverwalk Fine Art Fair (Naperville, Illinois)
www.napervilleartleague.com

Sausalito Art & Wine Festival
www.sausalitoartfestival.org

Sculpture in the Park (Loveland, Colorado)
www.sculptureinthepark.org

SOFA, Chicago IL
www.sofaexpo.com

SOLO
www.artexponewyork.com/solo/

Spectrumà Context à Pulse / Art Basel, Miami
www.artbasel.com

Mary Johnston

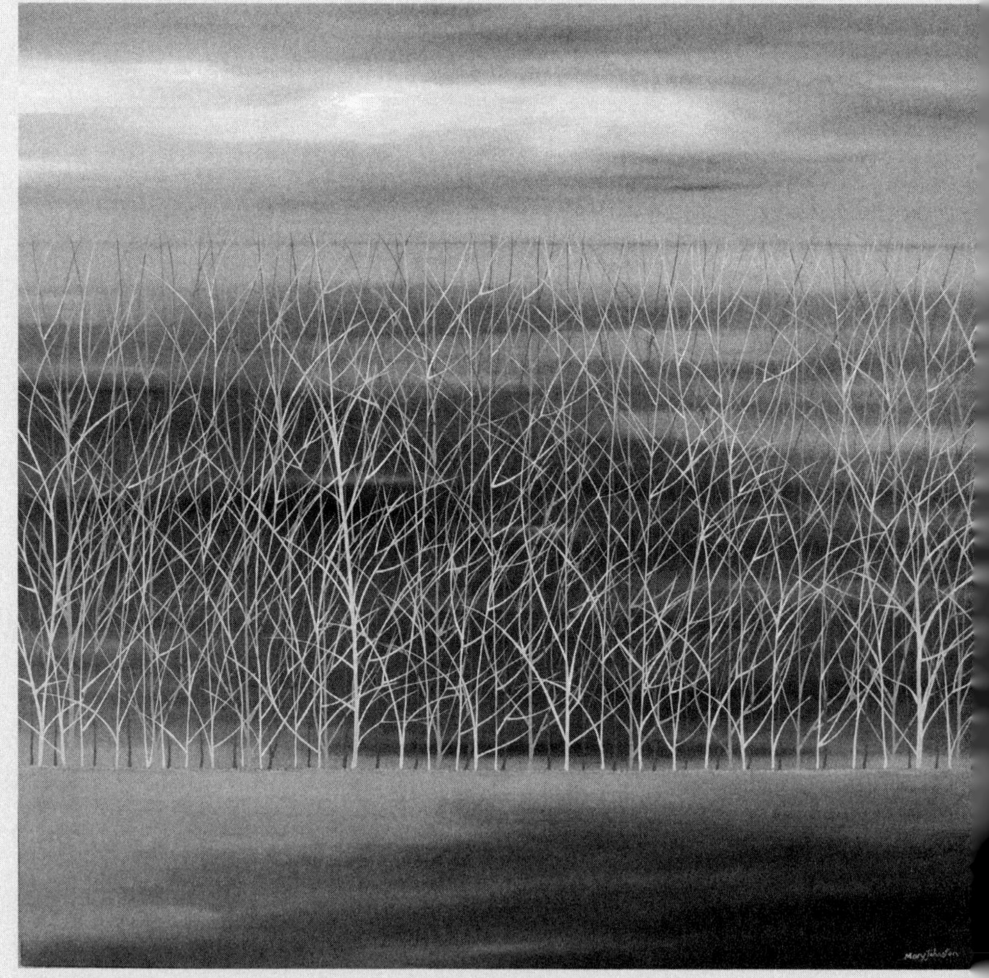

© Mary Johnston

The Importance of Featuring Art at Fairs, Conferences and Tradeshows

Mary Johnston is one of my top-selling artists. Not only are her large-scale contemporary oils rich, fully conceived, and beautiful, they seem to transport anyone looking at the art to a different place. Whether it's a large expansive sky, a peaceful water scene, green forests, or wind through the grass—you're there. You can feel the warm sun upon your face, you can hear the water lap upon the beach, you can hear the birds chirp in the trees and the branch break underfoot or the wind make music through the bending grasses. It's no wonder why so many buyers seek to have her work in their environments. Who wouldn't want to be transported to such beautiful, serene, and peaceful places?

Mary grew up on the Great Lakes surrounded by natural beauty, and spent her adult life exploring the natural world all over the the United States. When she wasn't appreciating nature's bounty, she was exploring other artists' interpretation of it. After graduating from the University of Minnesota, Duluth, she and her husband moved to New Jersey. Close to New York, she had the opportunity to explore many of the New York City art museums and galleries. It was in Bedminster, New Jersey, through the Somerset Art Association, she discovered and honed her own artist talents in watercolor and faux painting. She then moved several times—including a stint on the West Coast—that exposed her to the Pacific Ocean and the topography of the West Coast. When she, her husband, and her three children settled in Indiana in 2003 for her husband's new job, she discovered her current passion—oil painting.

She currently works out of her studio on the third floor above the Magdalena Gallery of Art in the Carmel, Indiana Arts & Design District, and is the consummate busy, working artist. She has built her business traveling throughout the U.S. attending tradeshows, conferences, art fairs, and being featured in galleries and art-consultant groups. If there is any artist who knows the value and ins-and-outs of conferences and tradeshows, it's Mary Johnston.

Mary has built her success and income on attending art shows. "Indoor and outdoor shows can become a major money-maker and very important part of your business as an artist," she says. But you need to have your market or buyer in mind. "Indoor and outdoor markets offer two different types of buyers," she says. "It's good to get a feel for both to find out where your market lies and how to exhibit at each type of show." She does her homework before attending and makes sure that work she exhibits appeals to the general buyer. "You might have some crazy, off-the-wall pieces that you're really excited about and want people to see, but if you're investing in a show and you're looking to sell, you have to go into a show with your buyers' needs in mind," she recommends.

Mary knows that shows can be costly, but they're worth the investment. "They're where you meet people. You have to put your work out there in front of the world if you want to sell," she says. She also advises artists to come prepared with their wholesale and designer prices, because trade professionals and gallery owners attend these shows with the intention of scouting new work. "I go to many shows each year and they're all important to my business," she says. But she also knows that you have to be willing to diversify. "Galleries sell my work as well, but you shouldn't rely on one source for sales. Each dealer's clientele is limited so having a presence all over the country is the best way to explode your art career. Exhibiting with a gallery or other platform can be a great way to get your work to a show to test the waters or work on a budget."

As far as recommendations go, Mary favors a few shows that she prefers. "Artexpo New York and One of a Kind Chicago have been my most successful indoor shows. I sell a lot of artwork and after doing these shows for many years, I have repeat buyers." And the shows are not only good for on-the-spot purchasers. "I also have buyers who have been eyeing my work for years until they can afford that big piece they've always loved. You have to have patience and perseverance and keep at it."

Mary's also had success at regional outdoor fairs and festivals. A Midwesterner, Mary knows her market and where her work will be appreciated. She tries to tries to attend such shows as the Edina Art Fair in Minnesota, Port Clinton Art Festival in Chicago, and the Ann Arbor Art Fair annually. And she recognizes the approach to outdoor festivals and fairs is different than indoor tradeshows. Because of the range of visitors, she advises, "You need to have pieces at every price point and you should sell from every price point. If 100,000 people come by your booth and you only sell one large piece, regardless of the monetary gain that's not a successful show." Again, like all professional artists and gallery owners often advise, Mary is a proponent of doing one's homework. "Find out which shows your work fits into and invest wisely."

To learn more about Mary and her art, visit www.maryjohnstonart.com

Eric Smith

Redwood Media

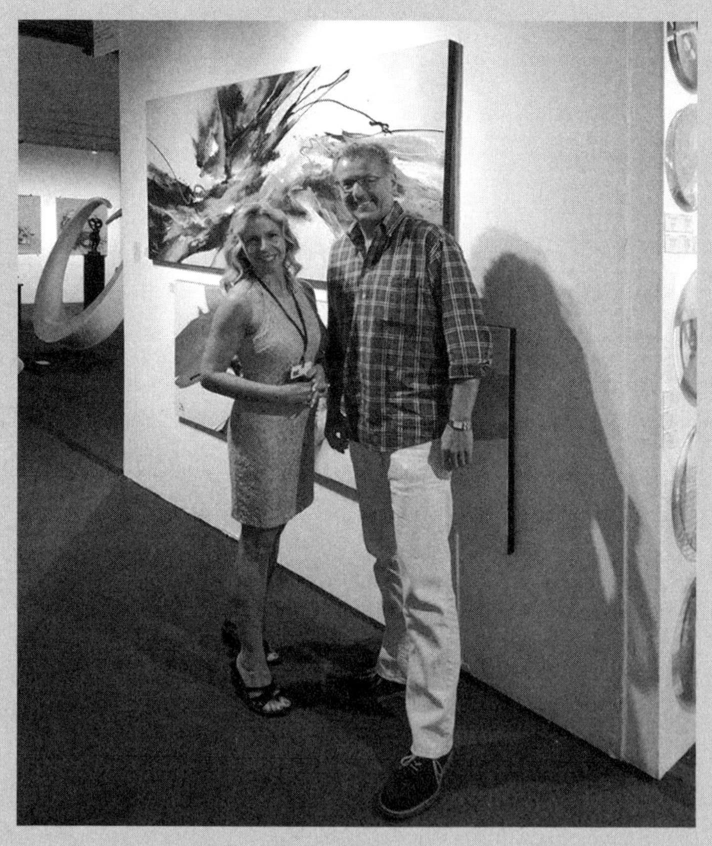

Showing Your Work for Maximum Impact

There is no one more qualified to talk about trade shows than my friend Eric Smith. Eric and I go way back. He asked me to speak on a panel at Artexpo New York the same year I debuted my ADC exhibition booth. Since then, my booth has grown (it's now one of the largest at Artexpo New York) and so has our friendship. When I was thinking of experts who could truly give artists the "insider secrets" to having a successful exhibit at a trade show, Eric was the first and only person who came to mind. There is simply no one who can honestly and succinctly tell artists what they need to do to prepare for a trade show more than Eric.

Who is this Eric Smith that I so esteem? Eric happens to be the CEO of Redwood Media Group, which owns Artexpo New York, Art Santa Fe, Art San Diego, Spectrum Miami, Spectrum Indian Wells, Red Dot Miami, and [SOLO]. Prior to leading RMG, Eric served as the Vice President of Summit Business Media, the leading producer of art-related trade publications, including *Art Business News*, *DÉCOR*, and *Volume* magazines. But Eric got his start in the art world over 20 years ago at the world-renowned national art retailer Martin Lawrence Galleries. As a director he managed over 20 galleries in California, Colorado, and Hawaii. His passion for modern and contemporary art led him to sell work from some of the world's top artists: Warhol, Rosenquist, Rauschenberg, Oldenburg, and Haring. His expertise in the art market, latest trends and forecasts, and what makes artists successful is a talent in and of itself. He is the go-to guy when someone is seeking a speaker at industry trade shows or simply a quote from an art expert for a major magazine. So I went to him, too. I wanted you to hear for yourself what it takes to make it in trade shows—and the art world as well.

"What makes an artist stand out at exhibition—anywhere really—comes down to two things: The work is both *consistent and unique,"* Eric says. "What did Lichtenstein, Picasso, Klein, Pollack, Chagall—you name the famous artist—all have in common? They were consistent and they created something unique. You can look at the work and know immediately who did it." What Eric is talking about is what is known as a "signature style." Sure, people can copy it, but by being the first to do something and doing it over and over again—that sets you apart. "Sometimes it may seem kitschy at first. Look at Rodrigue's *Blue Dog,"* Eric says. "This guy made a living painting a blue dog—that traveled through history, landscapes, and different art periods. He took his little blue dog and made it into a signature."

Speaking of dogs, Eric told me a story of how another painter of dogs failed to do the same—*at least at exhibition*. An artist in the [SOLO] pavilion of Artexpo New York packed her booth with every type of her artwork imaginable—landscapes, abstracts, and dog paintings. (Just an FYI: Every year at Artexpo New York, individual artists, who aren't represented by galleries yet and who are trying to break in to the industry at a lower price point, can display their work in the [SOLO] pavilion. For about $3,500, they can rent a small booth, curate the space, talk directly with buyers, and sell their work.) Eric approached the artist and said, "What are you doing? You can't show all these types of work at the same time!" Her response was one he often heard from novices: "I wanted to show all that I can do."

As Julia Roberts said so well in Pretty Woman, *"Big mistake, Huge."*

By filling up a booth with clutter, leaving no space for the viewer to breathe, you unwittingly look desperate to sell, and more importantly, like you have no idea what you're doing. "Buyers and collectors aren't stupid," Eric says. "They're informed. They don't want a one-and-done painting. They're looking to see if an artist has staying power and a signature—what I call ***consistency***—and that their work stands on its own—what I call ***unique.***"

Now, Eric isn't saying you can't experiment, grow, or transition. But, you save that for the studio. When you're at an exhibit, you want to present a streamlined message. You also need to be persistent. "Becoming successful is not something that happens overnight—for anyone," Eric says. "I remember this one artist who started off at a [SOLO] booth. His first year, he didn't sell a thing. But, his booth was well curated and he had some initial interest. People wanted to see if he'd be back. He came back, he sold a few paintings in the second year. By the third year, he sold every piece in his booth. He was consistent. The customers knew what to expect."

Eric estimates that there is a 30–40 percent success/return rate for new artists at his trade shows. Yes, that means 60–70 percent don't return for one reason or another. The ones that do stick with it seem to be prolific enough to keep producing work upwards of 20–50 pieces a year and who sell their work consistently—while being consistent and unique.

That being said, Eric doesn't want to discourage anyone. He knows exhibitors and artists are paying a lot of money to participate in the trade shows, and he wants them all to be successful. And he has a few tips to save them time, money, and disappointment. "Preparation is key," Eric says, "You have to come ready with handouts. The work has to be excellent—consistent. And, most importantly, you have to know how to hang your work. There is nothing worse than seeing poorly hung work. Presentation is everything. You need to give your art—and buyers—room to breathe."

Another key aspect of success is pricing the work. Eric recommends using what he calls the **TAPS** approach to retail pricing. "**T**itle, **A**rtist, **P**rice and **S**ize should always be clearly displayed," Eric says. "This," he says, "encourages the consumer to ask questions like: Where did the title of this piece come from? Who is this artist? Where is he or she from? Questions like these open up the piece for discussion and allow you or your dealer to engage the consumer, encourage sales, and get a feel for the type of pricing the market will support. A piece that you feel was priced on the higher end might be a no-brainer for an interested and seasoned collector. Or, perhaps you've out-priced yourself, given the reaction of passersby. Either way, you'll know for next time what works best."

Eric's best advice? "Be patient. Keep working. The most important thing is to be prepared and work together with your gallery, publisher, or trade show. Have a long-term plan. And remember, it takes a lifetime to become an overnight success as an artist!"

To learn more about Redwood Media Group and how to prepare for exhibitions, visit www.redwoodmg.com

Understanding Contracts

One of the best ways to avoid unnecessary conflicts or disappointment after unmet expectations is to have a contract in place with gallery owners, designers, or anyone else representing your work. Like all businesses and all industries there are always unethical, duplicitous, or corrupt people and agencies, whose sole purpose is to swindle someone out of their money and/or property. You have to protect yourself. You have to be scrupulous and ask questions. You have to follow your gut. You also have to listen to what a person says as much as what they do. If for any reason you have doubts or suspicions that the person who is trying to work with you is unethical do not get involved. That being said, every single person I have worked with in this industry has held themselves to the the highest of standards. Every gallery owner, consultant, and designer I know personally have contracts that include clearly defined roles and expectations, especially in regard to when an artist will be paid, how much, and under what terms. Some gallery owners ask for exclusivity, which is appropriate and can be to an artist's benefit. Knowing and understanding the terms of your agreement with gallery owners is crucial. For your benefit, I've included a standard contract that I use with my artists. It is also industry standard as well. If you're not offered a contract, or someone says to "trust" them, my recommendation is don't turn over any art without a contract.

Art Design Consultants Artist Agreement
Gallery and Online Sales Contract

Artist Name: ______________________________
Email: ______________________ Phone: ______________
Address:
City: ______________________ State: ________ Zip: ________
Website:
Representation: ☐ ADC Gallery ☐ ADC / Blink Art

Art Design Consultants (ADC) is pleased to offer you the opportunity to have your work for sale in our gallery and/or in our online store.

ADC Gallery Terms:
Contract Term: ________ Start Date: ________ End Date: ________

1. Contract term between ADC and the Artist is six-months as defined above.
2. ADC will receive a 50% commission on all sales originating in our gallery.
3. For gallery-only representation, the Artist agrees to sell represented artwork at the same price at every venue including personal studio, local and national galleries/ retailers and on the Artist's website.
4. For gallery-only representation, ADC offers non-exclusive representation of your artwork. Artists can sell independently and through other galleries locally and regionally.

a. Artist will offer ADC available works and notify ADC of any works that become unavailable.

5. ADC reserves the right to offer up to a 20% discount to industry professionals. Once the 20% is deducted, the 50% commission to ADC will still apply.
6. Artist will pay for shipping for all works to the ADC gallery located at 310 Culvert Street 5th Floor | Cincinnati, OH 45202. Artist has seven (7) days to ship the artwork once the contract term commences.
7. ADC agrees to pay the Artist within thirty (30) days of a sale (via company check). Artist will be paid after the customer has received the purchased item and the return period has lapsed.
8. ADC offers a 100% return policy for the customer. Customers have seven (7) days to return artwork after delivery.
9. ADC will pay for shipping back to the Artist at the end of the contract term if the works have not sold in the allotted time.

ADC Gallery Terms:

Contract Term: ________ Start Date: ________ End Date: ________

1. Contract term between ADC and the Artist is one (1) year as defined above.
2. Artist will coordinate with an ADC representative to select a minimum of six (6) works of art to which ADC will have exclusive sales rights during the year-long contract period.
3. Artist will provide all necessary artwork information including: professional photography, artwork description, media/materials description, measurements (including available variations), and retail price (including complete price list for size and media variations).
4. The Artist and associated artworks will be considered for inclusion in the magazine, Curated by Blink Art.
5. ADC will receive a 50% commission on all sales originating on our online store (http:// adcfineart.com).
6. ADC reserves the right to offer up to a 20% discount to industry professionals and/or special online promotions. Once the 20% is deducted, the 50% commission to ADC will still apply.
7. ADC will add shipping costs directly to the retail price of the artwork. Shipping fees will be deducted from the final sale price, after which the 50% commission to ADC will still apply.
8. Artist will ship artwork directly to the customer via ADC's UPS Ground pre-paid shipping option within seven (7) days.
9. ADC agrees to pay the Artist within thirty (30) days of a sale (via company check). Artist will be paid after the customer has received the purchased item and the return period has lapsed.
10. ADC offers a 100% return policy for the customer. Customers have seven (7) days to return artwork after delivery.

________________	________________	________
Artist Name (print)	Artist Signature	Date

________________	________________	________
ADC Representative (print)	ADC Representative Signature	Date

Payments and Receipts of Authenticity

Once you're a working artist, with connections and buyers, a beautiful thing begins to happen. You begin to get paid! And thanks to technology and the way we do things now, you can accept payments in all sorts of forms. We all know how cash works. You set a price and people pay it. The reality is though most people don't come cash ready to fine art events, and the likelihood of getting paid this way is slim. However, if you do get paid this way, you're going to want a receipt booklet ready. The receipt should include the date of purchase, the price, the location, and some sort of signature of veracity or authenticity. Most collectors or buyers like to keep the records of their purchases. You will want to keep a copy for your own records as well (more on this in the next section—Bookkeeping 101). Other ways to accept payment are personal checks or e-checks. Again, have a receipt ready to go. Online processing tools and credit card processing apps, like Square, are a must-have now. Every artist should have a credit card processing app of some sort. Square makes it easy. You can accept payments anywhere, and all you need is your phone. This is especially important at art fairs or solo studio events. If you have an online presence, you need to work with your webmaster (in most cases—that is you as well) to set up an online checkout that accepts credit cards and PayPal. PayPal charges monthly fees. So you may want to wait to set up a PayPal account, until your income exceeds the monthly charge to have the service.

Bookkeeping 101

"Making good judgments when one has complete data, facts, and knowledge is not leadership - it's bookkeeping."

— Dee Hock

I am going to go out on a limb here and say that most artists despise accounting. The very idea of sitting at a desk in front of an Excel spreadsheet is the thing of nightmares. But, let me tell you there is no bigger nightmare than working hard to earn money and only discover at the end of the day that you have none. Where did it all go? Well, there is a simple way to answer that. But, it involves tracking your expenses and income. And this is what this section is all about. Yes, it's boring. Yes, it's difficult to feel inspired by this. But, let me tell you, if your financial house is in order, so much else falls naturally into place. Life is too short to be stressed about finances. And, let me assure you, what you don't pay attention to, usually ends up controlling your life.

Remember, you're both an *artist and an entrepreneur* and you need to start spending a little time each day attending to the business of being an artist. Here's my best—and briefest—attempt at what you need to do to manage your business:

Litsa's Not-So-Secret Tips to Being a Working Artist/Businessperson

1. **Get in the right mindset:** ***You are a businessperson.*** The first and most important secret is that you have to start admitting and treating yourself like the businessperson you are. You have a product—the product is your art—and you have a consumer market. I hate to break this to you, but yes, these facts alone, make you a business owner.

2. **Name your business.** Since you're a business owner the first thing you need to set up is your business name. It's usually eponymous for artists. For example, Lisa Schuster's name is the same as her company: Lisa Schuster Art. Don't get too fancy. You want people to find you and the art you create. (More on brand building in Chapter Four).

3. **Acquire an EIN—Employer Identification Number.** An accountant can help you do this. Or you can go directly to the IRS website (link below) and set one up yourself following their step-by-step instructions. By doing this, you're letting the IRS know you're a business and will be accepting payments directly for your work. (You must do this. It is illegal, as you know, to accept payments without paying income taxes in the United States.)

www.irs.gov/businesses/small-businesses-self-employed/how-to-apply-for-an-ein

4. **Purchase and use an accounting software.** Selecting an accounting software like QuickBooks will let you easily keep track of income earned and expenses. You can track your business checking account, send invoices, enter payments received and money spent. It will also let you create reports to see where you are at and compare each year to see your growth. It will also make it a lot easier when tax time rolls around. You can print off reports that show gross income, expenses, and net income. (Tip: Entering customer addresses and emails into Quickbooks is a great way of building your marketing lists too. More on building marketing lists in Chapter Four.)

5. **Keep meticulous records of your expenses.** Keep all the receipts that you receive for payment of art supplies (paints, brushes, materials), business supplies (paper, pens, computer equipment, software, postage, shipping, studio space, etc.), web design, graphic design, workshops, conferences, travel expenses, meals, and track your mileage and car expenses (for work related activities). All of these expenses qualify as tax deductions.

6. **Keep meticulous documentation and records of your art.** My suggestion is to maintain a ledger of all of your art. List the name of the piece, the dimensions, specific details (if appropriate), locations of where the piece is displayed or stored, where it's been exhibited, for how long, who sold your work, the selling price, along with a photo of each piece.

7. **Keep your resume and biography up-to-date.** Keep your profiles online fresh and up-to-date. Invest in professional headshots (or take your own) and freshen your webpage and professional sites. Make sure you list your accomplishments, accolades, and new work interests.

8. **Join recognized artist organizations.** There are several regional, national, and international artist organizations that can help you keep up-to-date with changes in the industry, what other artists are doing, and where exhibitions are happening. Stay informed. Get involved. Network.

Investments

"Investing is laying out money now to get more money back in the future."

— Warren Buffett

Most artists don't think of the importance of investing or saving. However, like any business owner, you have to consider how you will make ends meet some day when you are no longer able to work—or in most cases—during the dry periods in your career. Yes, everyone, artists included, need a rainy day fund for when catastrophe strikes, but you also need a means to build income while you're not working. And, the best way to do that is to invest your savings. The good news is you don't have to be an investing expert to make good financial choices. Understanding just a few concepts can put you on the road to smarter investing.

It is a simple truth: Investing is generally better than not investing. While it's natural to want to wait until market conditions are "right," that's a call even professional investment managers find tough to make. A better strategy is to just get started.

Research shows that on average, even investors with bad timing earned twice as much as people who held their savings in cash over a twenty-year period. And those who stick to their investment plan achieve a higher net worth than those who don't. There isn't a magic formula – reaching your goals takes time, discipline, and a good investing strategy. Here's how to get started.

Start earlier rather than later allows you to benefit longer from compounding returns. If you're young and just starting out, now is the time to invest. Set aside a portion each week to put away. Even if it's small, it adds up over time. Do it automatically, if possible. Link your bank account to your preferred investor, and have the savings deposited automatically.

Work with a professional wealth management professional or investment firm to help you diversify your portfolio to help cushion market blows. You'll want a mix of stocks, bonds, and cash. Each of these traditional primary asset classes tend to fare differently in various market environments. For instance, stocks often perform well when economic growth is strong, while bonds may outperform when growth slows. By investing in all three, plus other investments (commodities, real estate, art, etc.) you're diversifying.

Francie Henry

Bank Executive

Francie Henry and I go way back. She's one of my oldest and dearest friends, and she's also a professional and personal inspiration. Francie has not only succeeded in a predominantly male profession; she has reached the pinnacle of it. Her insights and wisdom regarding how I should handle my finances and plan for the future have been invaluable to me personally and professionally. Since not everyone has their own personal financial guru as a dear friend, I thought I would lend Francie to you here. She's going to give you some meaningful, and easy-to-practice financial strategies here. Francie, take it away:

> *First things first, all people need to have a guide to help them develop their financial plan. Even if you have a strong background in finances it is not recommended that you develop your financial strategy yourself. A guide can be found in many forms from a website computer program to a financial professional. Depending on whom you are and how you learn and work, it is best to research all options and pick the one that feels right to you.*

Building your Financial Strategy involves 3 Steps:

Step One: Visualize

1. *Visualize financial needs like income requirements, risks that require insurance (health, home and car), tax planning issues.*

2. *Visualize your financial goals like retirement, education and investing.*

3. *Visualize a picture in your mind what you want to accomplish with your finances and then share it with a Financial Guide.*

Step Two: Uncover

1. *Uncover the various financial vehicles that can help you reach your goals (saving accounts, IRAs or Health Saving Accounts).*

2. *Uncover your required living expenses to uncover how much you can save on a monthly basis.*

3. *Uncover what to expect from government programs like Social Security or the Affordable Care Act and determine how they might affect you.*

4. *Uncover what type of investor you are and what kind of risk you are willing to take with your savings.*

Step Three: Develop

1. *Develop a savings plan.*

2. *Develop a retirement plan.*

3. *Develop an investment strategy.*

4. *Develop a financial discipline, review annually and learn to stay the course.*

The process described above involves a lot of work and thought. This work and thought is why most people procrastinate and never develop or accomplish their financial dreams. It is never to early or too late to start planning for your financial future. The key is starting the process, monitoring the process and learning to stay the course.

Action Steps

1. **Plan an open studio event.** Set a date. Set up an invite list. Set up a Facebook event page and share.
2. **Research a few juried competitions, art fairs, and tradeshows.** Make a list of ones that seem doable to either attend or submit work to in the next year.
3. **If you haven't already, set up a space or area in your home, studio, or office, to keep your records, receipts, and ledgers.** Do some organizing, sorting, and get your financial house in order.
4. **Follow Francie Henry's Three Steps to Developing a Financial Strategy.** Then sit down and create a budget, develop a retirement plan, and investment strategy.

Further Reading on Business and Investing

Rich Dad, Poor Dad by Robert Kiyosaki

The Essays of Warren Buffett: Lessons for Corporate America by Warren Buffett

The Intelligent Investor by Benjamin Graham

Think and Grow Rich by Napoleon Hill

It's your Business: 183 Essential Tips that Will Transform Your Small Business by JJ Ramberg

You are a Badass at Making Money: Master the Mindset of Wealth by Jen Sincero

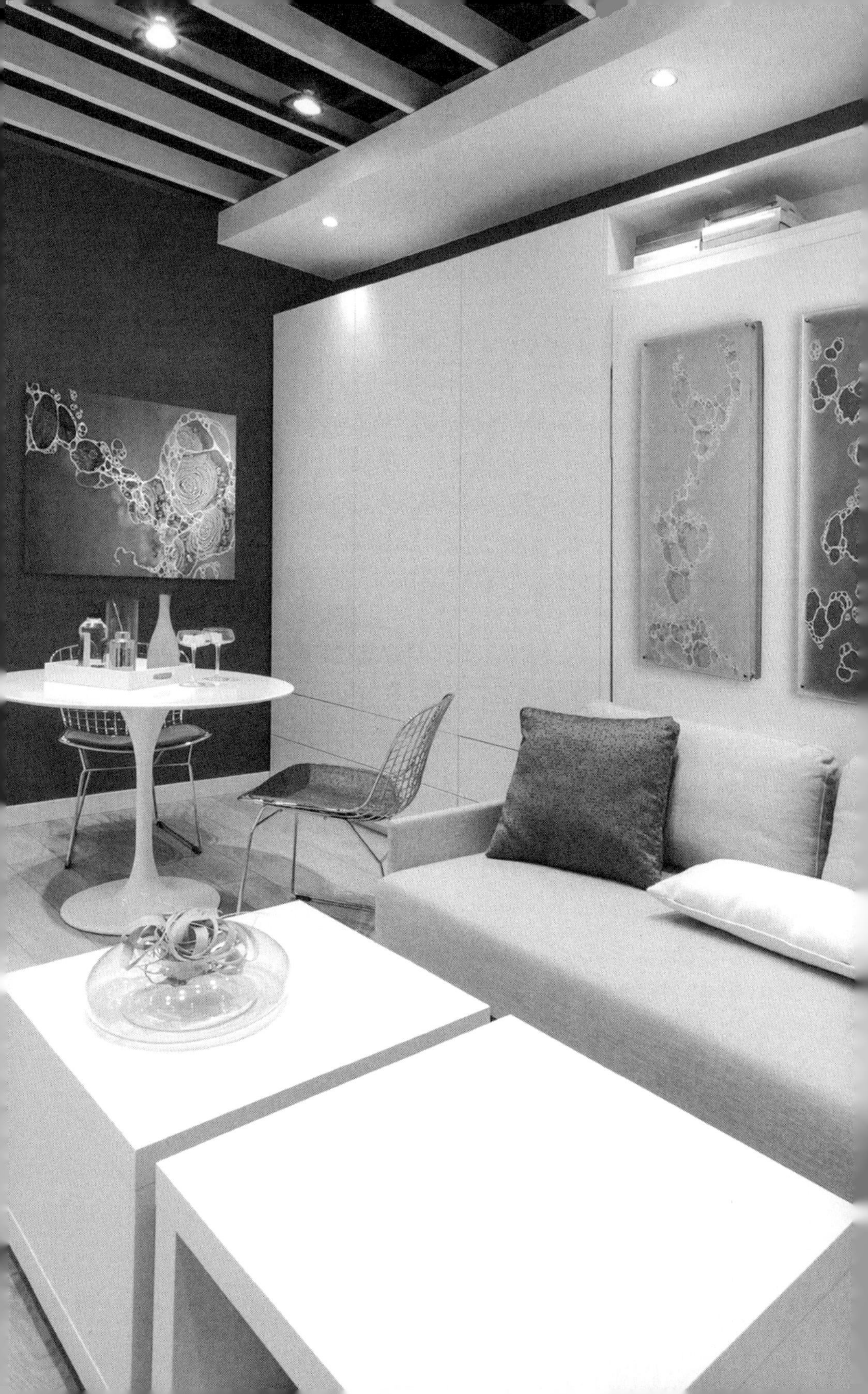

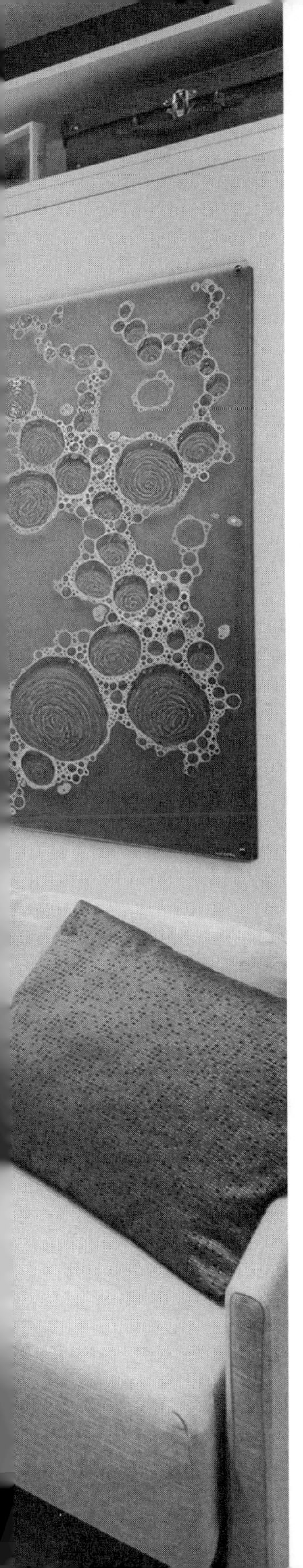

*"The **future** belongs to a different kind of person with a different kind of mind:* **artists***, inventors, storytellers- creative and holistic 'right-brain' thinkers."*

— Daniel Pink

Artist: Carla Goldberg

chapter four

BRANDING, MARKETING, AND RELATIONSHIP MAINTENANCE

"Your brand is what other people say about you when you're not in the room."

— Jeff Bezos

I saved the most important aspect of your business for last, and because of scope of this topic it gets its own chapter. There is no overstating this, if you want to be successful at selling your artwork and have a long, prosperous career as a working artist, you absolutely must do these three things:

1) **define your brand,**
2) **design and then implement a strategic marketing plan, and**
3) **build and maintain strong relationships through your defined brand and subsequent execution of your marketing plan.**

I could leave it at that. But, I know better. I know what you're thinking already. *What's a brand? I don't need a brand! I am an artist not a business! Marketing? I am not a marketer! I don't need to do that. If I just create great work, people will come to me.*

In a word: NO.

You can't underestimate the power of branding, marketing, and relationship building. It's how I have built and grown my business. It's how every successful business grows. It's everything! Without branding, marketing, and relationship building, I have seen many talented, hard-working, and amazing artists flounder. They've hosted solo gallery events. They've paid for booths at tradeshows. They've launched expensive websites. They've poured money into their studio. All well and good, but without a distinct brand, without a story to tell to captivate an audience, and without a killer marketing plan and execution of that plan to reach their target audience, their work went largely unnoticed. It's no surprise they grew despondent, and ultimately quit.

I don't want this to happen to you. And it doesn't have to happen. In this chapter, you're going to learn a lot. Consider it a crash course in branding, marketing, digital marketing, marketing analytics, consumer trends, and relationship building. Does this sound overwhelming to you? I promise you I will break it down so that even a person with absolutely no prior business knowledge or business acumen can understand it. No jargon, I promise.

The Difference Between Marketing and Branding

Before I go any further, and before I launch into a discussion of the importance of defining one's brand (or as I like to call it in the art world, your "signature style"), I have to be clear on an oft-made mistake when it comes to understanding branding and marketing:

They are not the SAME.

Let me repeat, marketing and branding are two distinct aspects of business. People tend to lump them together when talking and I am not going to do that. I know that each is important and distinct in its own way. One can have a marketing plan without branding (though, it won't be successful). However, one can't have a successful business without a distinct brand or a signature style. Every single aspect of your business depends on a clearly defined brand.

What is a brand?

Branding is behind everything you do. And branding should underlie every marketing effort. (A marketing effort is basically another way of saying "an attempt to reach buyers through various channels," i.e., social media, advertising, direct mail, etc.) Branding tells people a story—a consistent story. It is not, contrary to popular opinion, simply a logo, a special font, a design layout, or a business card. Yes, those are aspects of branding design, but behind all that is the message, style, and story your organization is trying to convey to the consumer. A brand communicates the characteristics, values, and style or attributes of a person, organization, or in your case, your artwork. If implemented effectively and consistently, it becomes so iconic one can easily recognize one's "brand" or "style" within seconds. And more than that, as soon as they see this style and brand, their brain automatically connects words, phrases, ideas, beliefs, and yes, even stories, to that brand.

"Art is a vast, ancient interconnected web-work".
—Camille Puglia

Pretty powerful, right?

However, a brand doesn't *say buy me, click here, sign up now, sale,* or *join me* at this event (that's marketing). Rather a brand says:

This is me. This is who I am. And because it's who I am, you connect to it too on some basic level. You too are part of this brand. You too are defined in some way by your connection to this brand. You support me. You recommend me to friends. You're loyal to me.

Your brand is the first and lasting impression a customer or a potential buyer has. Your brand communicates all you want the buyer to know. It's strategic and well-thought out. It also determines who is going to be a loyal customer or not. By defining your brand and story, you're defining your target audience.

What do I mean by *target audience*?

Say you're a car manufacturer, and you have decided your brand is going to be uncompromising luxury and performance—only the best mechanical parts, only the finest leather, and details. Right there, see what you've done? You've done it. You defined your target audience. Your audience is attracted to luxury. They only want the finest of everything, and therefore they have the wallets to do so. Your brand attracts your audience. Say you paint dogs. Your "target audience" will be dog lovers. Say you paint dramatic seascapes. Your audience, when it desires seascapes, will come to you. They know you can deliver the goods. And the opposite holds true. If you try to be all things to all people, you don't have a brand. And without a brand you don't have a target audience. Without a target audience you don't have buyers to market to.

So what makes branding so different from marketing?

A marketing effort might include a commercial, a Facebook ad, an email, a few social media posts, and a newsletter. Those things will bring a customer to the galley. But, the brand is what they want. What they are attracted to. If the brand hype lives up to one's expectations—the sculpture is in fact the ultimate art piece of their dreams—then the owner becomes a lifelong customer and a person who will forever sing the praises of their preferred "brand." Good branding is like evangelization. The message grows and spreads, even when the brand isn't in the room or nearby—and it will last for generations if done well.

As I have said many times already, all working artists are entrepreneurs. And that means you're running a business. And all businesses must sell to survive. How you sell your work defines your brand. In fact, every thought, every piece, every ad, every email, every Facebook post, every event should reflect your brand or your signature style.

Simply put, your brand is a *solemn promise*. It's a promise to your trusted buyer. You're telling them what they can expect from you, now and in the future. You're not going anywhere. Your customer can count on you to deliver the goods. It also differentiates you. It sets you apart from everyone else doing the same thing. It's as unique and special as you are.

Okay, so now that you understand what a brand is, you're ready to define yours. I can help you with that. Let's do a few exercises to get started.

Steps to Help You Understand Your Brand

1. How would you describe your artistic style? Traditional? Modern? Whimsical? Quirky? Bold? Try to find three words that describe your work. Just three words. (Some examples might be: Honest, Immersive, Daring or Joyful, Unrestrained or Luminous, Rich, Unguarded.) Try it yourself. If you get stuck, take three or four of your best works and see if there is a theme, a style, a word that comes to mind when you see each of them. *(Tip: Get a stack of Post-its and write down a word that describes your work on each Post-it. Do it as fast as you can for one minute. See how many words you come up with. Then one-by-one, take Post-its away that don't seem to fit your work perfectly until you're left with three distinct words that define your style.)*

Words that describe your style:

1.

2.

3.

2. What is your "mission" statement as an artist? Try to create one mission that distills in one crisp, unified thought what you're trying to achieve with your work. My mission is "to create beautiful environments." Every decision I make, every thought I have, every interaction I have whether with an artist, a client, or a vendor, keeps this mission statement in mind. It's more than a "tagline"—it's a way we do business at ADC. It sums up my goals, my achievements, and my style. All of my employees are behind my mission, too. Everyone knows it and participates in this vision of mine to create beautiful environments. Now what's yours? Do you want to dare people? Do you want to soothe them? Do you want your work to transform people? Challenge people? Ask yourself what you're trying to achieve. Ask yourself what you hope your audience feels when they see the work? You're getting closer to your mission.

My mission is . .

3. What are the features of your art? Expensive materials? Organic materials? Bright hues? A special, one-of-a-kind medium? What sets your work apart?
What makes it stand out?

4. What qualities do you want your audience to associate with your works? (Cutting edge? Edgy? Serene? Beautiful? Thought-provoking? Engaging? Eye-catching? Deeply felt?)
Write them here.

Testing Your Brand

Now you should have a general idea of what you think your artwork/signature style is. This is a great step. However, I have to break it to you, it's just the beginning. Now you need to do some consumer testing to see if how you perceive your brand is how others perceive your brand. This takes some time and some homework on your part. You need to get some feedback from known and unknown sources. Show your work to friends and colleagues and test your theories, definitions, and thoughts. Do their words sound like your words when they are describing your art work? Are the feelings you are trying to provoke in your audience having that desired effect you were hoping for? This is called consumer research/feedback. You need to figure out if your idea of your brand is meeting expectations of your consumer. You can do this several ways. You can send out a survey. You can post a photo or two of your artwork and ask your friends to describe the work or how it makes them feel. See if it matches your self-perception. If it does, fantastic! You're ready to move on. If not, you need to go back to square one and tweak your mission and defining words a bit.

> **"Storytelling is the mother of all 'pull' marketing strategies. It encourages dialogue, engagement and interaction among equals—an exchange of meaning between people. Yet many companies and brands are still relentlessly pushing messages out, hoping that with enough repetition, something will stick."**
>
> **—Bill Baker**

Creating Your Artist Statement

Now you are ready to draft what is commonly referred to as an "Artist Statement." An artist statement offers prospective buyers, clients, gallery owners, and anyone who visits your website or studio a view into your life as an artist and the work you create. You don't need to get personal (overshare) or write a novel. The artist statement is usually no longer than one page in length. It informs the reader of what you're trying to achieve and uses clear, jargon-free, descriptive language to describe the work. It answers questions like: *What inspires you? What is a particular series based on? What elements in your artwork set you apart from other artist doing similar work? Who are your major influences—artists, musicians, writers, etc. What process or technique, especially if unusual, does a consumer need to understand about your work?* You want to be a specific as possible. When appropriate, it might be a good opportunity to share a seminal moment that determined your fate as an artist. Using a brief story or anecdote can create a powerful and memorable moment that helps you and your work stand out.

"Marketing is no longer about the stuff that you make, but about the stories you tell."
—Seth Godin

Write a rough draft of your artist statement here:

Now that you've created an Artist Statement, you'll also need to condense this down into an Elevator Pitch. When you're at networking events or have a brief amount of time to discuss yourself and your work, you're going to need a working elevator pitch that shows your passion for your art, what you've already done, and where you want to go. Rehearse it in front of the mirror a few times before you actually use it and run it by a family member or a friend first too. Usually a pitch is no longer than a minute long. But, it can be as brief as twenty seconds. As business owners, we often get so excited about what we do that we talk too long or give too much detail in an elevator pitch. Here are three simple questions that can help you highlight the most important details to include in your pitch:

1. Create one sentence that describes what you create/do.

2. Give one example of what you've done so far:

3. Conclude with who your ideal clients are or who you market to:

Now take all of that information and put it into a paragraph and present it to someone *who knows nothing about you.* Finally, solicit feedback. Ask a friend if they now understand what you do and how you want to grow your business. Once you've got that down, stand in front of a mirror and practice, practice, practice so that you can deliver this pitch with passion and clarity. Remember, with a busy person, you've often got one shot to impress!

Write your elevator speech here.

Now You're Ready to Execute Your Brand

Now that you have a clear vision of the work you create, it's time to start taking steps to get the word out and, yes, now you're finally ready to create a logo, print business cards, and start designing marketing materials, ads, and even a website. Here are some things you need to consider when branding.

1. You need a signature logo.

An artist's logo is usually their name. It should be the first thing a buyer sees on your website, marketing material, and clearly defined on your artwork as well. If you're a modern, abstract artist your font choice, color choice, and overall design should reflect that. I recommend working with a graphic designer if that is not your skillset. By conveying certain words, feelings, and ideas to graphic designer, you will be able to work with him or her to execute a name logo that is right for you. There is nothing more off-putting than an amateurish, comic-sans, clipart-esque logo. Your brand is the first thing someone will see when they go to your website. If you're going for bold, loud, and intense, but your logo is full of pastels and serif fonts—you're not "on brand." If you want to look professional, you have to act professional. Hire an expert. *(Tip: There are some apps now that help you quickly and affordably create a brand logo. Tailorbrands.com is a useful website. You just type in the words your trying to convey, the name of your brand, and answer a few questions, and they will automatically produce several sample logos for you. You can even purchase a style guide and other brand materials from them.)*

2. Plan to integrate your brand into EVERYTHING.

Your signature logo should appear everywhere your art work is and it should be consistent. You should also place your brand on letter-head, in your email signature, on portfolios. Wherever your work is, your brand logo should be there too.

3. Distill your Artist Statement

Distill your Artist Statement down to a memorable, meaningful and concise statement that captures the essence of your brand, signature style.
Now rewrite it here:

4. Design templates and create brand standards for your marketing materials.

Use the same color scheme, logo placement, look, and feel throughout everything you do. If you worked with a graphic designer, he or she may even pull a style guide together for you. It should include Pantone or HTML color codes (So all colors are the same and consistent everywhere—in ads, on your website, posters, etc.), font choices, sizes, layouts, and a variety of logo sizes with varying degrees of resolutions and shapes. *(Facebook, Instagram, LinkedIn, and Twitter all have different specs.)*

5. Be consistent.

Branding is nothing without consistency. In fact, the entire point of a brand is to be consistent—your customers, clients, buyers, and gallery owners are counting on it.

Marketing: Getting the Word Out

We have branding covered. It's the foundation of every great business. However, it's just one part of what makes a business great. One of the most difficult challenges every artist faces is not to make a name for themselves, but getting others to recognize that name! That's where marketing comes in. You need to get thc word out. And you need to do this efficiently, effectively, and consistently. The way you do this is to create a marketing plan and strategy, and then implement that strategy consistently throughout your career.

"It's like everyone tells a story about themselves inside their own head. Always. All the time. That story makes you what you are. We build ourselves out of that story."
—Patrick Rothfuss

Marketing is your connection to your buyer. It's also the vehicle that takes your brand to where you want it to go. There are more ways than ever to reach your market. For years the Rule of 7 ruled the business-fundamentals day. The Rule of 7 is simply the belief that in order to make a sale, a customer has to be "touched" at least seven times by some sort of marketing—whether it's a billboard, a radio ad, a television ad, a direct mail piece, a coupon, a phone call, or a walk through a store—before one finally felt secure making a purchase—or in most cases— "finally got the message" to make a purchase. The reality is there is so much branding and marketing "noise" these days, it takes far more than 7 touchpoints to make a sale. When I open my email each morning I have more than 200 emails competing for my attention. When I drive into work, I hear radio ads, pass countless billboards, and stores and businesses with signs—and they're all competing for my attention. Then when I pick up my phone to check my social media accounts, I see more ads, more posts. I also read magazines, books, and newspapers—and watch television. Yes, all seem to be promoting something for me to buy. Like most of you, my entire day is spent "filtering" out a barrage of marketing. With so much marketing going on—almost everywhere we go—you see how difficult it is to stand out? You are not just competing with other artists or galleries for attention and sales—you're competing with everything and everyone to get a moment of their time. So how do you overcome this?

Well, if you can't beat 'em, join 'em.

Yes, that means you need to be everywhere, all day, every day, and you need to be consistent. You need to make it so your potential buyers have as many opportunities as possible to be "touched" by you. How do you do it?

Marketing.

Marketing is the vehicle that takes your brand/product/art to where the people are. It's your website, it's the content on your website, it's the blogs you write, the information you share, the emails you send, the direct mailers you send, the social media accounts you manage, the ads you purchase, the SEO (Search Engine Optimization) you utilize to attract more followers, and the events you host in order to build and maintain personal relationships. In this section, I will go in detail about what you need to do to establish a strategic, step-by-step marketing plan:

1. Build and optimize your website.

We already established your logo and brand. You should have a ready-to-go style guide and overall idea of the look and feel you want to convey to your audience. Now you need to apply these things to create your online presence. You need a website. And let me assure you, website design is more than just "looking pretty." Your website is YOUR BRAND. It's your audience's first impression of you. It needs to be functional. It needs to be concise. (The average person clicks-thru or out of a page in less than three seconds!) Give your audience a reason to stay or give them enough information as possible with as few words as possible. You need to immediately grab your audience's attention. For artists—it will be your work. Your pages should not appear cluttered. The work should be well curated (just as you would for a tradeshow). If you're not tech-savvy, hire a web designer to help you. Some finer points:

> **"Teach yourself to work in uncertainty."**
> **—Bernard Malamud**

- **Invest in photography.** Since you're showcasing artwork it's also imperative that you have high quality photos of yourself, your art, your studio, and completed projects. Be sure to have professional headshots as well as images of you and your work environment, along with action shots that show, for example, you working in your studio will help with portraying who you are to your clients and potential clients. Beautiful photos are worth the time, expense and effort, and they'll make you look polished and reliable.
- **Make it easy for people to contact and reach you.** Visitors come to your website to learn about your business, but they also want to know the person behind

the scenes. By creating a streamlined one-click contact section, you'll ensure that they can easily find and connect with you. Make sure to include your email address, business phone number, and links to social media pages. *(Tip: Avoid those annoying email security contact pages on your website. Gallery owners, like myself hate these because we have to wait for you to respond. Many times, if I'm looking to buy art and need information quickly, and I see this, I simple move on to another artist and that artist loses a potential sale.)*

- **Include customer feedback.** When promoting your art business, nothing beats featuring great testimonials from loyal customers and happy gallery owners. For example, my gallery's website is adcfineart.com features photos and heartfelt statements form our clients. Contact your favorite collectors and ask for feedback—you'll be amazed at what you'll receive.

2. Focus on your content. Make sure it is excellent.

Every marketing major knows the oft-repeated statement: "Content is king." And it is. The content you have on your website is what will ultimately attract your clients. Google's search algorithms are designed so that relevant, timely, and consistent keywords drive users to your site. It's not just about selling either—it's about informing. Your site has to "offer" something to attract buyers to you. And the blogs and information you write will drive potential buyers to your website.

3. Set up and maintain a blog.

There is no better way to drive people to your site than to write informative, inspiring, or entertaining blogs that showcases your work, helps other artists, helps clients understand some aspect of art better, answers a question, or entertains or inspires your audience. If done correctly and consistently, your website will soon become an "attraction"—somewhere your audience wants to go to when they are online. If you're consistent and gain subscribers, you will also build a following, which means people will be coming back to see what you're up to. (Remember when I used that "garden" analogy way back when I was describing your career as an artist? Well, content marketing is your full watering can. By pouring content out you are helping your career to grow.)

4. Set up various channels for your web content: eBooks, guest blogs, webinars, vlogs, and podcasts.

Just like every flower needs a different amount of water at different times during its lifecycle, so too does your career. Setting up a website and writing a blog (or posting a video blog—vlog) once a week, isn't going to get the job done. And it may only reach one type of potential buyer. You need to know what types of content there are and when to use them—and how often. For example, if you are just getting started, and you are trying to grow awareness you need to diversify your content. What are some examples? You can write a short eBook or offer a small print of your work for free if someone clicks on the link and gives you their email. (This is a popular way to build mailing lists. If you don't know this already, you must BUILD subscribers. They have to give you explicit consent for you to email them. They must provide their email and subscribe. It's the law). Another way is to write an eGuide, or a write articles and submit to popular online

"Nobody who ever gave his best regretted it. "
—Geore Hala

magazines that can in turn share your website information and drive people to your site. You could also offer to "guest blog" on another artist's site who has a similar audience you're trying to attract. Some artists may ask that you return the favor. It's a win for everyone. Once you're past the "awareness" phase, you move into, what marketers call the "consideration" phase. People know who you are and want to hear more from you as they "consider" buying from you. Perhaps you can post video of yourself at work, or in a documentary style interview. You can also host live webinars and webcasts. Another popular way to reach people is podcasts. Invite other artists for you to interview. Or share information about a topic that interests or inspires you. Give other artists helpful tips, or buyers tips. Again, it's simply another "touchpoint" for a potential buyer to find you.

"Surround yourself with people who are going to motivate and inspire you."
—Charles H. Marcus

5. Define Your Distribution Channels: Social Media, email, direct mail, and advertising.

"I set up a website! I blog once a week! What more do I possibly have to do!"

-Oh honey...in the words of Karen Carpenter: *We've only just begun.*

Yes, content is king. Yes, branding is massively important. Yes, your website looks beautiful, but, it will all go to waste if it just sits there in cyberspace. If you build it, they decidedly won't come. Let me assure you. As important as all this is without distribution channels (paid and unpaid), as well as a clear understanding of how each works, your content goes to waste.

Social Media

"Oh, yeah I have a Facebook page! I even Tweet sometimes."

Super. You're on your way! But, that's not enough. In the world of social media marketing, again consistency pays. And having a strategy, plan, and regular execution of that plan is absolutely imperative. If you're just getting started and don't have the budget for a marketing or social media manager, you're going to be on your own for this and it can be overwhelming. However, there are ways to streamline and simplify this process. The first and foremost way is to set up accounts in various platforms, Facebook, Twitter, Google+, LinkedIn, Vango, Instagram, and Pinterest. (If you haven't already done so, do this now. I'll be right here when you get back.) Once you have done this, now you can streamline your Instagram, LinkedIn, Facebook, and Twitter accounts by setting up a Hootsuite or Buffer account, which is a social media "dashboard." In other words, it allows you to set up posts in advance. It also connects your social media accounts so that you can distribute to your various channels from one location. That being said, you don't want to share ALL THE SAME INFO on each platform. Each platform is different, has a different audience, and a different way of communicating. They are different sites that have different purposes and your messaging needs to reflect that.

"Avoid having your ego so close to your position that when your position fails, you ego goes with it."
—Colin Powell

However, one strategy that does work across all social media channels is using photographs.

Lucky you! You're an artist! So by regularly posting your work, you're going to easily appease all the different platforms. As a general rule, posts with pictures get higher clicks and engagement across the board. You also have to consider timing—as in when you send out your posts. Over the years, market analysis experts have figured out the best times of day to schedule posts (which you can automate on your social media dashboard). Here's a little cheat-sheet from sumall.com that tells you when the optimal time to post on each site (when buyers are most active).

Twitter 1-3 p.m. *weekdays*

Facebook 1-4 p.m. and 2-5 p.m. *weekdays*

LinkedIn 7-8:30 a.m. and 5-6 p.m.
Tuesday, Wednesday, and Thursday

Instagram 5-6 p.m. *weekdays*

Pinterest 2-4 p.m. and 8-11 p.m.

Google+ 9-11 a.m. *weekdays*

Here's a "cheat sheet" Social Media Calendar for you to copy and fill out.

AY	DATE	TIME	MESSAGE	LINK	CAMPAIGN	IMAGE
onday						
	1/1/18	9:00 am	sample message here	www.facebook.com	selling campaign	Image of artwork "Untitle #1"
	1/1/18	12:00 am				
	1/1/18	3:00 pm				
	1/1/18	6:00 pm				
esday						
	1/2/18	9:00 am				
	1/2/18	12:00 am				
	1/2/18	3:00 pm				
	1/2/18	6:00 pm				
ednesday						
	1/3/18	9:00 am				
	1/3/18	12:00 am				
	1/3/18	3:00 pm				
	1/3/18	6:00 pm				
ursday						
	1/4/18	9:00 am				
	1/4/18	12:00 am				
	1/4/18	3:00 pm				
	1/4/18	6:00 pm				
iday						
	1/5/18	9:00 am				
	1/5/18	12:00 am				
	1/5/18	3:00 pm				
	1/5/18	6:00 pm				
turday						
	1/6/18	9:00 am				
	1/6/18	12:00 am				
	1/6/18	3:00 pm				
	1/6/18	6:00 pm				
nday						
	1/7/18	9:00 am				
	1/7/18	12:00 am				
	1/7/18	3:00 pm				
	1/7/18	6:00 pm				

Spend a few hours one day of the month and fill out, plan then and automate your posts. It will save you time and you won't worry about those times when you're not available to post. But here are some other things to consider:

Don't forget to be spontaneous too!

I should mention, as great as it is to have your posts scheduled, you should also be spontaneous and share whenever you can or feel the need to—do so. Especially if it shows a personable, likeable aspect of you. People are on social media to be "social." If you're at an event or your working on something—share it! Tag friends and locations! By doing this you'll be opening up a variety of new ways to reach more people.

Respond and engage!

Don't forget that in all of your posts and putting "stuff out there" you need to respond and connect. Another important aspect is following and engaging with others. By liking, commenting, and sharing, you're letting people know you're there and are interested in them. This endears you to people and they will in turn follow you. Spend some time each day "engaging"—following, liking, reposting, and sharing—and watch your followers grow. That being said, be careful! Remember your "brand"/signature style is linked closely to you. Anyone can get a website, rant on a blog, post on Facebook, or send

> **"Continuous effort--not strength or intelligence—is the key to unlocking our potential."**
> **—Liane Cordes**

e-blasts. How you use these powerful media tools however, is what will set you apart. When you present yourself in the best light, you will earn your customers' loyalty, create a marketing message that sizzles and ultimately boosts your art business and bottom line.

And sometimes you have to pay to play!

Some of my artists have had HUGE returns experimenting with paid advertising on social media. You can set up a daily ad budget and post images and a few words of content. You can also promote popular posts. The best part is that you set the budget. If you can only spend $5 a day, then that's all you get. It's fairly easy to use too. Go to your social media settings and click on "Create Ad" links and the sites will walk you through it. (Remember to keep the receipts and factor this into your overhead!)

Nicholas Teetelli

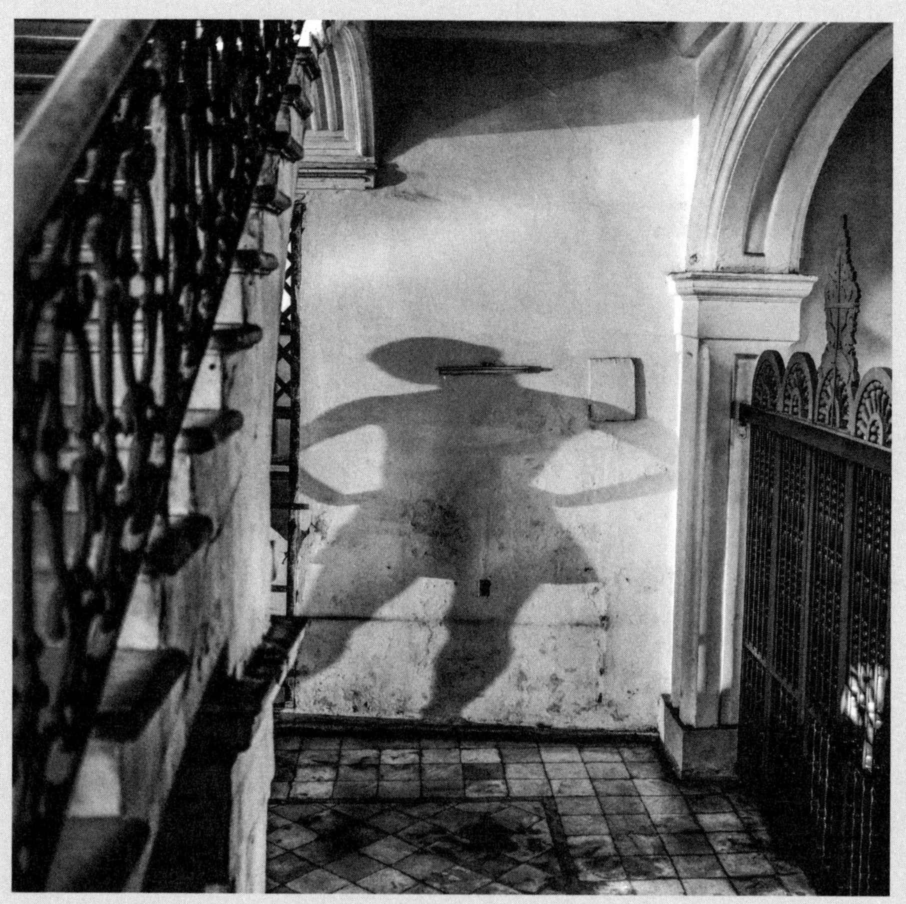

© Nicholas Teetelli

The Power of Ad Campaigns on Facebook

There is no better story of success using ad campaigns on Facebook than Nicholas Teetelli's. He is a marketer's dream. Transitioning from the corporate world to fine art photography, he used social media to grow his audience and ultimately sell work. And, he did it with little to no prior experience—in both the art world or social media. "Being 'an old dog' I was somewhat resistant to the Facebook concept, however, also being in the technology business for the past two decades, I knew better," he says. "As an aspiring artist, the single most important initiative, from my perspective, is marketing. After all, if people don't know you exist or know that your art exists, well, you're not going to get very far these days. So I decided to invest in myself, my brand as an artist, and make a serious effort to get myself out there."

Nicholas set up his Facebook page for his business, and became aware of the incredible tools at his disposal to help set up ad campaigns and target his audience. "I cannot overemphasize the importance of utilizing these features properly, and paying attention to them. If you're just going to post on your Facebook page and hope you will get noticed or get people's attention, you are totally wasting your time and effort," he says. "You need to set up your campaigns (posts) and boost every one of them. So, in short, you will need to have a budget that you are willing to invest to gain traction. I boost every one of my campaigns, typically anywhere from $20 to $50 each. I select my target demographics: gender, age, location, interests, and as I get the demographic results back from Facebook each day, I revisit, tweak and adjust my campaigns to maximize target reach."

Nicholas had almost immediate results. "In two short months, I had accumulated an international following of nearly 10,000 people, and now just a few months later I have almost 40,000 followers. The first month my artwork postings were receiving 'Likes' in the low hundreds, into the second month high hundreds, and more recently, likes into the thousands, with one of my art images receiving nearly 13,000 likes," he says. And that was just in two months!

But, Nicholas is quick to advise to not rely on paid ads alone. "While I attribute a good portion of the success to my boost investments, they alone cannot do it for you," he advises. "Your posts have to be interesting, personable (I mix in some personal-level posts... my life, my daughter, and what is going on in my life as well), to show people I am no different than my audience and that allows me to connect with people more effectively. I get dozens of comments every day, to which I respond to every single one individually—no bulk replies."

Nicholas' final piece of advice: Engage. "You need to engage your audience on a personal level to be successful, it takes a lot of work and commitment, but it's worth the investment."

To learn more about Nicholas Teetelli, visit www.teetelli.com

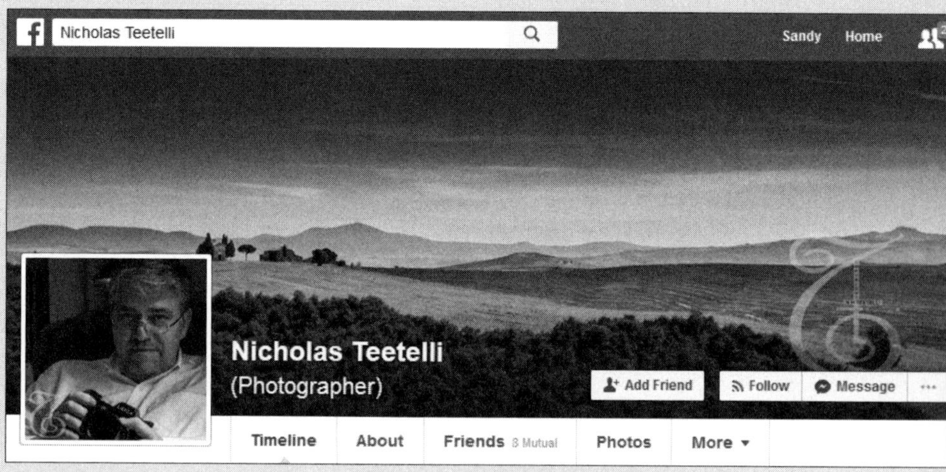

A word about # (Hashtags)

#DontUnderstand #WhattheHeckareYouTalkingAbout

Ok, unless you've been living on a different planet the past five years, you can't go a day without hearing about hashtags. A hashtag is simply a way to categorize a topic in social media—mainly on Twitter and Instagram. Although, Facebook now can be searched by hashtag too, people rarely use them there. Hashtags make it easier for people to search for other social media posts about those same topics. For example, if you type #photography or #oilpainting or #design into the search box at the top of any Twitter or Instagram page and hit Enter, you'll get a list of tweets or instas, most of which will be related to those topics. You can find cool people and art this way. And the best part: People searching these topics can find you this way!

"Now that I know better, I do better."
—Maya Angelou

On Twitter, given the character count (140 characters or less) you usually can't use more than two hashtags. But, on Instagram, you can really see the engagement power of hashtags. You can use up to 30 hashtags on Instagram! 30! Some marketers/business gurus say this is comparable to "spamming." Many experts say that using 11 hashtags fosters the best engagement (more followers, more likes, more comments, more "touchpoints," and more links or drivers to one's website). However, the two main points I want to make about hashtags are:

1) **Use them,**
2) **but, use them effectively.**

It doesn't matter if you're using one or thirty, if you're putting your work or posts in the wrong category or wrong topic, they're never going to be discovered. Popular hashtags like #love #peace have millions of posts. And people are literally posting these hashtags every minute. Your hashtag appears in order of when it was posted. It's not only rated by popularity. (Although, the posts with the most likes or comments will be featured as "most popular" at the top of the page). My point is, you want your hashtags to be strategic. You also want to create your own. That way, when you're on Instagram and continually use a hashtag for a particular series of your work, when someone clicks on that hashtag they will see only and ALL your posts from that series. Instagram will immediately filter out all of your other posts. Amazing! Be sure to check these tags aren't being used already. Encourage fans and followers to use your hashtags too, and you'll learn who your fans and followers are, because posts from other pages will appear under your hashtag. *(Tip: Create a list of hashtags and save in your Notes app on your phone. Then every time you post all you have to do is copy and paste your #hashtags, instead of retyping them every time).*

"It is not the language of painters, but the language of nature which one should listen to."
—Vincent Van Gogh

KX2

Ruth Avra & Dana Kleinman

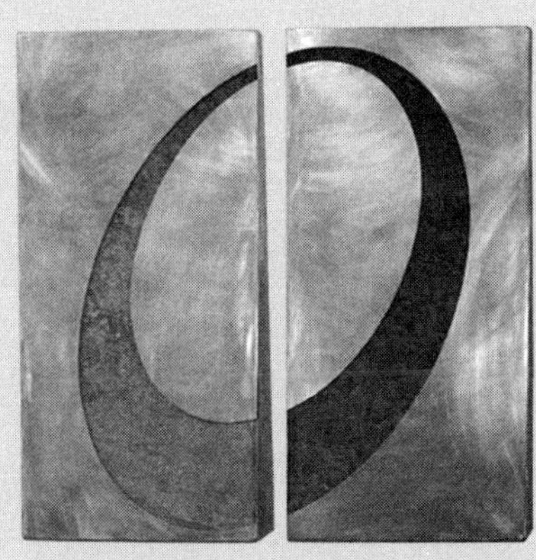

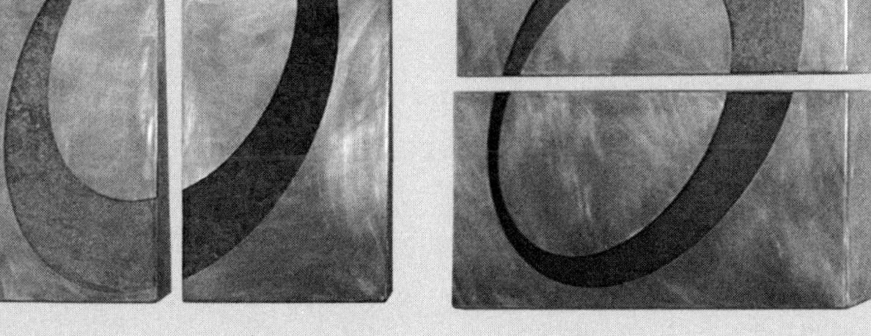

The Power of Instagram

"Instagram has turned out to be a great social media tool for us. With any new social media, we tend to hold off for a little bit since it can be a lot of work to learn and then maintain. But after encouragement from other artists, we gave in about a year ago and found ourselves sucked in pretty quickly. Instagram is the perfect tool for artists since it is all image based. Not only is Instagram great for exposure of our own work, but we enjoy following other artists, galleries and designers, and find daily inspiration. We have also been contacted about sales and commissions through this platform just in the short time we have been on it. And it is beneficial for us to see what pieces people seem to respond to more than others by looking at the number of likes."

KX2 Ruth Avra & Dana Kleinman
Find them on Instagram: @kx2art

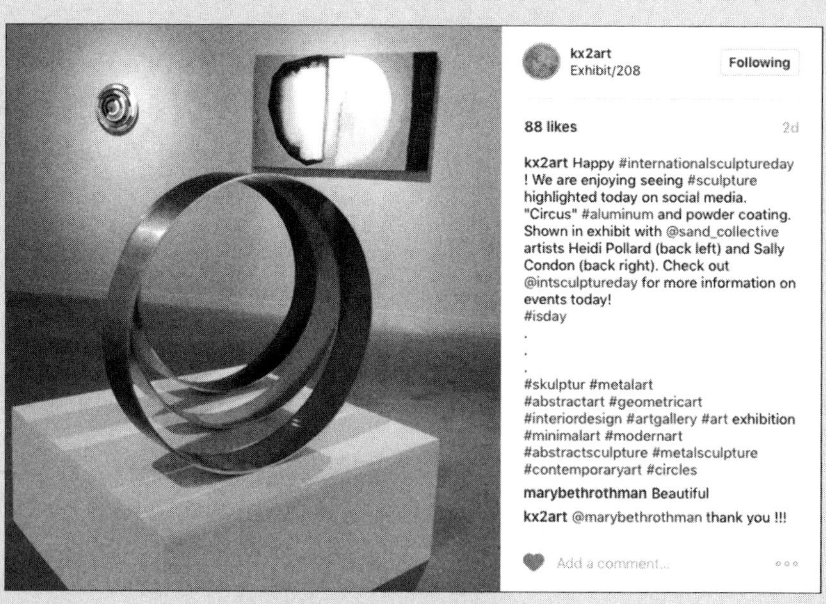

Let's put a Pin in It

Pinterest is one of the leading social sites for consumers. Do you know you're most likely to purchase something if you pin it? By curating a beautiful Pinterest board, with distinct categories—by color, style, design, and subject—as well as pins outside of your "wheelhouse" that show what you're interested in or what inspires you, will drive more people to your site. You can also pin blogs you've written, favorite galleries, favorite artists, favorite books. The sky's the limit. Play around with it and have fun.

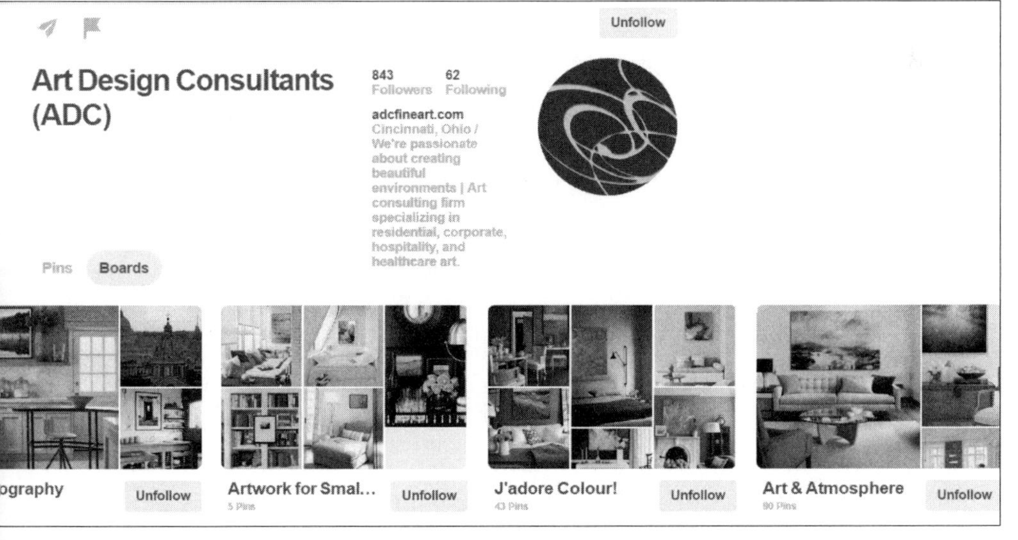

Random fact and something to think about!

The average person checks his or her phone every six minutes, that adds up to about 150 times per day! This is a huge opportunity to engage with people and become an essential part of their daily lives. You don't want to miss the opportunity to be where your customers are!

Kevin Grass

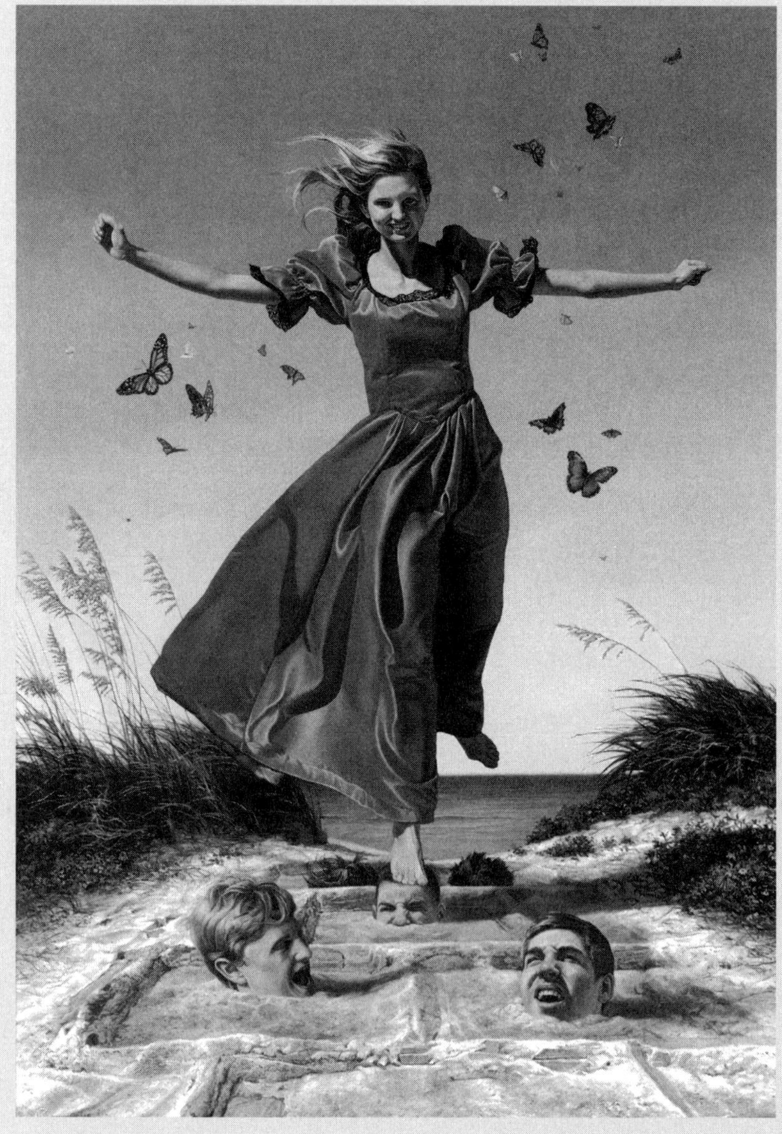

The Power of Twitter

"We use Twitter and Facebook to make potential collectors more aware of Kevin's paintings and to drive buyers to our solo booth at the SPECTRUM art fair during Art Basel/Miami. Building a steady following via social media marketing helps entry-level collectors purchase giclée and paper prints. When this audience can afford the original works, they will have been following Kevin's progress for a while and will know that he is a talented artist whose paintings show his personal commentary on social issues in our society." *—Michaela Oberlander, Marketing Manager for Kevin Grass Fine Art*

Follow Kevin on Twitter at @fineartfan or visit www.kevingrass.com

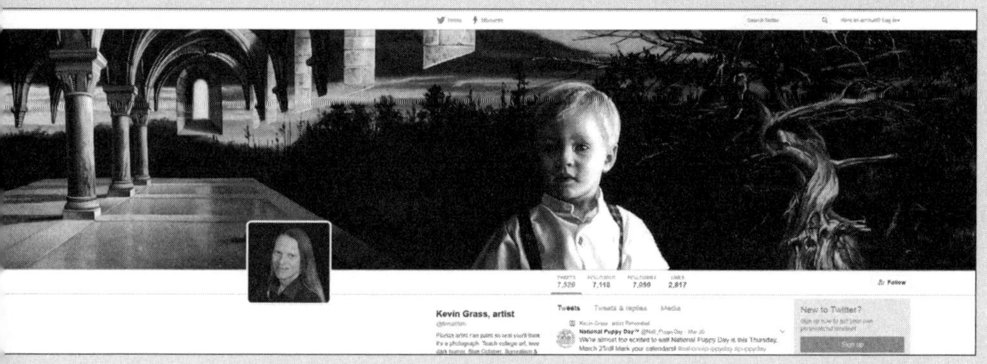

Email Marketing

One of the most successful ways I've had in keeping in touch with clients and artists alike has been with my e-newsletter. Email is easy, effective, and a great way to stay connected to and GROW your client list. Email is also commonly used for announcements, newsletters, and promotions. However, just as I mentioned above, timing is everything—and so is frequency. Every day is too much for my audience. Once a year? Too little. Also, as I said earlier content is king. Keep it short, effective, and clean! There should be no grammatical errors. Have someone review your email before you send it out. Make sure all the dates, prices, and key information are correct. And most importantly, make sure the subject line is catchy. If you don't give the reader a reason to open up and answer the email, they won't. Ask a question. Or say something bold and leave them hanging, so they have to click through to see the rest of your message. Mix it up. If you're always writing: EXCITING NEWS! Guess what? It's probably only exciting to you at this point. They have heard this all before. If you're only sending emails to toot your own horn or announce your accomplishments: Again: Snooze fest. You may be excited and proud, but your audience is thinking: *Oh here we go again…a note from Mr. Wonderful. It can't be all about YOU!* You have to give your audience a reason—several reasons to like you, or come back to you. Have a weekly feature of art work, or technique discussion. Offer your audience information that will enhance their life. They will click. Then when you do need them to respond, they will. They'll be used to clicking on your emails because they'll find them useful and relevant to their lives.

"Every artist was first an amateur. "
—Ralph Waldo Emerson

Cat Tesla

Cat Tesla

The Power of Newsletters and Social Media to Boost Art Sales

"Email newsletters and social media have been extremely helpful to my art business. Staying in touch with collectors and showing them images of "behind the scenes" works in progress, inspiration, and invites to special showings are a critical part of my art business. The people that follow you and love your work always want to know more. I've sold many artworks off of FB and Instagram even before they were finished, as well as images of new works featured in newsletters." —*Cat Tesla*

To learn more about Cat and her art, visit www.artbycat.com

Wednesday, December 28, 2016

The Top 10 Things Overheard in My Art Booth in 2016

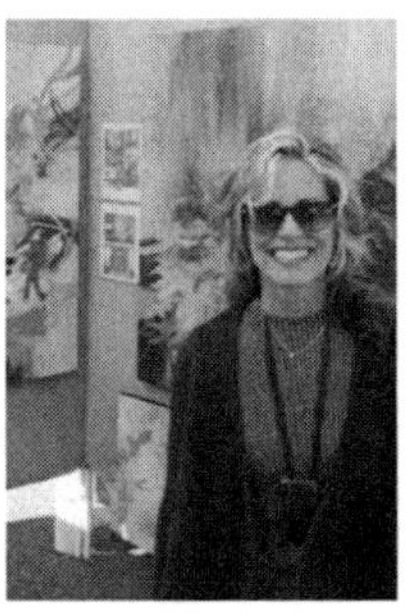

Just when I think the past year couldn't possibly be topped, the things people say at art shows continue to amaze me!

(Insert drumroll here). . . here are my "top ten" conversations, questions, and comments overheard in my art booth in 2016:

1. My wife would have you bring the entire van full of art over to the house, but then I'd need a bank loan.
2. Are these jewelry boxes? (asking about my "Outside of the Box" series)
3. I'm looking for the scruffy guy with the beard who does wood sculpture.
4. You look like your work - soft and beautiful.
5. Were you having a stroke or causing a stroke when you painted this one?
6. You gotta love an artist who has the guts to do this.
7. These are just stunning, Cat! Yours is the only card I took from the show.
8. You're not afraid of color, are you?
9. That looks like what will be at the pearly gates.
10. You're a nice looking couple; maybe you can get a job at this show?

About Me

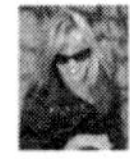

ARTIST: CAT TESLA

It is said that a cat has 9 lives. I'm on my 3rd. For me college was a toss-up between art & science; I chose the latter. My 1st life was a decade as a genetic counselor seeing patients in high-risk prenatal & cancer clinics. My 2nd life a hybrid of genetic clinics by day, painting by night, traveling to art shows on weekends. Trapped by the golden handcuffs of healthcare & a steady paycheck, my emotional state swung from burn-out to fatigue to resentment to boredom. It was time to go. My 3rd life as a full-time artist had begun. I'm a painter & can often be found sketching ideas on yellow sticky notes, cocktail napkins, & the edges of grocery lists. Ideas come & they come often. Design is everywhere. Inspiration isn't far behind. I am guilty of doing too many things at once. Personality tests describe me as pioneering, creative, visionary, & a self-starter. Oh, & tenacious. I was born in the Chinese Year of the Rabbit - 1963 - & for those curious, my parents didn't name me after an animal. "Cat" is short for Catherine. Thanks for visiting my blog where I'll provide a peek into my life as an artist, sources of inspiration, previews of my artwork.

View my complete profile

Visit my website

www.artbycat.com

artist to artist

Cindy Avroch

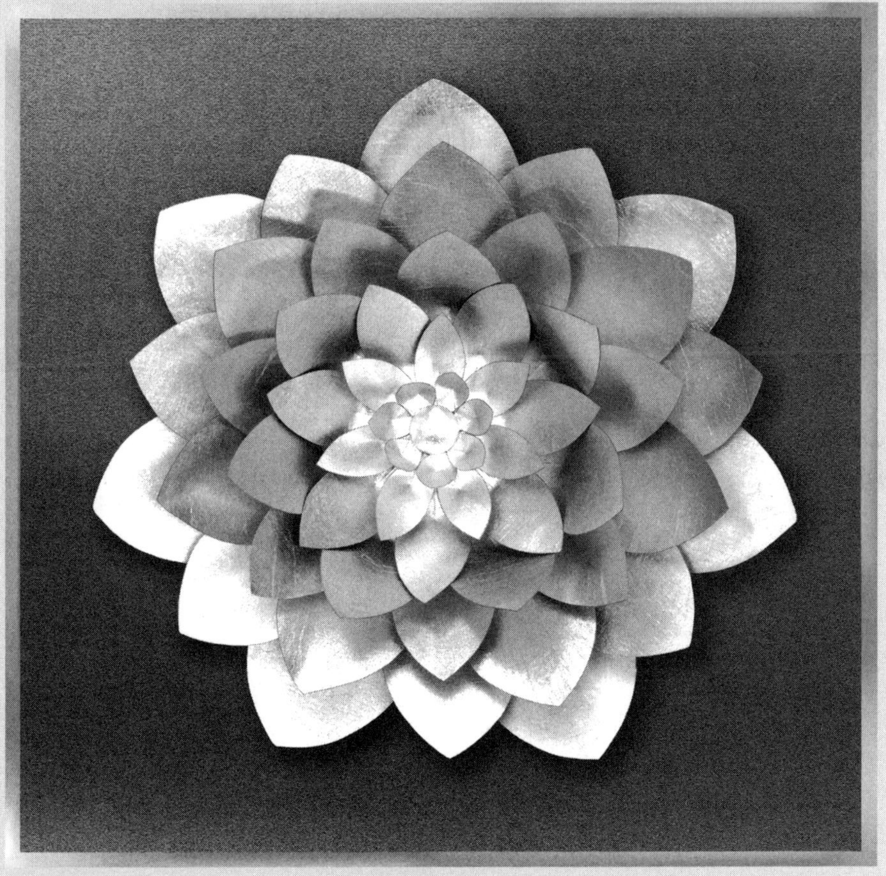

The Power of Newsletters to Enhance and Strengthen Relationships

One of the highlights of my career as a gallery owner is following the fascinating journeys and explorations that my artists and friends take on their own paths to success. One artist I absolutely love to hear from (and await her newsletters with anticipation) is Cindy Avroch. Cindy is a multi-talented artist who has found massive success in just the past five years as a working fine artist. One of the ways she's done this is through the use of newsletters to connect with her growing audience.

"I've been using Mailchimp to send out e-newsletters for the past couple of years. I cross-populated my mailing list from my LinkedIn contacts, gmail contacts, and solicited help from a friend in the PR business," Cindy says. She prefers to work with a software platform like Mailchimp or Constant Contact, because they have ready-made templates and easy-to-use features and analytics built in. "I just have to plug in the information—content and pictures—each month, and I don't have to worry about formatting or design each time," she says. All told, she spends about one to two hours a month on creating the content and pushing send.

Cindy doesn't overcomplicate it or overthink it. She thinks of the newsletter as a way to keep in touch with "friends." She uses a conversational style and will update her friends/audience on any number of pieces she's been working on, pieces she's sold, and even how the weather is effecting her creativity. She also always has a section called "Cindy's Picks" in which she highlights events going on the New York City. "I don't want it to be all about me," she says. "You need to offer your audience something they can't get anywhere else." She and her husband also travel quite a bit, and she likes to visit and then highlight the galleries she visits. But she doesn't feel like she needs to write a novel about everything she sees. "You need to keep it short and sweet," she advises, "and don't complicate it. There is always something new to share, new to talk about, new work to show." Cindy rarely feels stuck when searching for content to share. She spends a lot of time checking out other artists' blogs, fashion and design magazines, and staying abreast of art trends. "Whether it's a fashion trend, a color trend, a home furnishing trend, there's tons of info out there to choose from to write about: events, holidays, personal milestones. I try to mix it up and keep it interesting," she says.

Engagement like this has a purpose well beyond staying connected. "Though I can't trace a sale directly to a newsletter I've sent, I can say, that I've had galleries contact me and several people will give me feedback on a piece I am working on right away," she says. "I also know that galleries are paying attention. They may watch you for a year to see how you're handling your career and marketing—and what types of work you're producing. Newsletters are just another way to keep them on your radar."

To learn more about Cindy and her art, visit www.cindyavrochfineart.com

Direct Mail

Do not overlook the power of sending a carefully designed invite or promotion to an event through the mail to your clients. Nor, as I have mentioned several times before, should you ever hesitate to mail a handwritten and thoughtful thank you note to a customer. Every touchpoint is an equally important one.

Paid Advertising

As I said before you can pay for ads on social media platforms, but you can also pay for placement in magazines and other publications. Our annual publication *Blink Art Resource* was designed to give artists an opportunity to get their work in front of top designers, art consultants, and galleries in North America. Leading trade professionals use Blink to source artwork quickly and efficiently - resulting in beautiful environments that satisfy clients. The book can be used all year, as well as its online store.

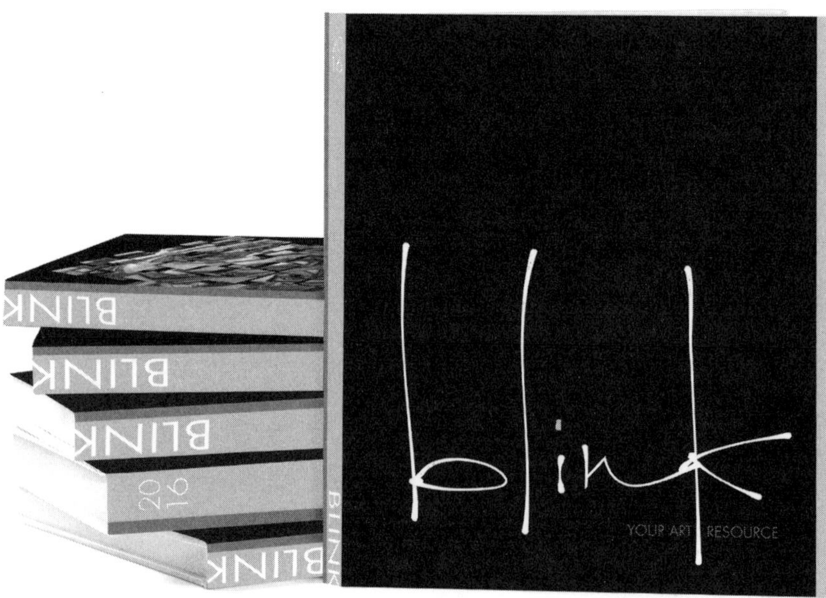

Artists pay for promotional space in the book. Here they can showcase their best work, and provide their website and contact information. In addition to having their work featured in the printed *Blink Art Resource,* artists can also enjoy an incredible online presence equipped with an online catalog and online artist portfolios. You have to remember, however, that advertising, like attendance at tradeshows, takes time. Buyers want to see if you have "staying power" and that you're more than a "one and done" type of artist. Yes, it's a financial commitment. But, remember the "Rule of 7"—even if a customer can't trace their reason for buying a piece directly to an ad placement, it no doubt served as a "touchpoint" at some point. And another rule of advertising and marketing to consider: If you're not there, someone else will be.

For more information, visit www.adcfineart.com.

Search Engine Optimization (SEO)

While it's true that the content you create is king, it is, again, only useful if it finds its way into the right hands. Google and other search engines use SEO to "index" your pages so that your content can be found by your clients/customers/visitors when they go on a search engine and type in a what they're looking for. Even though it doesn't seem like one, you need to think about SEO as another integral marketing channel. And like all marketing channels, in order for SEO to work, YOU need to optimize it (okay that's jargon). Translation: You need to make your content stand out! When I say stand out, I mean, there are a list of rules or algorithms that Google and other search engines use to index and categorize your work. Whether its blogs, landing pages, or social tags, you need to create a "keyword" list. In other words, keywords are the words or phrases that you know your target audience will be searching for when they go to search engines. Once you've created your keyword list, you have to make sure that exact word and phrase shows up multiple times in blogs, content, and your landing pages. You also need to use them frequently. The way that SEO works is the more a keyword phrase is used and often, the more it will rise in the "search engine."

"Words are how we think; stories are how we link."
—Christina Baldwin

Nicholas Yust

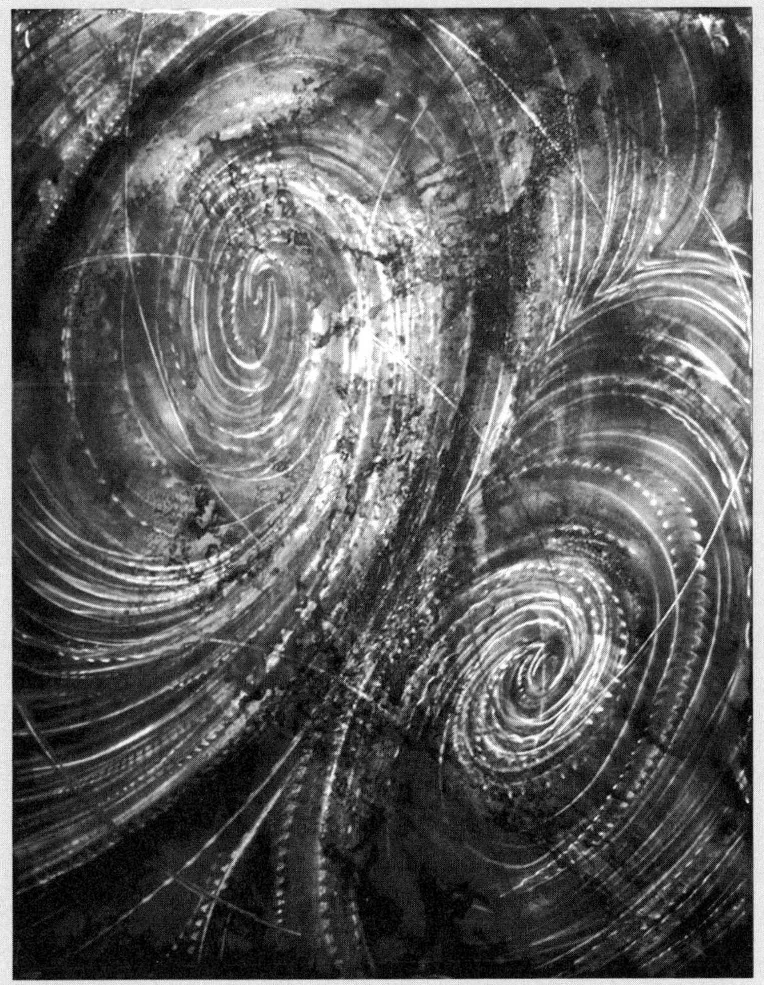

The Importance of a Well-Designed Website, Keywords, and SEO

One of the most successful artists I know who has perfected engagement and using SEO marketing is Nicholas Yust. While he has an engaged and huge following on Facebook and Instagram that helps boosts his visibility, these social media sites are not the only thing that's driving visitors to his website. There is a lot more going on behind the scenes. Nicholas has figured out the best way to drive users to his site is through SEO. "I have a professionally built website, a great design platform, and carefully selected SEO keywords that promote the kind of art I do. This drives everything. On average I am getting 300 unique and new visitors to my website every day," he says.

When choosing his "keywords" he is strategic. He knows his market and therefore chooses words that he knows his target audience would most likely type into a search engine when looking for his work. "Currently, I have small specific keyword groups that are more geared toward large scale corporate artwork audience, as well as keywords that describe the type of work I do—copper sculpture, metal, art, sculpture," he says. Knowing who his market is and what it is they're looking for helps him choose the words he uses on the site effectively and in all the content he produces.

While he has used Google AdWords to boost traffic to his site, he's says that most of the traffic is organically driven (in other words, no one is clicking on ads to find his website). Because he has so effectively chosen his keywords, his website has naturally become highly ranked. How does this happen? Well, there is a formula at work here. Google, Bing, Yahoo!, and other search engines rely on algorithms that determine a site's ranking and where it will appear (as in the the top or the bottom of the search page). In response to this, Nicholas has become strategic. "We're very specific with our website wording, and we also stay current with what's going on. Search engine algorithms change all the time and we make changes on our site regularly to reflect them," he says. "All websites need to be mobile friendly now. If they're not, your ranking will drop. You also have post frequent and relevant content. If you want to be successful, you have to stay on top of it."

"Once you have SEO figured out, you're going to notice an increase in followers on Instagram and Facebook," Nicholas adds. While social media does drive visitors to a site, that's not the reason Nicholas focuses his attention on it. "For me, there is not a big ROI on social media. I would say I sell one original piece a month through Facebook. And this is miniscule compared to my other marketing efforts. So why do it? "Social media use is more for a credibility factor," he says. "Having a presence there helps an interested person see who they're buying from. They want to make sure I'm a legitimate artist. They want to see that I am still active and relevant in the artist and fine art community. It's a way to show that I am doing residential work and have experience working with Fortune 500 companies." He also does it to connect and give back to his followers as well as keep them engaged and informed. He does have some helpful advice though. "Don't get into politics, and don't share too much personal information. Keep your work relevant to your work as an artist. And, when possible, give back," he says. Nicholas offers thousands of dollars a year in scholarships for his design contests he hosts on his Facebook page. He invites art students to submit design images, and he and a peer jury select the winners. The winners not only receive a scholarship, but if they're interested in having their work produced and marketed, they will receive a royalty off of their sold works. "It gives artists an opportunity to generate an income and earn a credential or two, and in return, those interactions generate a lot of likes, shares, admiring of the art, and continued engagement," he says.

To learn more about Nicholas and his art, visit www.nicholasyust.com

Measuring and Analyzing Your Data Regularly

> **"Great works are performed not by strength, but by perseverance."**
> **—Samuel Johnson**

No one particularly likes to do this, but it's a necessary part of the process: You have to measure and analyze results of all of your marketing efforts. Why? Because you need to know if they're working. You need to see how things grow over time. **You can't just be focused on dollar amounts or likes or hits.** You have to constantly look at the big picture and assess where you are at. There is no sense in doing something, over, over, and over only to have the same poor results. The definition of insanity is doing something over and over and expecting different results. If you're not looking at results and you're not taking some time each month to measure and assess, you don't know what's working and what's not. As soon as you start executing your marketing plan, you need to start tracking what's working and comparing. If you've gone to one tradeshow for ten years, spent an enormous amount of money to get there, but come home with crates full of paintings and only a couple of business cards—something is not working. It's time to do some research. What can you be doing differently? Also, is there a show that you've had more success at? Wouldn't it make sense to allocate more dollars there?

Scott McHenry

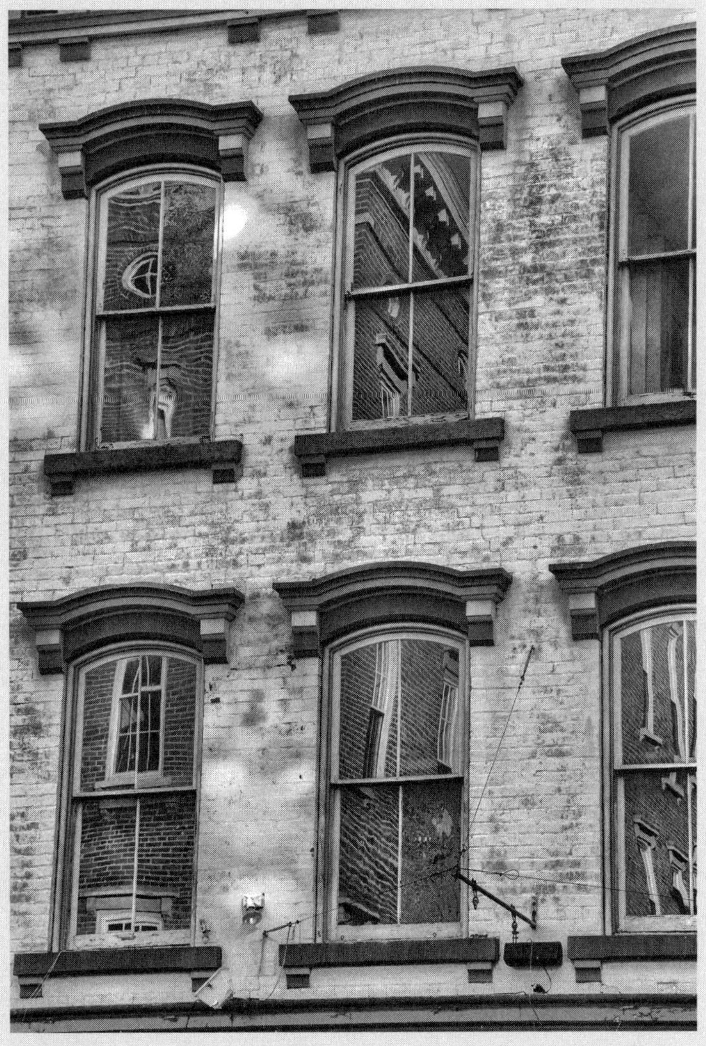

© Scott McHenry

The Power of Using Measurement Tools and Proper Use of Social Media

"I use my business page on Facebook as my main social media platform. Unlike a lot of artists I have set up my art as a business. I think most artists don't really consider cost of goods sold, return on investment or marketing. They are what I call 'secret artists.' With Facebook I am aiming to do two things:

1) *Be a constant presence on social media. I make three to five posts per week about upcoming shows or simply a photo with a short story. I have found that people tend to view the photo and not read very much so it might be a catchy title or one or two sentences.*
2) *Drive people to my website. I want them to ultimately make a purchase and look at my entire portfolio.*

They key is to be consistent and constant. I boost posts when I wreally want people to take action in some way or remind people of my complete list of products and services. Usually, it only takes one sale to more than pay for a boost. I am successful at that about 75 percent of the time.

I also use the Insights page to research how my posts are doing and who and where my followers are. My website has a stats page that I can analyze how many people go to my page and what they looked at. Then I use Google Analytics which is linked to my page for further analysis. I study the results and then adjust accordingly."—**Scott McHenry**

To learn more about Scott and his art, visit www.scottmchenryphotography.com

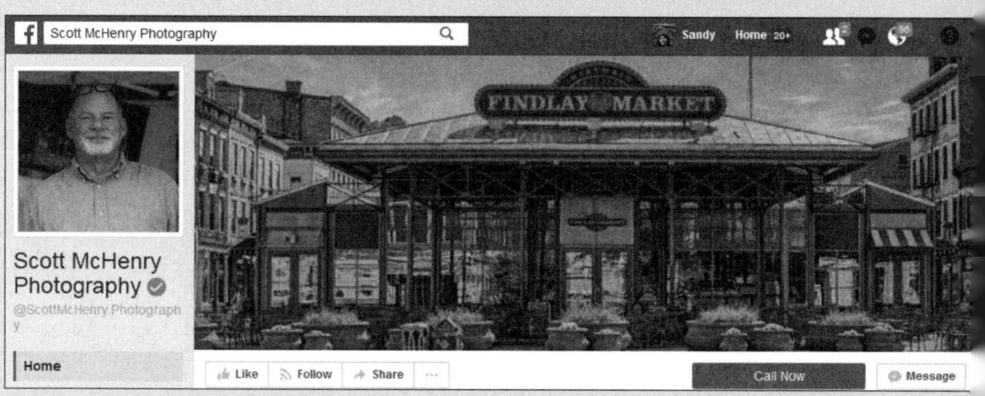

Maintaining Relationships in Real-Time

The Importance of Networking and Community Involvement

While social media is a wonderful way to stay connected, you don't want to overlook the power of connecting face-to-face with clients, gallerists, and other artists. Most artists I know prefer solitude, however, you absolutely need to schedule time in your calendar for real—live—people, in real time. Trust me, I know: When you're responsible for everything from sales to sweeping the floors, life as a business owner and artist can become lonely. You must find ways to connect with other people if you want to survive. You have to put yourself in places to interact with others. Here's what I recommend:

1. **Surround yourself with great people.** The people you surround yourself with will shape you more than anything else. Spend time with talented, experienced, and growth-minded people. Schedule a lunch once a month with someone who challenges you, inspires you, or pushes you. Put a time on the calendar each month to reach out to a gallery owner you work with. Call them, say hello. Ask them how they are doing. See if they need anything. It will keep you on their radar.

2. **Find a mentor that has been successful and can give you advice.** Make a list of five people in the art industry that you admire. Write a letter, an email, or send a Facebook message. Tell them your story (again keep it to the point). Be direct, sincere, and authentic. What can you bring of value to them, too?

3. **Get involved with your community.** Participate in local arts and business events; rent a booth at business trade shows and home and garden shows to get to know designers. Join your city's Chamber of Commerce, attend networking events, host networking events, and lend art to high-end commercial furniture dealer showrooms in exchange for referrals. Another great way to get exposure is to partner with local charities by donating a portion of your sales for a fundraiser.

gallery owner to artist

Jason and Bonnie Mansour

Art Leaders Gallery

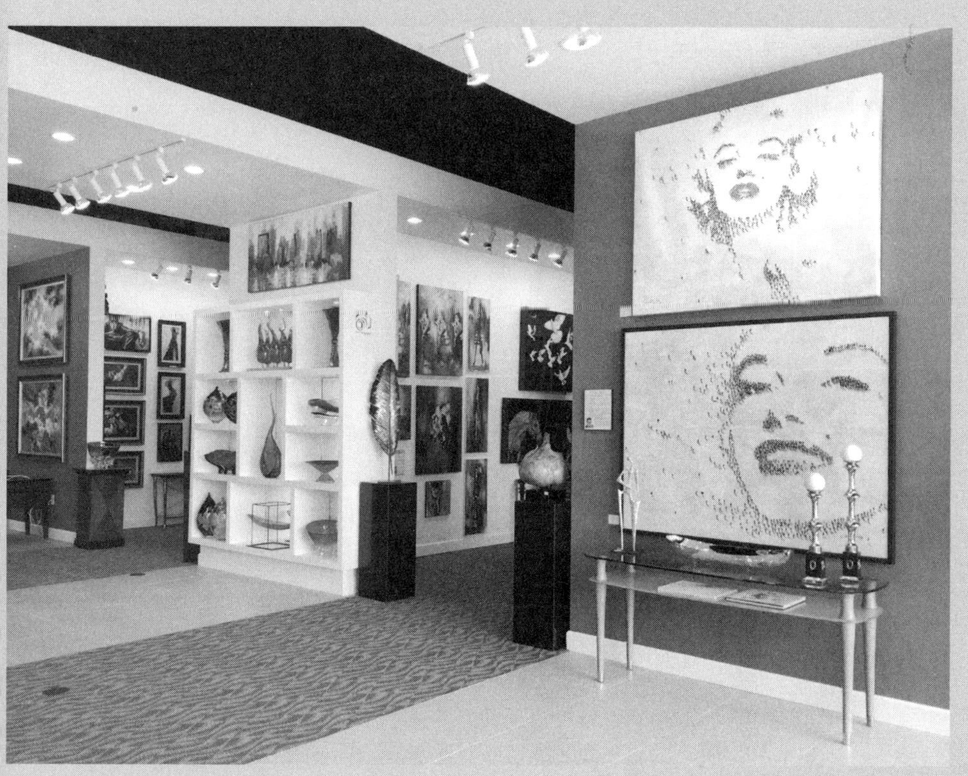

The Importance of Marketing

When I think of a dynamic couple that's shaped a thriving business, I think of Jason and Bonnie Mansour at Art Leaders Gallery. Committed in business and marriage, Jason and Bonnie have formed a foundation that's resulted in twenty-five years of gallery success. I met Bonnie during an Artexpo in New York and was immediately drawn to how honest and real she is. An influential businesswoman, seasoned art dealer, and wonderful friend and mentor, Bonnie holds nothing back. There is no pretention in her approach to art. She knows what she is doing and she's seen it all. Whenever we get together we're able to talk about life, art, business, work balance, and the realities of all of it.

Bonnie is an assiduous worker that has perfected a trifecta of techniques in building a strong clientele, seamless branding, and a gallery image. Everything this power couple does—from the beautiful storefront, to an extensive 12,000 square foot gallery, is entirely reflective of restless efforts and exquisite taste. Art Leaders hosts a full-service e-commerce website, multiple social media accounts, and countless gallery events all for the sake of promoting their artists.

I asked how she and Jason manage it all and she was honest about the work entailed, "We have a full-time marketing person and an exceptional team to relay our extensive offerings which span an entire collection of original oil paintings, hand-blown glass, sculptures, and monthly shows and events. That's an entire year's salary dedicated to promoting our artists' work. This sets us apart from a lot of galleries," she admits. "We know how difficult it is for artists to get their name and work out in front of collectors and interior designers so we're working hard for them." Bonnie offers an incredible service that most artists simply couldn't afford on their own; Art Leaders offerings are beyond a complete package. "A marketing and public relations firm would cost tens of thousands of dollars per campaign to promote the work we do all day, every day for our artists," she says.

The Art Leaders team takes a full-press approach to marketing and relationship building. "We dedicate a lot of time to social media—Facebook, Instagram, Pinterest—direct email marketing, and direct outreach to our clients personally. It all works hand-in-hand. You can't ignore any one aspect," she says. "We also cross market with the artists we represent and it benefits everyone. I won't work with an artist that isn't loyal to the gallery or is only looking for a one-way partnership. There is so much time, energy, and money poured into running a business like this, and it's nice if they promote the galleries working for them by listing their names on their own websites or social media platforms. It's a small thing, but it can help with the relationship."

Another part of the marketing approach that the Mansours take very seriously is the development of an e-commerce website. Bonnie credits a lot of their successful growth to Art Leaders web presence. "We just had a client who ordered a piece online because she saw the artist's work at another gallery, but couldn't remember the name of it. She went online and searched images of the art and found us. She then bought more works of art when she came in. She would have never have discovered us without our website." Online presence absolutely drives physical visits to Art Leaders Gallery. "I hear it all the time from clients that say they went online and were so impressed by our website and online galleries," she says. The Mansour's have many fundamental elements for success, Bonnie notes, "Remember this: Image, quality of artists represented, customer service, and building lasting client relationships is key." With over two decades in the industry and an esteemed reputation, Art Leaders Gallery continues to blossom and impress.

To submit your work to Art Leaders Galleries, visit www.artleaders.com.

artist to artist

Kevin Caron

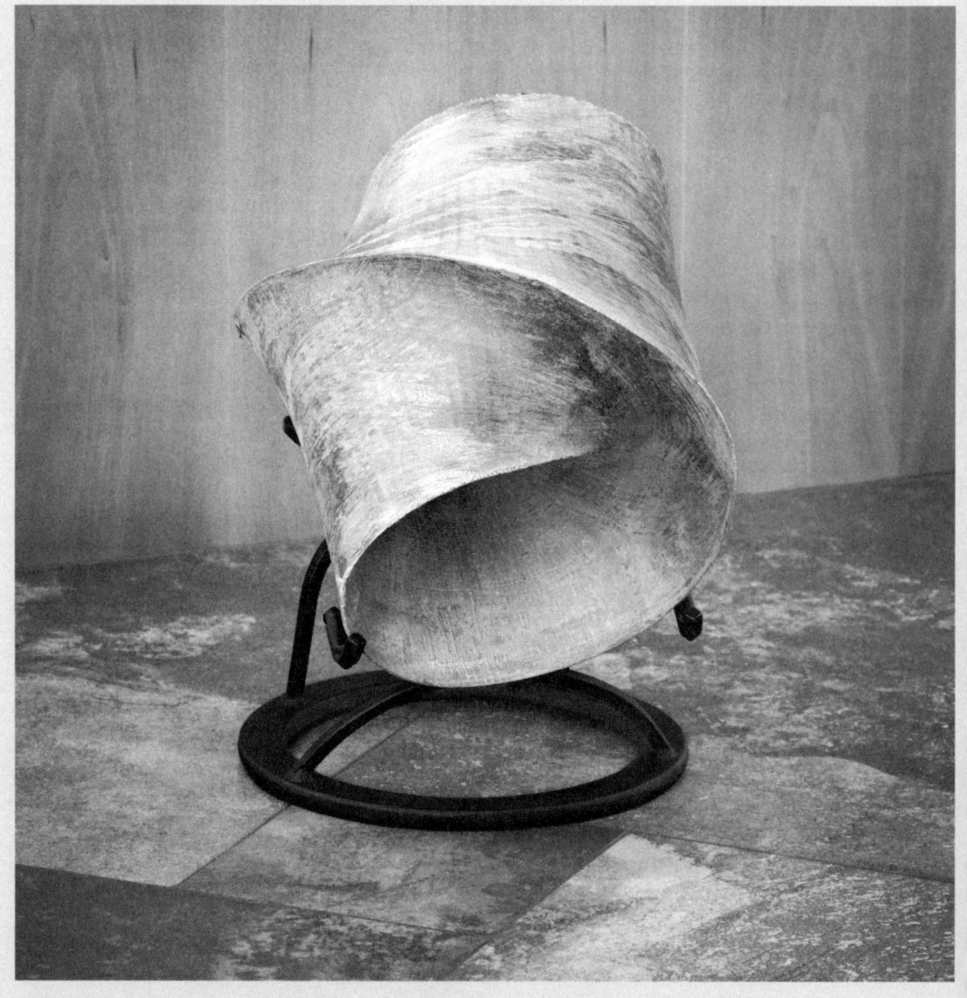

© Kevin Caron

The Power of Youtube

Kevin Caron, one of our most successful sculptors, started a YouTube channel (http://www.youtube.com/kevincaron) about ten years ago and has grown an incredible following, while growing his business. He started making short videos with a still camera and only posted videos sporadically at first. The plan was to cover what was going on in the studio that week. However, at first "no one cared," he said. What changed?

Consistency.

"We eventually got a regular schedule going – being predictable seems to build audience, but still only posted a new video weekly. It also became clear that people were more interested in how-to, instructional videos, so that became the focus," he says.

As expected, it took patience and diligence. After just one year, the channel began to take off. But, at the time a year to grow an audience took some perseverance and some looking on the bright-side when subscriptions were slow. "What kept me going was that the videos gave me an opportunity to speak, something I needed to be good at for public art presentations."

Ten years later, Kevin has more than 44,000 subscribers and 450 videos. (See! Posting just once a week adds up.) He now has more than 11.8 million views. Besides building a subscription following, he has also benefited in several ways. He says:

1. I have gotten a lot more comfortable in front of a camera and a crowd.
2. I also earn recurring revenue ($500 - $600 a month) from YouTube advertising.

3. I get a lot of love from Google, which has led to many sales and commissions. Everyone knows Google is the top search engine. YouTube is #2, and Google owns it. I believe the addition of a video every week to my website as well as my YouTube channel keeps me high in a search.
4. I get many thousands of dollars of free equipment from companies that want to expose their products to a qualified audience. (We are very careful how we handle this)

Besides those incredible benefits, which has increased his bottom line as well as his exposure, he's also come away with a few other pieces of wisdom to share. He advises:

1. Replying to comments is critical. Have a standard of what is and isn't acceptable. For me, if anyone makes a personal attack on anyone or uses foul language, they are banned.
2. You need to post regularly. You can schedule posts and midweek is always better than weekends, Mondays or Fridays.
3. Keep your videos short. It helps, too, to have enough subjects to cover if you just look at one aspect at a time. For instance, if you're a painter and want to share tips, focus on color selection in one video, application technique in another, etc. You may be able to break those down even further into more topics.
4. Don't worry too much about production values because YouTube viewers don't expect much, but make sure the sound is clear—turn off the background radio—and include action. Just talking isn't very exciting to watch.

5. Always include a call to action at the end. Once they've finished watching, what do you want viewers to do next? Go to your website? Call you? Find you on Facebook? Have a clear idea of your goals so you know what you want them to do.
6. Organize your videos into playlists and be sure to write a descriptive title with valuable keywords as well as a description and keywords themselves. This helps people find you.
7. Promote your videos on social media. If you struggle with what to post to Facebook, Twitter, etc., here's a good thing to let people know about! You can also embed your videos on your own site, which keeps it updated, too.
8. Have a plan and give it a chance. I usually give a marketing initiative six months before evaluating its value.
9. Watch your statistics. YouTube offers incredible analytics. Figure out what people want and give them more of that as long as it is in keeping with your goals.

To learn more about Kevin and his art, visit www.kevincaron.com

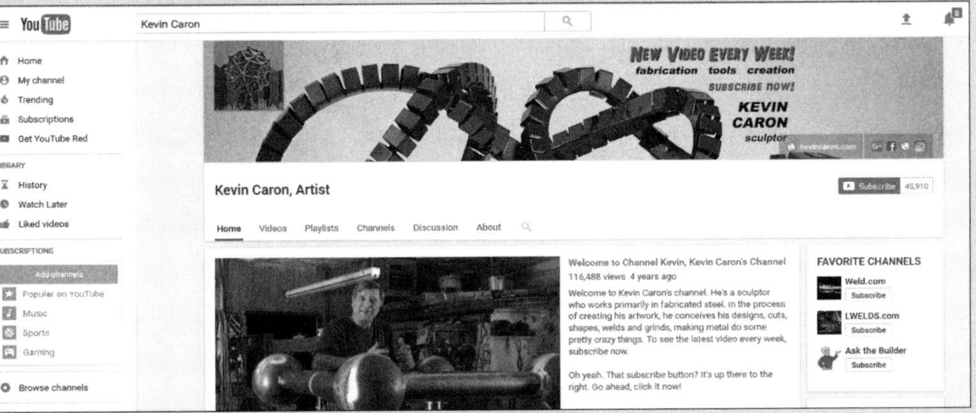

Online Opportunities to Market and Sell your Artwork

In addition to the various channels to market your work, there are plenty of sites online that give you yet another channel to promote and sell your work.

Artful Home

Artful Home is a platform through which artists reach hundreds of thousands of possible buyers. What began as a print publication in 1985 has become a huge marketplace for original artwork including everything from paintings to sculpture and functional artwork. Artists provide Artful Home with an inventory of ready-to-ship pieces and restock upon request. Especially successful artists are featured in their quarterly publication which goes out to industry professionals as well as individual art buyers. Artful Home's many years of experience and huge distribution list for their publication have made them a well-respected art-buying resource.

To learn more visit www.artfulhome.com.

Amy Meya

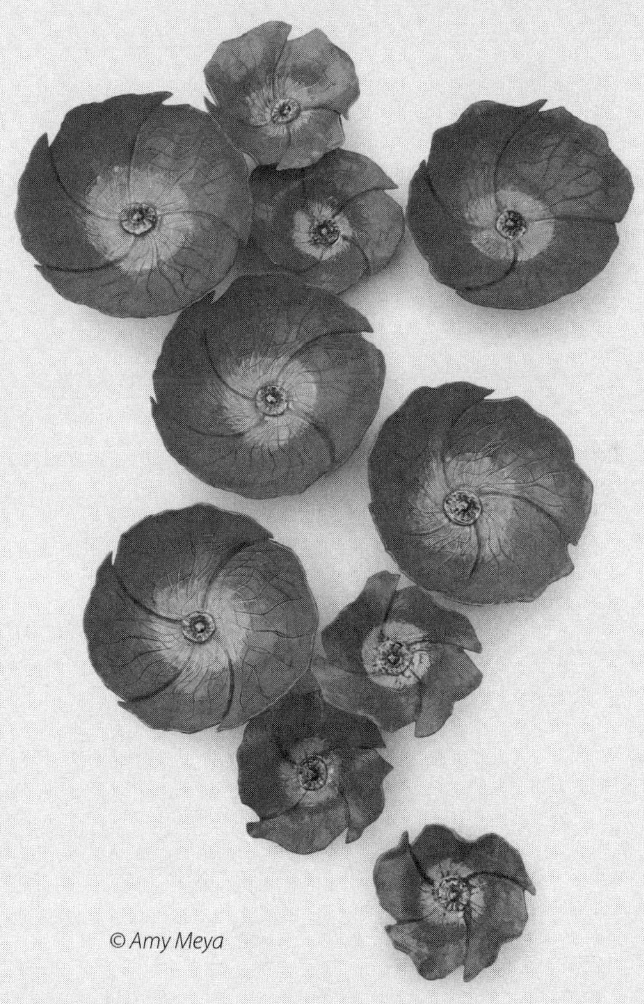

© Amy Meya

The Power of Seeing Work as a Product

"I have been a full-time artist (which means making a living selling my artwork) since 2008, when I did the Buyer's Market of American Craft for the first time. That show really launched my career. From there I met many art galleries that purchased my work wholesale, and reordered work when it was sold out. However, this was also the beginning of the big economic turn down, so things were changing.

Artful Home always attended this show and I met them there in 2011, I believe, they suggested that I apply to be on their site and I did so, successfully. I have been with them for a few years now and in the past two years my sales have exploded.

I did a lot of research on what was selling, and what in particular was selling in my genre—wall sculptural pieces. From there I seemed to have found a niche that designers are looking for and it has become so busy that I have neglected a lot of my galleries, which is unfortunate. This year I hired a local artist to do some glazing for me so I can keep up with the production side. I hope to create enough of a back stock to begin to develop new work. Working production for an outfit like Artful Home is wonderful for the bottom line when your designs are hot, but you have to keep the creative juices flowing for the next trend, and when they create such enormous volumes of sales it is hard to find that balance sometimes.

Artful Home is a really great way to sell your work, but you have to be able to make the same pieces over and over again, which for a potter is a simple task, maybe not so much for a painter, or other type of artist. It has really taught me how to produce my work as a product, which is something a lot of artists resist, but for me, I look at it as design work, there are a lot of successful designers whose work speaks over decades, or even centuries." —*Amy Meya*

To learn more about Amy and her art, visit www.amymeya.com

artist to artist

Renato Foti

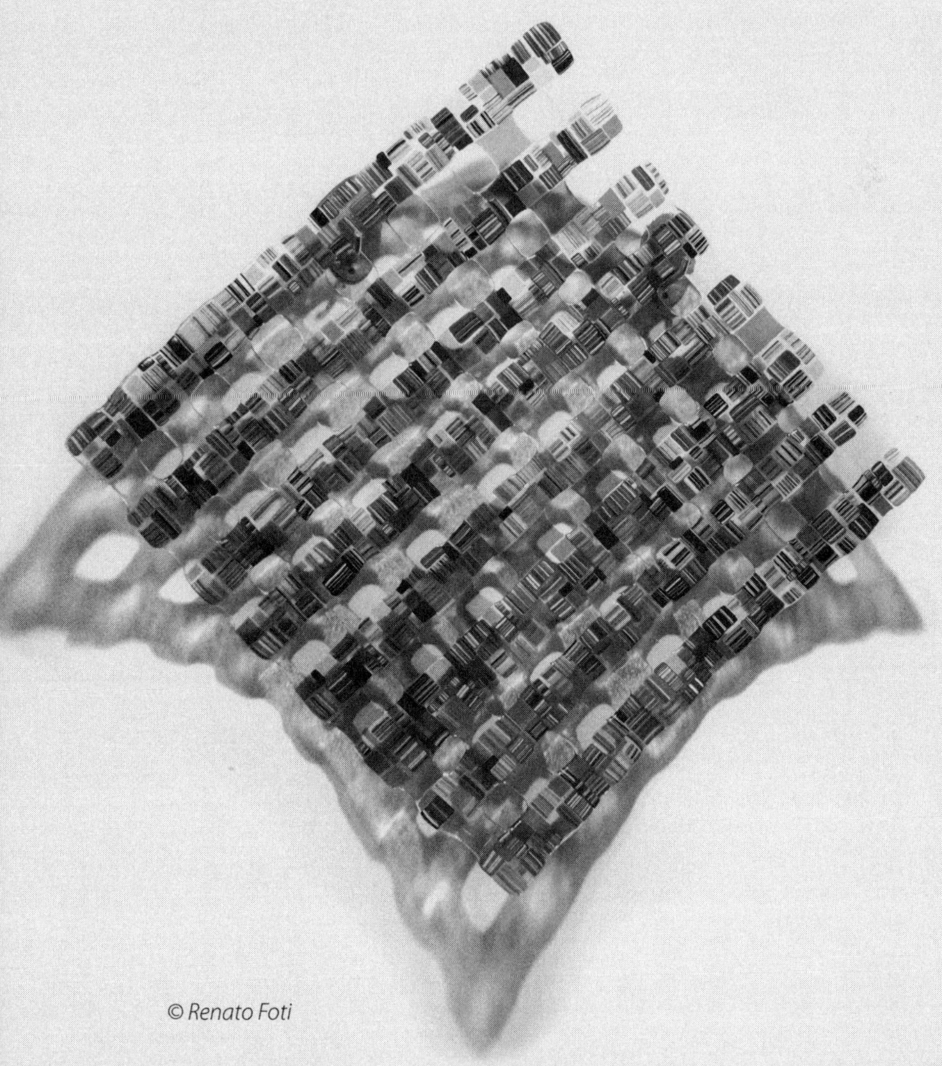

The Power of Artful Home for Marketing

"Artful Home is one of the first real Internet companies doing art, and they also do hard print catalogs. Having been working with them for many years, I'm typically one of the featured artists in the catalog. Your work gets in front of so many people, professionals and art collectors across the country. It really gets your name out to people that typically you'd never reach. Artful Home is one of my largest clients. It's such an important part of my business now. They have a great reputation for both artist and client service, which benefits everyone in the end."—*Renato Foti*

To learn more about Renato and his art, visit www.renatofoti.com.

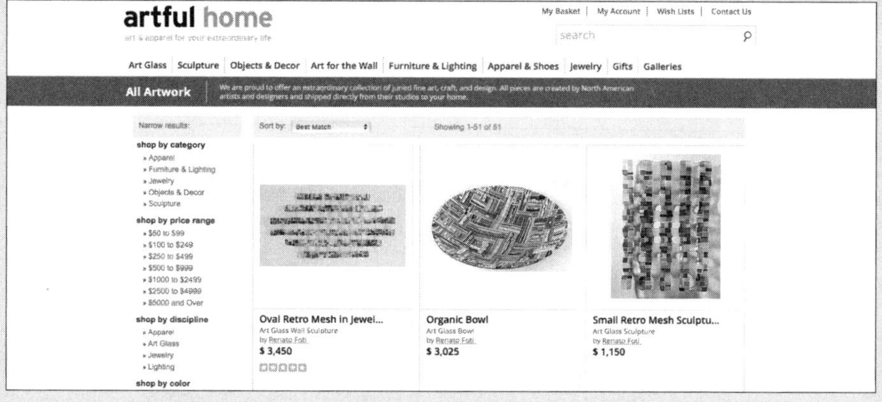

Blink Art Resource

Blink Art Resource is an annually published art resource guide distributed specifically to art and design industry professionals including galleries, consultants, and interior designers. Each year 11,000 copies of the publication are circulated all over the country, and a digital marketplace provides an online portfolio for each artist as well. Rather than the usual commission-based structure, Blink is a once-per-year investment that offers members the opportunity to tour national art shows including Artexpo New York and SPECTRUM Miami.

To learn more visit www.blinkartresource.com.

Lea de Wit

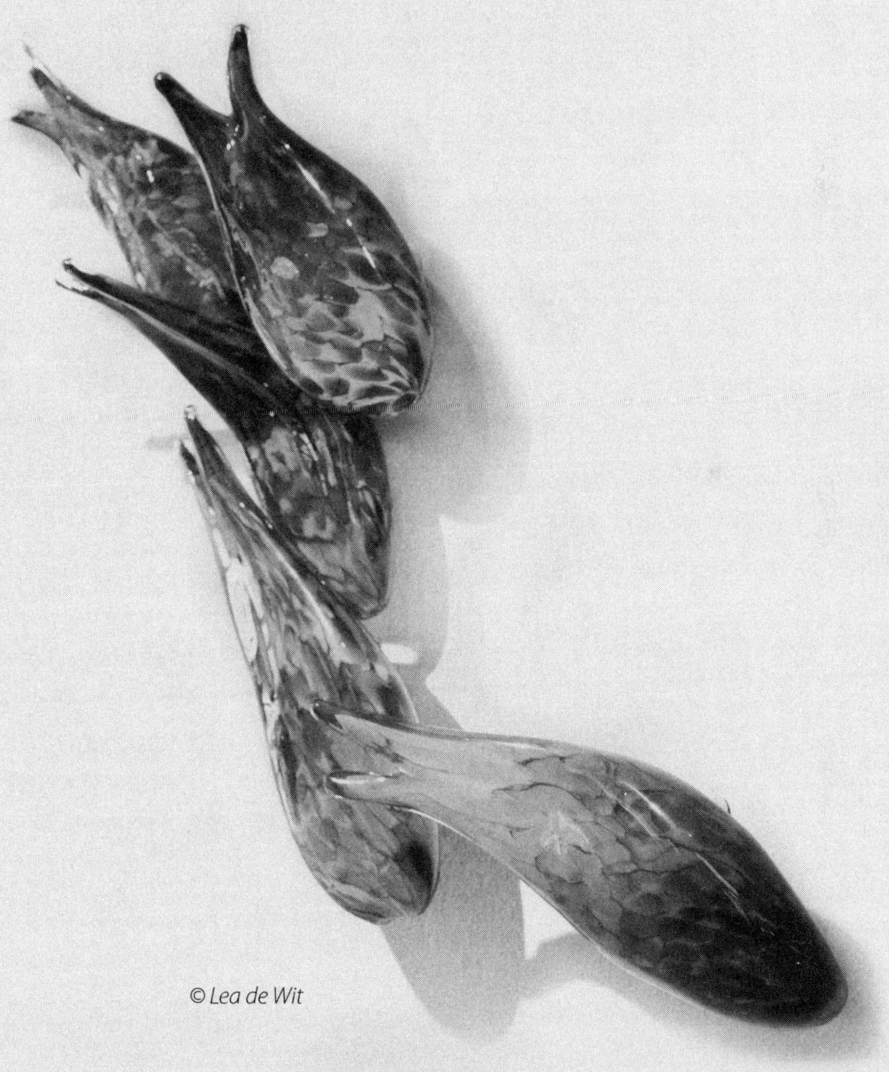

© Lea de Wit

The Power of *Blink Art Resource*

"I have been choosey over the years about which print and online resources I should invest in. Because my overhead expenses in making hot glass work are so ridiculously high, I typically don't have a huge amount of money to invest into these types of marketing efforts. Of the resources that I have selected to invest in, I have partnered with Blink Art over the last few years because I have gotten great returns on my investment. In the first year, I generated revenue from commissions that were twenty times my initial investment. This year's ad placement looks like it's going to yield commissions that will gross at least ten times my initial investment and I am not even in my busiest quarter of the year yet. Because of this success, I have already committed to my third year with Blink Art. Through Blink Art, I have been contacted by many new art consultants and designers across the country. I am happy to say that I now have representation in areas of the country that I wouldn't have otherwise had the ability to reach. Through this representation, I have been awarded three healthcare art commissions with two more pending. The relationships I've cultivated through Blink Art allow me to spend more time in the studio making work because I have representation that's promoting my art. It's a smart use of my resources." *–Lea De Wit*

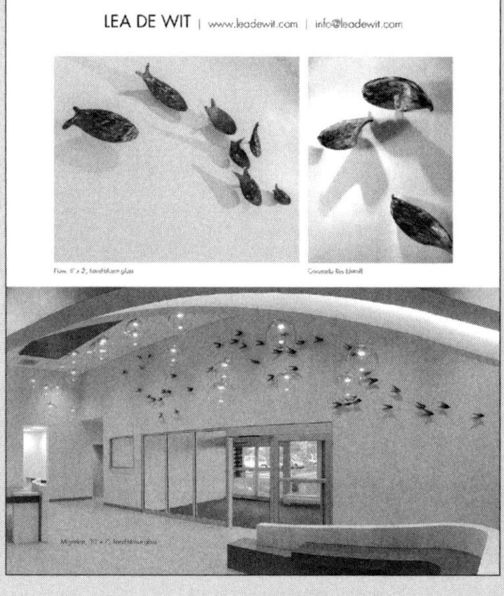

To learn more about Lea and her art, visit www.Leadewit.com

Codaworx

A collaboration platform connecting artists and design professionals, Codaworx allows artists, designers, architects, and developers to upload samples of their artwork and finished design projects. Anyone can peruse finished projects and artwork samples, allowing artists to show off their portfolios to the right people, and allowing designers to find the perfect artwork for their projects or the perfect artist for a commission. The website provides different ways to search based on who you are. The image-heavy pages are full of inspiring spaces and artwork. Good photography is a must.

To learn more visit www.codaworx.com.

Curated by Blink

Curated by Blink is the brand new quarterly catalog, which my company ADC Art Design Consultants, Inc., launched in 2017. Having a strong desire to make art more accessible to residential buyers and collectors across the country, I wanted to launch a catalog to showcase original artwork from over a three-hundred different esteemed artists (and growing). *Curated by Blink* catalog is distributed to over 10,000 homes and businesses nationwide, featuring artist stories, behind-the-scenes articles, design inspiration, and how-to guides for living with art.

To learn more visit www.blink.acdfineart.com

Etsy

Etsy is a digital marketplace for creatives offering buyers everything from laser-cut vinyl lettering and personalized sunhats to original paintings and fine crafts. Etsy allows users to create a "shop," list available or commissionable products, and communicate directly with individual buyers. Etsy requires a small listing fee for each item listed and a small fee for all sales, making it a great bang-for-your-buck as a seller.

To learn more visit www.etsy.com.

Saatchi

Saatchi Art is a digital art gallery offering artists 70 percent of sales, paid shipping, and secure online payments. Saatchi offers a social community to members as well, allowing individuals to follow others, favorite artwork, and enter competitions. Saatchi distributes a publication full of new and seasonal artwork, offers free advisory services to buyers, and puts out a great blog.

To learn more visit www.saatchi.com.

UGallery

UGallery is a digital exhibiting platform dedicated to connecting artists with buyers of all budgets. UGallery has sold work in every state in the country and 45 countries all over the world. When a piece is sold, they send shipping materials to the artist so the pieces go straight from studio to client. UGallery also covers all shipping costs and even promotes the work on Amazon. The customizable search function is great, providing buyers a no-stress process for finding the perfect piece.

To learn more visit www.ugallery.com.

Zatista

Zatista is a digital platform for exhibiting only original works of art. They work with designers and art consultants to find the perfect work for each unique project. Zatista's specialty is original artwork, with an exception for limited edition photography and printmaking. They have guest curators bring their unique expertise to the company and even offer an "Art 101" section to help new buyers discover their taste in art.

To learn more visit www.zatista.com.

Publishing Your Art

Another way to boost your annual income and your exposure as an artist is to publish your work. Publishers work with artists to distribute prints of their work to a vast market of trade professionals and art lovers. Publishers will return a percentage of sales to the artists, which can be substantial when you get into larger prints, giclées, or prints on canvas. One of my publishers is Editions Limited. They are the leading publisher and distributer of fine art reproductions. They offer print-on-demand services and they also feature work on their website. Another fantastic online and print-on-demand resource is Fine Art America. Resources abound in this area.

Editions Limited

Editions Limited is a wholesale publisher and distributer of fine art posters and also maintains a full gallery with a large inventory of paintings, prints, and sculptures. Editions Limited serves a wide range of customers, from wholesale market buyers, residential art buyers, framers, art consultants, designers, corporations, hotels, hospitals, government agencies and art collectors.

To learn more visit www.editionslimited.com.

Joanne Chappell

Editions Limited

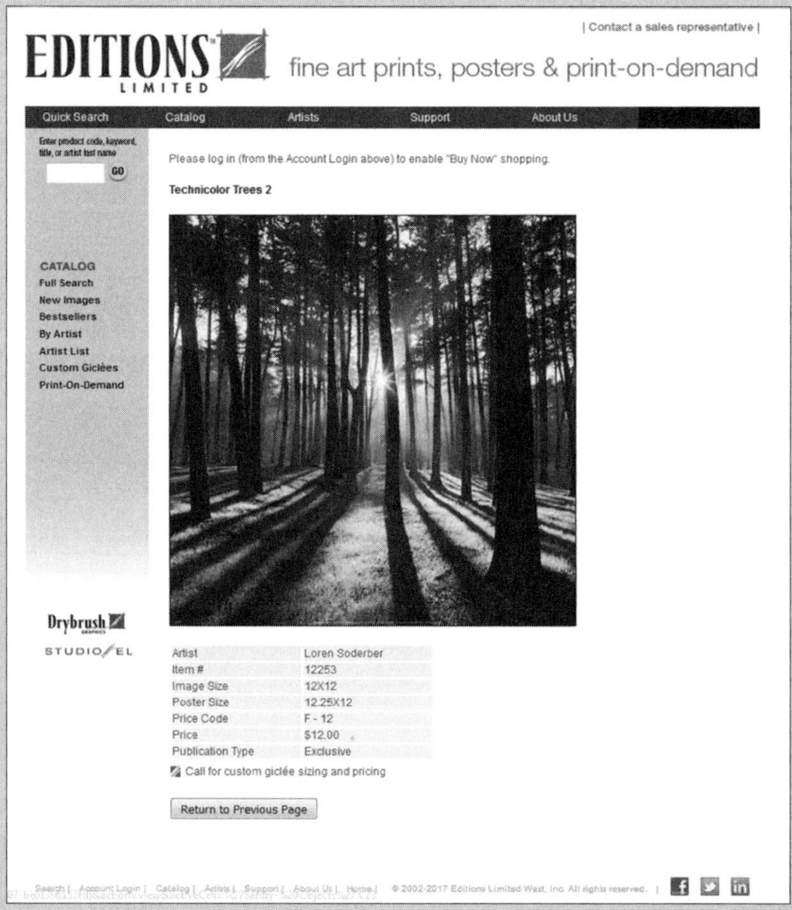

What Artists Need to Consider When Submitting Work

When I think of mentors—no, legends—in the art world, the first person that comes to mind is Joanne Chappell. Joanne has been a mainstay in the art world since 1968. As the founder and owner of Editions Limited who publishes and distributes a large inventory of paintings, prints, and sculptures, she knows firsthand what the mass-market, corporate, and healthcare industries are looking for. "We do a lot of installations for healthcare and senior living facilities," she says. And after nearly fifty years of working with businesses seeking large quantities of artwork, she has recognized a few recurring requests and themes. "We are looking for their work to be generic. No artist wants to hear this, but it's true. But, when I say generic, I don't mean it in a bad way. I just need artwork that will appeal to a large audience. Landscape and nature inspired art that can pretty much be anywhere. If an artist can redefine the landscape and make it more colorful, more emotional, and not just some banal photographic image that's what sells," she recommends. "Something else that carries a big interest is abstract art—especially the kinds that focus on texture and dimension."

How does Joanne find the work to publish? Two ways. Artists can submit their work personally or she actively goes out and seeks it. "I am constantly looking at gallery emails and I also spend a great deal of time online looking at artist's websites. I also go to a lot of art shows to scout out new talent," she says. She recommends that artists keep their websites current and focus on keywords. "I am often looking for something specific, so if your website is easy to navigate and look at, as well as easy to find based on the category, I'll most likely find what I am looking for," she says. But, she's not opposed to artists sending her work directly. "I look at every email personally. I try to respond to every single request," she says. "Of course, I can't accept everyone, but if people are polite and have done their homework, it makes it a lot easier on both of us."

To learn more visit
www.editionsl

Don Wunderlee

© Don Wunderlee

Success Selling Prints with Editions Limited

"I was very honored to be one of the artists to win a multi-year publishing award with Editions Limited through Art Comes Alive, an annual competition hosted by Art Design Consultants. Todd Haile of Editions Limited has worked very closely with me to build out a collection of sixteen pieces of my original artwork. Editions Limited is recognized for superior quality print-on-demand products and their printing standard is quite amazing. Visitors to my studio often confuse the prints for paintings, the reproduction quality is so good. In the first year I have sold over 200 prints through Editions Limited."
–Don Wunderlee

To learn more about Don and his art, visit www.wunderleeabstracts.com

Fine Art America

Fine Art America is the world's largest art marketplace and print-on-demand technology company. They've been helping artists sell prints, home decor, apparel, and other products since 2006 and are home to hundreds of thousands of artists, photographers, graphic designers, illustrators, and iconic brands. With just a few clicks, artists and photographers can upload their images to their website, set their prices for hundreds of different print-on-demand products, and then instantly sell those products to a global audience of online, mobile, and real-world buyers. Fine Art America fulfills each order on behalf of the artists, taking care of the printing, framing, matting, packaging, shipping, collecting payments from the buyers, and sending profits to the artists.

To learn more visit www.FineArtAmerica.com.

Karen Hale

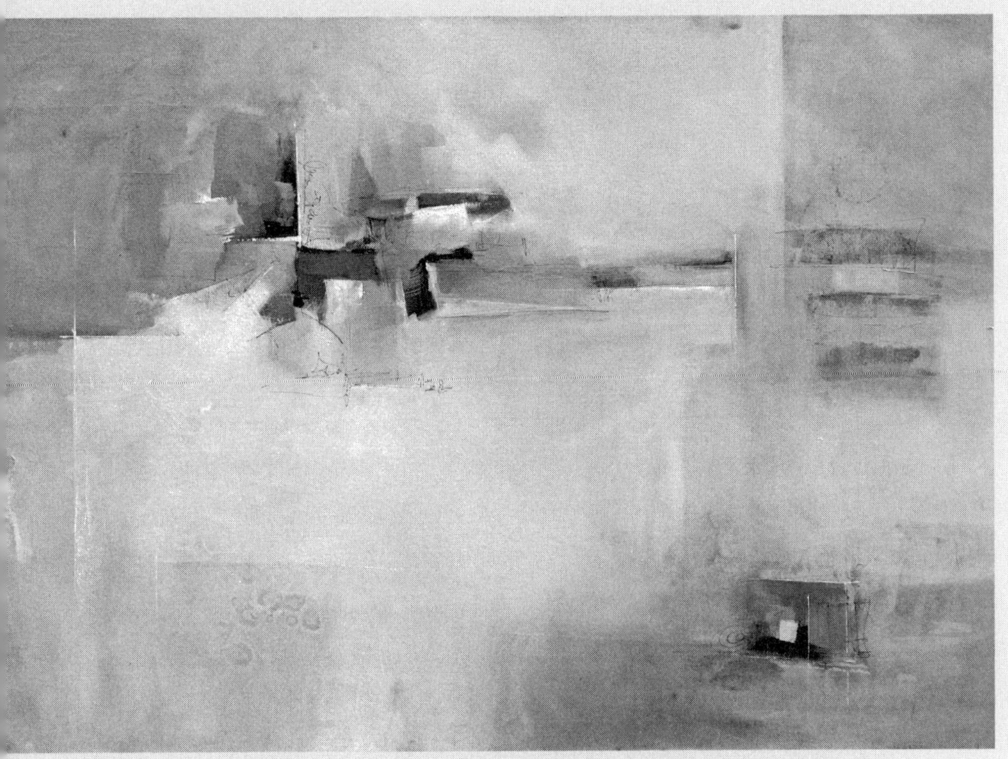

How Fine Art America Works for Artists

"About five years ago I realized that the art buyer was moving to online sites to purchase and decided to become part of that movement. I think I found Fine Art America (FAA) while doing research and at the time it was free to upload an unlimited number of images. They have grown enormously over the years and offer printing on over a dozen surfaces from prints on paper and canvas to home decor items and ship all over the world. There are other forums that you can use on their site but I personally am only interested in the print aspect.

A couple of years ago they changed their policy so if you want to upload more than 25 items you must pay a nominal annual fee. When you upload an image there is a list of questions, definitions, prices, images, etc., that you must complete. It is up to each artist to determine what payment they will require. Fine Art America then adds their amount so the client sees the total.

When you sell an item you are notified by email. In this they tell you what kind of order it is and what the payment will be. They pay after the 15th of the month after the item is delivered.

In my business I concentrate on producing original paintings. I feel it is important to offer a print option to my clients but I really don't want to take the time, pay for, or store prints or giclées. This is a viable option for me to give to clients who want a print of some sort. I recently had a decorator purchase four pieces that were similar for one of her jobs. I try to upload as large a file as possible so that the buyer has a wide variety of sizes in which to choose. I think the rule of thumb is 100 pixels to inch of printable area.

I do have a link to FAA on my website and tell my patrons about FAA if they seem interested but it is up to them to follow through. It's not a huge success but just one more web presence and another choice for my patrons." –*Karen Hale*

To learn more about Karen and her art, visit www.karenhale.com

Trademark, Copyrights, and Other Legal Matters

If you plan on selling, publishing, or reproducing your artwork, you absolutely must protect yourself. Forgery, plagiarism, and the actual stealing and passing of your work off as another's own is a real possibility and threat to your career. You don't want to be paranoid, but you have to be smart.

First, most artists don't know the difference between trademark and copyright. Copyrights are reserved for works of "authorship"—that means paintings, books, photography, sculpture, songs, poems—basically anything created by an individual. You must copyright every single thing you create. Your website should also have a Copyright note on it on each page. By copyrighting your work, you're making sure that anything you write or publish is your property and can't be stolen, copied, or reproduced. Trademarks on the other hand are for things like your logo, brand name, or slogan. By securing a copyright or a trademark you're ensuring that no one can use your work or your brand without your written permission—and in some cases—without payment.

Your work is "copyrighted" the second you make it and send it out into the world. Just by signing a work, or having a Copyright note on your website, you're legally protected. Copyright uses the symbol ©. Just by putting this symbol on any original piece of work that you have created, you're telling the world it's copyrighted.

Though you can legally register a copyright, it's not always necessary unless you're publishing a book or a book of art. To do so, you must go through the U.S. Copyright Office through the Library of Congress. Copyright registration provides legal protection for the life of the author plus seventy-five years. That means all the money earned by a publisher or subsidiaries must be transferred to the original copyright owner, and then their heirs for seventy-five years after the creator's death, unless otherwise noted in contracts.

A trademark is a different story. You must register a trademark for your own protection, and you do that through the United States Patent and Trademark Office. Unlike copyrights, trademarks last forever, but depending on the type, you may need to use it or renew it. When you create a trademark, you are permitted to use the TM sign to signify it as a trademark. If your trademark is registered with the U.S. Patent Office you are able to use the ® sign next to the logo, brand, or slogan. Warning: If you use this symbol without registration, it is illegal and punishable.

As you progress in your career and your work is more distinguishable, and therefore more popular, you may need to be on alert for forgeries, copies, and individuals passing your work off as their own. If this happens, be sure to contact a lawyer. You do not want to fight a copyright or trademark case on your own. When in doubt, seek legal counsel for all copyright and trademark questions you may have throughout the life of your career.

Hiring Help

There may come a time in your career, when you are making enough money to afford all of your living expenses, all of your supplies and business expenses, and have ample amount left over. My suggestion is, if this is the case, invest in yourself—your time. And how do you get more time to create and work and produce more? You get that time by hiring someone capable who can help. You may find you dread marketing, social media, promotion, and event planning. In that case, you may want to hire an assistant who can help you with all of your marketing and sales needs. Perhaps you just need an assistant to help you with daily tasks—someone who can respond to emails, keep up with your business requests, and respond to your clients. Figure out what you can afford and place an ad. You will need to consult an accountant to figure out the finer points of hiring an employee. You will need to pay taxes on that employee and you'll need to fill out the appropriate paperwork to do so. (Again, a software like Quickbooks will help with these details.) Also, I might add, you don't want to hire the first person who responds to your ad. Hiring the right person for the job takes time. You want to hire not only a talented and experienced individual, but you want to hire someone with an interest in the work you do and a positive, can-do attitude. This seems obvious, but as an employer, I can attest that taking the time to listen to what an interviewee is telling you can pay dividends in the long run. You don't want managing another person to be one more task you have to do. Remember you're hiring someone to HELP you. Take your time, follow your gut, and ask questions that will help you get to know your potential hire a bit better. Once you do hire someone, LET THEM DO THEIR JOB. Don't micromanage or become needlessly stressed out at "how" someone does something. Check in or set up times that don't interfere with your scheduled work time in your studio to follow up on tasks.

As I have mentioned before one of the biggest hindrances to anyone's career is burnout. If you feel overwhelmed, stressed out, and incapable of managing all the day-to-day business aspects you may need help. No one, and I mean no one, gets through this life without some help from others. If you want your career to grow and you want more time to focus on your work, then you need to invest in some outside help. And once you do, let them help you.

Action Steps

1. **Create a marketing strategy for the next year.** Using the guidelines in this chapter get out a calendar and plan a couple of open studio or gallery events, schedule regular blog posts (pick a day and time that works best for you to write a short piece), set some dates for your email marketing campaigns, as well as some direct mail campaigns.

2. **Look into some paid advertising opportunities.** Do you have a piece or a post that is particularly popular? Try promoting it on Facebook and see what kind of response you get. Play around with the demographics and target audience.

3. **Evaluate your website. What keywords have you selected?** Are they used throughout your site? Is it mobile friendly? Is the content up-to-date and relevant to your subject matter?

4. **Get involved.** Seek out a group or organization where you can spend some time with other artists or mentors.

5. **Research online selling opportunities.** Spend some time looking through sites like Artful Home, Editions Limited, Ugallery, Etsy.com, Curated by Blink, etc. Is there a site you can publish your work right now?

Further Reading on Living Life as Artist and Entrepreneur

Content Inc.: How Entrepreneurs Use Content to Build Massive Audiences and Create Radically Successful Businesses
by Joe Pulizzi

Content Chemistry: An Illustrated Handbook for Content Marketing
by Andy Crestodina

The Best Damn Web Marketing Checklist, Period!
by Stoney deGeyter

The Creative Artist's Legal Guide: Copyright, Trademark and Contracts in Film and Digital Media Production
by Bill & Ellen Seiter

How to Say it: Marketing with New Media
by Lena Claxton & Alison Woo

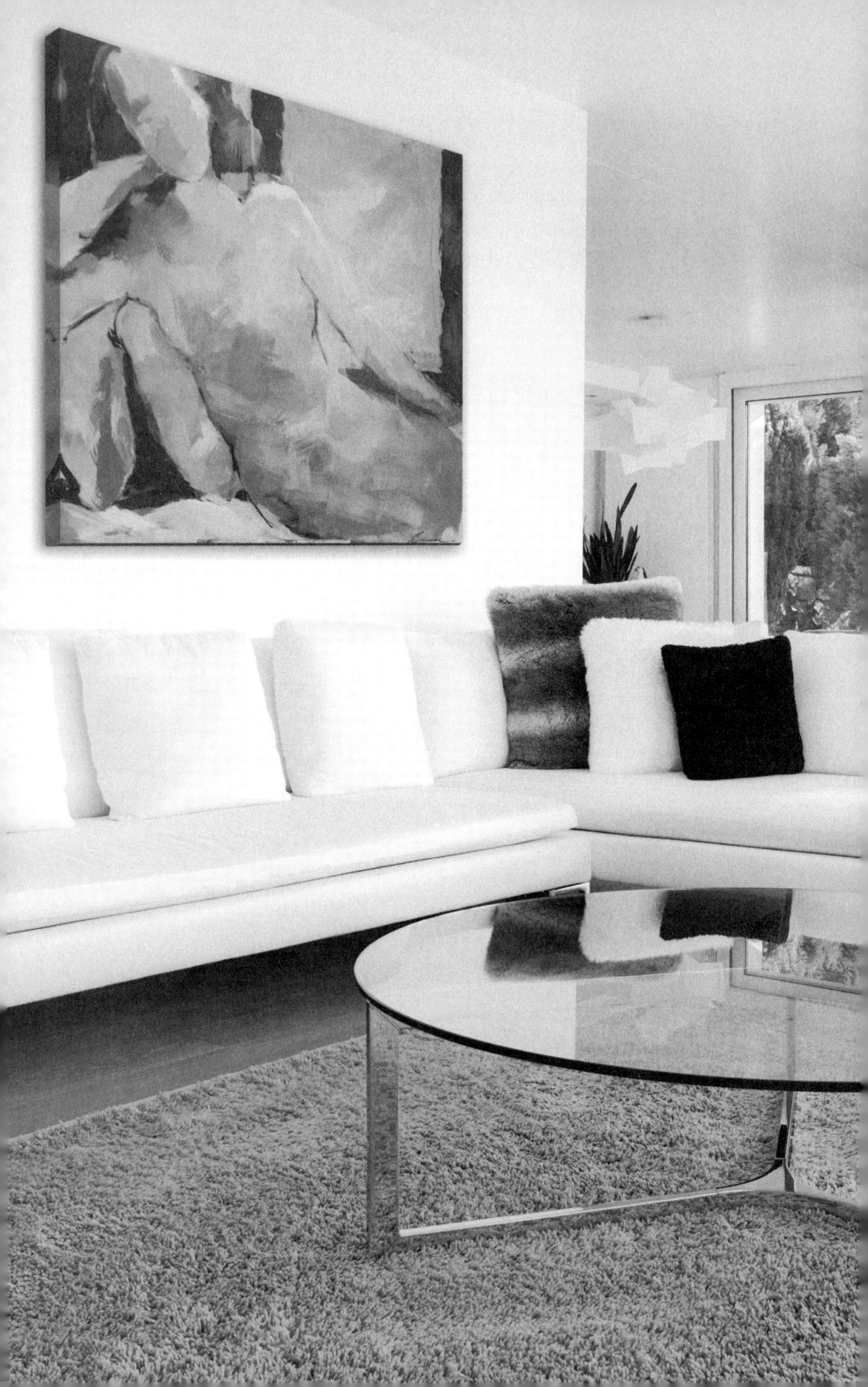

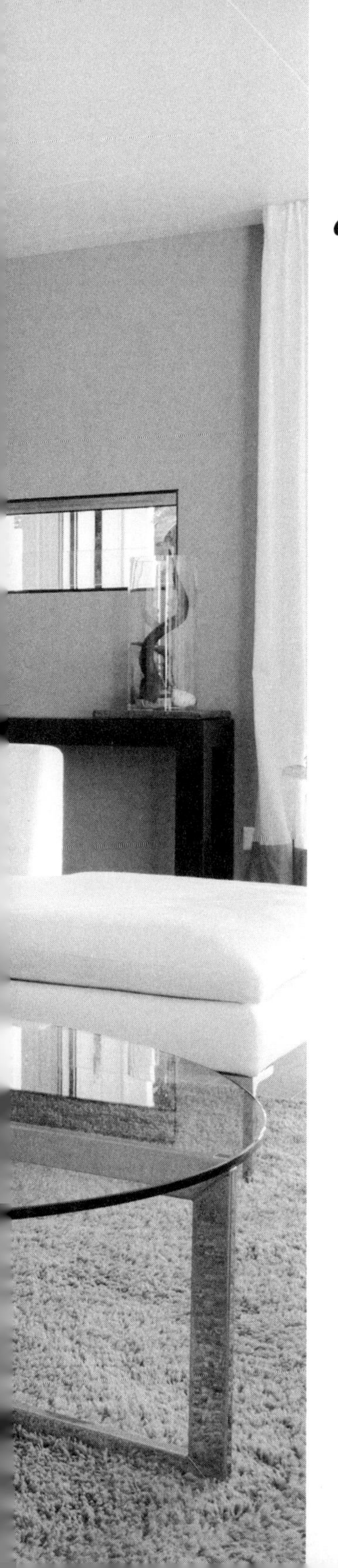

"If you ask me what I came to do in this world, I, an artist, will answer you: I am here to ***live out loud****."*

—Émile Zola

Artist: Beau Wild

conclusion

YOU HAVE WHAT IT TAKES

"Creativity takes courage."

— Henri Matisse

Conclusion

And I would like to add that life as a creative takes:

Faith

Hope

Heart

Strength

Passion

Love

Persistence

Inspiration

Humility

Friendship

Encouragement

Wisdom

Patience

Yes, you're going to need it all.

Becoming an artist, what you're truly meant to be, is not a task for the meek. It will take an iron will. It will take an intrepid spirit that knows, somewhere deep down, that all one needs to do is leap and everything else will fall into place. So I encourage you: Take that leap. Just do it. Start somewhere. Anywhere. Just make sure that whatever you do make sure that you start. Start today. Don't let this book be the end. Let it be the beginning. Come back to it as often as you like. Revisit the activities. Read when you need to feel inspired. But, don't get too caught up in the details if you start to feel stressed or overwhelmed. Just take every day—every moment—at a time. Start small. Make incremental changes and you'll start to see that they add up.

It will be the greatest joy of my life if one day I get a letter from someone who said "I just did this one thing, and it helped so much." Or, "Because of this book, I started something I never thought I could."

Oh, how badly, I want you to start! Start as if your life depends on it. (I might add, it does.) This life, this one, beautiful, precious life you have is yours and you can make it whatever you want it to be. You can create it—every hour of every day—into the life you want. And that's what I want for you.

An artist's heart is a tremendous one. It feels so much. It longs for so much. It has so many dreams and hopes. I encourage you to keep that heart beating, keep that heart longing, keep that heart dreaming. But, I want you to pace yourself too. I want you to use the tools that I've given you in this book and all the expert advice from your peers and use it to help you achieve those dreams and those aspirations.

Most of all, I want you to remember that part of your journey as an artist isn't just financial or occupational; it's also emotional, mental, and spiritual. By seeking new ways of spending your time and applying your talents or personality assets, you can create a life uniquely your own. You can expand your perspective, find new joy, and discover what gives you a sense of fulfillment and purpose.

When you were a kid, did you dream of spending your days in a crowded office or fighting through traffic both ways on your commute? Did you envision halfheartedly serving the ideas of your boss or being forced to play corporate politics? Did you think you would be scraping together crumbs just so you could afford to take your family on one vacation a year? When you were a kid, did you imagine being an adult would be better than this?

It can be. Being an artist and entrepreneur is about far more than money, flexibility, or self-reliance. It's the opportunity to create something out of nothing—a miracle. Become a miracle maker. Your place as an artist can't be filled by anyone else. The world is waiting for your skills, your ideas, your smile. Are you ready to step up? It's time to claim your place in the art world. And here's my final secret: It's already there waiting for you. All you have to do is show up.

In the meantime, I'll be waiting to hear from you. I know you can do it.

Contact me at Litsa@adcfineart.com

Acknowledgments

If someone had told me a year ago that I would write a book, I would have said, "Oh, right, that's not happening." At fifty-three and with three children, a growing business, community work, and laundry (yes, loads of laundry), I knew it wasn't going to happen. But then I realized that 2017 would be a special year, because I'd be hitting a milestone in my life and career. Yes, 2017 marks my twenty-fifth year as an entrepreneur! So I decided that instead of buying myself a designer watch to commemorate the occasion (although that would have been nice!), I would do something much more meaningful instead: *I'd write that book.* But, not just any book. I wanted to write a book that would include all that I have learned over the years (from failures to successes). More than anything, I wanted to create something to help and inspire others who had also devoted their lives to art.

To make this dream of mine to write, edit, and publish a book in less than a year's time a reality, I have so many people to acknowledge! A big thank you goes to Mary Curran Hackett, our Senior Content Strategist, for "getting my voice" from the get go. You are a truly gifted writer and have taken this book farther than I would have been able to do myself. To Kate Messer who photographed me for the back cover (she chose the white dress over the red one too!) and to the many contributors of this book who have given time to share their knowledge of the art world. I also want to acknowledge my incredible team at ADC/Blink – especially the talented Sandy Eichert who designed the book in record time. A thank you goes to Maxwell who edited it and to Elizabeth for her amazing photoshopping skills on my cover photo (to make me look ten years younger!). I also want to acknowledge Chelsea, Nicole, Christian, Sara, Dave, Kevin, Tessa and Roger who contribute to the success of our business every single day.

I also want to thank my clients who believe in the power of art. There are too many of you to list here! By giving us the opportunity to put art in your homes, offices, hospitals and hotels, you not only have created amazing spaces with beautiful art, but you have supported a small business and ultimately helped many artists and their families as well.

To my parents, Petros and Sofia, thank you for taking the ultimate risk by bringing your young family to "the land of opportunity" fifty years ago so we could follow our dreams. To my sister, Sylvia who shares my journey and my passion for art, and who is my best friend, thank you for always being there for me. To my beautiful girls, Sophia, Angel, and Hanna, thank you for your love and encouragement. And finally to my sweet husband, Van Spanos: You believed in me long before I learned to believe in myself. I am so grateful for your love.

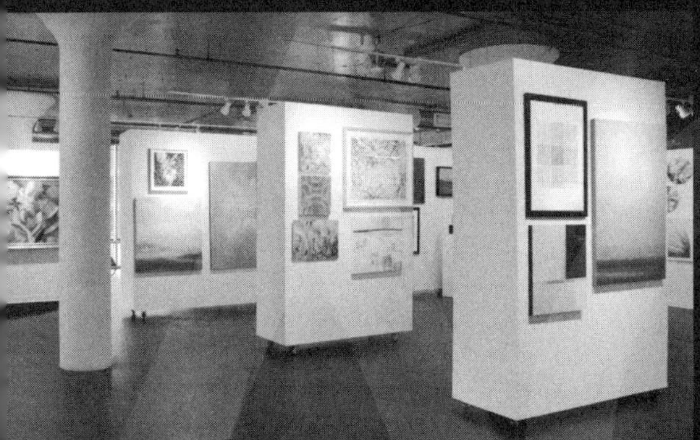